HARBRACE
COLLEGE
WORKBOOK
FORM 10C

Writing for the
World of Work

HARBRACE COLLEGE WORKBOOK FORM 10C

Writing for the World of Work

Sheila Y. Graham
Late of the University of Tennessee

Melissa E. Barth
Appalachian State University

Harcourt Brace Jovanovich, Publishers
San Diego   New York   Chicago   Austin
London   Sydney   Toronto

TO THE INSTRUCTOR

Welcome to Form 10C of the *Harbrace College Workbook.* Like Forms 10A and 10B, Form 10C is designed to be used either independently or in conjunction with the Tenth Edition of the *Harbrace College Handbook.* Form 10C is unique, however, in focusing on the world of work: all of the examples and exercises deal directly with the working world and illustrate the writing skills students will need as they pursue their careers. For this edition, all of the explanations and exercises have been re-examined; well over half of the exercises have been entirely rewritten, and most of the other exercises, as well as most of the explanations, have been significantly revised. **Section 31, Logical Thinking,** is new.

Arrangement   The materials in Form 10C are arranged in sections that parallel the sections of the *Harbrace College Handbook,* Tenth Edition. In Form 10C for the first time, the numbers and letters denoting subdivisions within the sections also correspond exactly to those of the *Handbook*, with three exceptions: **Section 5** on case, **Section 7** on verb forms, and **Section 12/13** on the comma. Because of the special emphasis on certain skills in this version of the *Workbook*, an organization somewhat different from the *Handbook* seemed necessary in these three sections. You will note also that the section numbering system of Form 10C jumps from **Section 33** to **Section 35,** omitting the *Handbook's* **Section 34** on the research paper, a subject beyond the scope of most courses in which the *Workbook* is used. However, although Form 10C omits the research paper, **Section 35, Business Writing,** incorporates many of the skills required of students who will be writing the traditional college research paper, most notably subdivisions **35c(1)** and **35c(2)** which deal with the process analysis report and the documented report.

   Section 1 of Form 10C covers the main points of grammar and punctuation; it is, in other words, a practical minicourse in the grammar and punctuation of sentences. Some students may be able to move directly from **Section 1** to the later sections that treat word choice and sentence effectiveness (**Sections 20** through **30**) or even to the sections that go beyond the sentence to longer units of composition (**Sections 31** through **33**). Other students will need additional review of basic areas—such as agreement, tense, and the uses of the comma and apostrophe—that is supplied in the intervening sections (**2** through **19**). Of course, the needs of the class or the individual student will determine how much time is devoted to **Sections 2** through **19** and how many of the exercises in each section are assigned.

Exercises   The subject matter of the exercises is the world of work. The exercises cover such topics as the importance of work, the job market, writing and speaking on the job, and work-related issues such as leisure time and women in the working world. Form 10C provides many more exercises related to basic areas of grammar and punctuation than are found in the other forms of the *Workbook;* students should not run out of exercise material before they have mastered a specific skill. For example, fifteen exercises deal with the use of the comma (six in **Section 1,** six in **Section 12/13,** and three in **Section 17**); twelve exercises stress the use of sentence-combining techniques to achieve an effective style.

Writing   Form 10C includes not only sections on writing paragraphs and essays but also a section **(35)** on the special kinds of composition students will need to have mastered in order to succeed in the world of work—for example, letters of application, letters asking for adjustments, memorandums, and reports.

The Dictionary   Proper use of the dictionary is stressed throughout Form 10C: in the study of nouns, adjectives, adverbs, and verbs, and in the sections on capitalization, abbreviations, italics, and numbers. But unless each member of the class is familiar with the dictionary, the best place to begin teaching and learning dictionary skills is **Section 19,** "Good Usage and the Dictionary."

Spelling   Although most students receive little formal instruction in spelling after elementary school, correct spelling is important to success in college and in other work. Form 10C does not presume to be a complete spelling manual, but it does emphasize throughout use of the dictionary to avoid various kinds of misspellings, and it covers all major spelling rules. In addition, it presents a list of words that are frequently misspelled in professional writing. Perhaps even more important, the "Individual Spelling List" at the end of the *Workbook* offers a chart on which students can record the words they misspell in their writing assignments and the reasons for the misspellings.

Acknowledgments   Although I did not have the opportunity to know the late Sheila Graham, who for so many years wrote and revised the various forms of the *Harbrace College Workbook,* as I worked on the revisions for Form 10C I came to respect her knowledge and her commitment to students. I am grateful for all the guidance I have received in rewriting Form 10C, especially from my editors, Thomas Broadbent and Cate Safranek. Among the others at Harcourt Brace Jovanovich to whom I owe thanks are Martha Berlin, Jamie Fidler, and Schamber Richardson. I also owe a debt of gratitude to several mentors at Purdue University: Muriel Harris, with whom I worked in the English Department's Writing Center, and Agnes Lokke, who introduced me to the pleasures of teaching business and technical writing. In preparing this edition of the *Workbook* I have been greatly helped by the thorough critiques of Professor John N. Snapper and of Professor Suzanne S. Webb, Texas Woman's University. Finally, I would like to thank my friends Mr. Foonman and Mr. Tigger, and my computer, HAL, without whose late night encouragement none of this work would have gotten done on time.

Melissa E. Barth

Note: Each of the forms of the Harbrace College Workbook is available in an Instructor's Edition as well as a Student Edition. The Instructor's Edition is an exact replica of the Student Edition, with answers to all exercises overprinted in a second color.

TO THE STUDENT

You learn how to write chiefly by correcting your own errors. Corrections made for you are of comparatively little value. Therefore your instructor points out the errors but asks you to make the actual revisions for yourself. Your instructor usually indicates a necessary correction by a number (or a symbol) marked in the margin of your paper opposite the error. If a word is misspelled, the number **18** (or the symbol **sp**) will be used; if there is a sentence fragment, the number **2** (or the symbol **frag**); if there is a faulty reference of a pronoun, the number **28** (or the symbol **ref**). Consult the pertinent explanation (see the guides inside the front and back covers), master the principle underlying each correction, and make the necessary revisions. Draw one line through words to be deleted, but allow such words to remain legible in order that the instructor may compare the revised form with the original.

In certain cases your instructor may require that you pinpoint your errors by supplying the appropriate letter after the number written in the margin. For example, after the number **12** in the margin you should take special care to supply the appropriate letter (**a**, **b**, **c**, **d**, or **e**) from the explanatory sections on the comma to show why the comma is needed. Simply inserting a comma teaches little; understanding why it is required in a particular situation is a definite step toward mastery of the comma.

Specimen Paragraph from a Student Theme

Marked by the instructor with numbers:

3   Taking photographs for newspapers is hard work, it is not the

12   romantic carefree adventure glorified in motion pictures and novels. For

18   every great moment recorded by the stareing eye of the camera, there are

      twenty routine assignments that must be handled in the same efficient

28   manner. They must often overcome great hardships. The work continues

24   for long hours. It must meet deadlines. At times they are called on to

      risk their lives to obtain a picture. To the newspaper photographer, get-

2   ting a good picture being the most important task.

Marked by the instructor with symbols:

cs   Taking photographs for newspapers is hard work, it is not the

,/   romantic carefree adventure glorified in motion pictures and novels. For

sp   every great moment recorded by the stareing eye of the camera, there are

twenty routine assignments that must be handled in the same efficient

ref   manner. They must often overcome great hardships. The work continues

sub   for long hours. It must meet deadlines. At times they are called on to

risk their lives to obtain a picture. To the newspaper photographer, get-

frag   ting a good picture being the most important task.

Corrected by the student:

3   Taking photographs for newspapers is hard work; it is not the

12 C   romantic, carefree adventure glorified in motion pictures and novels. For

18   every great moment recorded by the ~~stareing~~ *staring* eye of the camera, there are

twenty routine assignments that must be handled in the same efficient

28   manner. ~~They must often overcome great hardships. The work continues~~ *newspaper photographers must often*

24   *overcome great hardships and work long hours to* ~~for long hours. It must meet deadlines.~~ At times they are called on to *meet deadlines.*

risk their lives to obtain a picture. To the newspaper photographer, get-

2   ting a good picture ~~being~~ *is* the most important task.

CONTENTS

GRAMMAR

MECHANICS

PUNCTUATION

SPELLING AND DICTION

EFFECTIVE SENTENCES

EFFECTIVE WRITING

SENTENCE SENSE   ss 1

1

Develop your sentence sense.

A sentence is made up of a subject and a predicate. The subject tells who or what the sentence is about, and the predicate says something about the subject.

> Subject   +   Predicate
>
> People   +   once had few choices in careers.

The subject is often a noun or pronoun—a word such as *people* or *they*. The predicate contains the verb. The verb expresses an action, an occurrence, or a state of being. From now on, the subject of the sentence will be underlined once, and the verb will be underlined twice.

> People once had few choices in careers.   [*Had* is the verb; it expresses an occurrence.]

Order of Sentence Parts   The usual order for the two main sentence parts is subject, verb (S—V). But in most questions, in many emphatic sentences, and in sentences beginning with *there,* the order of the sentence parts varies.

> USUAL ORDER   Today's world offers many careers.
>
> QUESTION   Have you investigated various career opportunities?   [A part of the verb precedes the subject.]
>
> EMPHATIC   Many are the possibilities.   [The subject comes last.]
>
> THERE   There are books about careers in the library.   [The verb precedes the subject.]

The order of the main sentence parts is very important in a language like English because the function of a word often depends on its position in the sentence. In the following examples, *employer* is a subject in the first sentence and a part of the predicate in the second; on the other hand, *employees* is a part of the predicate in the first sentence and a subject in the second. Only the *position* of these two words tells you what part they play in the sentence.

The <u>employer</u> <u><u>praised</u></u> the employees.

The <u>employees</u> <u><u>praised</u></u> their employer.

Both the subject and the verb will be explored in depth in the following pages of Section **1.**

Main Sentence Parts   Exercise 1-1

NAME _____ SCORE _____

DIRECTIONS In the following sentences, the subject is underlined once and the verb is underlined twice. If the main parts of the sentence are in the usual word order, write *1* in the blank; if they vary from the usual order, write *2* in the blank. When you have finished the exercise, answer the questions that follow it.

EXAMPLE
What would you have done to make a living during the 1700s?   *2*

1. Your career in colonial America would probably have been

   farming.   _____

2. In the early days of our country most families farmed for a

   living.   _____

3. Every member of the family had a job on the farm.   _____

4. There were many chores to be done each day.   _____

5. Families were, of necessity, quite large.   _____

6. A few people in a community worked in a general store.   _____

7. Have you seen a record book of one of these early stores?   _____

8. A book in the Cades Cove Community of Tennessee shows

   the purchases of a typical family in the area.   _____

9. What products did most families buy?   _____

10. Typical purchases were things like tobacco, coal oil, coffee,

    and shoes.   _____

11. Most families paid for their purchases with products from

    their farm.   _____

12. During the 1800s the <u>Agricultural Revolution</u> <u>spread</u> to North America. _____

13. Fewer <u>people</u> <u>were</u> then <u>needed</u> on the farm. _____

14. <u>Springing up</u> everywhere <u>were</u> <u>factories</u>. _____

15. Many <u>people</u> <u>found</u> jobs of various types in the factories. _____

QUESTIONS

1. How many sentences have the main parts arranged in the usual order? _____

2. Which sentence varies from the usual order for the sake of emphasis? _____

Rewrite sentence 7 in the usual word order.

Rewrite sentence 14 in the usual word order.

1a Use a verb in every sentence. When you look for sentence parts, find the verb first.

Every sentence has a verb, even the one-word sentences that trainers use to communicate with their dogs: *Stay. Fetch. Sit.*

Function   Like the words spoken by a dog trainer, most verbs express action. But other kinds of verbs express occurrences or states of being.

ACTION   Most people now *work* eight hours a day.

OCCURRENCE   Many people *choose* their careers during their teen-age years.

STATE OF BEING Sometimes people *become* unhappy with their careers.

Note: The verb may appear as part of a contraction: *I'm* (I *am*), *we're* (we *are*), *he'd* (he *had* or he *would*).

   Sometimes a word looks like a verb because its meaning is associated with action, but it functions as some other sentence part—quite often as the subject or a modifier. Take the word *work*, for example, which is an action word but which may serve as a subject, a verb, or a modifier.

SUBJECT   *Work* is important to most people.

VERB   People *work* for reasons other than pay.

MODIFIER   The five-day *work* week may become obsolete.

To distinguish between *work* as a verb and *work* as some other sentence part, try putting an article (*a*, *an*, or *the*) in front of the word; if the sentence still makes sense, then the word is probably functioning as some other sentence part, but if the sentence does not make sense with the article included, the word is functioning as a verb.

SUBJECT   [*The*] Work is important to most people.

VERB   People [*the*]   work for reasons other than pay.

MODIFIER   *The* five-day work week may become obsolete.

Transitive and Linking Verbs   Many verbs serve as transitive verbs; they pass their action along to the object or objects. (See also **1b(1).**)

TRANSITIVE   Fortunately, people can change their careers.   [Can change what?

            Careers receives the action of the verb.]

TRANSITIVE   An internship showed me the need to change my career plans.

            [Showed whom what? *Me* and *need* receive the action of the verb.]

5

Other verbs—like *be, seem, appear,* and *feel*—introduce material in the predicate that gives more information about the subject.

LINKING I was grateful for the internship program. [*Was* links the subject with

a complement, *grateful,* that says something about the subject.]

Helping (Auxiliary) Verbs   Often the main verb—which shows the action, occurrence, or state of being—is accompanied by one or more helping verbs—usually forms of *be* (*is, are, was, were, has been, will be,* and so on) or *has, have, do, can,* or *could* (see the Appendix for a more complete list of helping verbs). The helping verb or verbs (also called *auxiliary verbs*) may come immediately before the main verb or may be separated from the main verb.

Fortunately, people today *can change* their careers. [The helping verb, *can,* immediately precedes the main verb, *change.*]

They *do* not *have* to remain in the same career forever. [The helping verb, *do,* is separated from the main verb, *have,* by *not.*]

Have you *found* your career yet? [The helping verb, *have,* is separated from the main verb, *found,* by the subject, *you.*]

Notice that a verb like *have, has, be, can,* and *do* work either as the main verb of the sentence or as a helping verb. In the second example above, *have* is the main verb; in the third example, it is the helping verb.

Note: The helping verb, like the main verb, may be a part of a contraction: *can't* find (*can*not find), she*'s* coming (she *is* coming), we*'ve* gone (we *have* gone).

Phrasal Verbs   The main verb may also be accompanied by a particle—a word (or words) like *to, in, with, up,* and *of* that adds to or changes the meaning of the main verb.

We *put* our names on the list of applicants for the job. [main verb]

We *cannot put up with* the company's delay much longer. [The main verb, *put,* is accompanied by a helping verb, *can,* and the particles *up* and *with.*]

Compound Verbs   Often a sentence has two verbs connected by *and, but, or,* or *nor.*

We *applied for* summer work but *did* not *hear* from the company for a month.

We *waited* and *waited* for some word.

Form   Verbs can change their form to show number (one or more) and tense (the time of the action, occurrence, or state of being). Singular verbs in the present tense usually end in *s* or *es,* and past tense verbs usually end in *d* or *ed.* (The dictionary shows all unusual changes in verb form.)

A person usually shows a natural inclination to work with people or with things. [singular number; present tense]

People *show* their preferences in many ways.   [plural number; present tense]

She *has decided* on a career in counseling.   [past tense shown by *d* ending of main verb; singular number shown by helping verb, *has*]

They *have selected* accounting as their major.   [past tense shown by *ed* ending of main verb; plural number shown by helping verb, *have*]

Identifying Verbs

Exercise 1–2

NAME _____ SCORE _____

DIRECTIONS   The following famous quotations about work illustrate the various functions of verbs—to express action, occurrence, or state of being. The subject of each verb is already underlined once; you should underline each verb twice. (Most sentences have more than one verb.) Then make a list of the twenty-five verbs that you have located in these quotations.

EXAMPLE

Work is the refuge of people who have nothing better to do.   —OSCAR WILDE

1. I thought [work] was a very bad thing that the human race had invented

   for itself.   —AGATHA CHRISTIE

2. I'm [I am] a great believer in luck, and I find the harder I work the more

   I have of it.   —THOMAS JEFFERSON

3. When a man tells you that he got rich through hard work, [you] ask him

   whose.   —DON MARQUIS

4. [You] never give away your work. People don't [do not] value what they

   don't [do not] have to pay for.   —NANCY HALE

5. Apparently we all work for ourselves, but in reality we are always working

   for others.   —DR. WILLIAM STEKHEL

6. A human being must have occupation if he or she is not to become a nui-

   sance to the world.   —DOROTHY L. SAYERS

7. I never forget that work is a curse—which is why I've [I have] never made

   it a habit.   —BLAISE CENDRARS

8. A society in which everyone works is not necessarily a free society and may

   indeed be a slave society. . . .   —ELEANOR ROOSEVELT

LIST OF VERBS

1.	14.
2.	15.
3.	16.
4.	17.
5.	18.
6.	19.
7.	20.
8.	21.
9.	22.
10.	23.
11.	24.
12.	25.
13.	

Identifying Helping Verbs and Particles   Exercise 1–3

NAME _____ SCORE _____

DIRECTIONS   In the following sentences the main verbs are underlined twice. Find the helping verbs and particles that go with these main verbs and also underline them twice. Then write the entire verb or verbs in the blank.

EXAMPLE
People should study the job market and match up their skills with the available posi-

tions.   *should study, match up* _____

1. A person may learn about a job opening from a friend or acquaintance. __

    _____

2. You can sometimes come up with a job because of the Help Wanted section

    of the newspaper. _____

3. Public or private employment agencies can also help the job hunter. _____

    _____

4. Public employment agencies do not charge for their services, but private

    agencies usually do ask for payment. _____

    _____

5. Once you hear about a good opening, you should contact the employer or

    personnel director immediately. _____

    _____

6. The applicant for the job may write a letter or call for an interview with

the potential employer. _____

7. Because an application letter does give the employer a first, and usually

lasting, impression of the job seeker, you should always take the time to

make yours perfect. _____

8. The letter of application can serve as your letter of introduction. _____

_____

9. The letter must mention the job and the applicant's special skills. _____

_____

10. The last paragraph of your letter should request an interview and should

give an address and telephone number. _____

_____

Main Verbs, Helping Verbs, and Particles   Exercise 1–4

NAME _____ SCORE _____

DIRECTIONS In the following sentences the subjects have been underlined once. Underline the complete verbs twice—that is, the main verbs and, if there are any, the helping verbs and particles. Some sentences have compound verbs. Write the complete verb or verbs for each sentence in the blank.

EXAMPLE
The applicant may send in a résumé with the letter of application.

_____ *may send in* _____

1. Sometimes the résumé is taken to the interview rather than mailed in ahead

   of time. _____

2. A résumé explains in outline form the applicant's education, skills, and job

   experience. _____

3. A résumé is usually confined to one or two pages. _____

   _____

4. The name, address, and telephone number of the applicant normally lead

   off the résumé. _____

5. The educational record and employment background of the applicant,

   as well as certain other information—activities, honors—make up the body

   of the résumé. _____

   _____

6. The résumé also lists three to five references. _____

   _____

7. These references should know about the applicant's qualifications for the

   job. _____

8. Have you ever written a résumé? _____

   _____

9. A résumé should be filled out and read over carefully by the applicant.

   _____

10. Most applicants type their résumés and make additional copies to use in the

    future. _____

Forms of Verbs   Exercise 1–5

NAME _____ SCORE _____

DIRECTIONS   In each of the following sentences, one verb has been omitted. Fill in the blank with the present tense (present time) of the verb written in parentheses after the sentence. If you think that the subject, which is printed in italics, is plural, or more than one, then drop the s ending from the verb or change the form to *are*.

EXAMPLES

Most college *courses* ___*present*___ more theory than practice.   (pre-

sented)

The *practice* ___*comes*___ with the job.   (came)

1. *People* _____ their work in different ways.   (saw)

2. Some *people* _____ their careers are the most important

   part of their lives.   (thought)

3. Other *people* _____ their families are more important than

   their jobs.   (felt)

4. Many *arguments* _____ over the importance of work.

   (occurred)

5. "Idle *hands* _____ the devil's workshop" is a familiar say-

   ing.   (was)

6. Another well-known *expression* _____ "All work and no

   play makes Jack a dull boy."   (was)

7. *One person* _____ that work is a person's reason for

   being.   (said)

8. Another *person* _____ that work is something a person does

   to make enough money to do the important things in life.   (claimed)

9. The *importance* of work _____ on the individual's values.

(depended)

10. Still, most *people* _____ many hours a day at work.

(spent)

11. *Workaholics* _____ it difficult to quit working.   (found)

12. The *workaholic* _____ on at the office long after the end of

the eight-hour day.   (stayed)

13. Such a *person* rarely _____ a vacation.   (enjoyed)

14. The workaholic's *characteristics* _____ inability to accept

failure, guilt about level of productivity, and almost constant worry about

performance.   (included)

15. For the workaholic, all *relationships* and leisure *activities*

_____ unimportant when measured against success at

work.   (became)

16. There _____ more *workaholics* than most of us realize.

(was)

17. Most *workaholics* _____ before they reach retirement age.

(died)

18. *Heart attacks* among workaholics _____ extremely com-

mon.   (was)

19. Of course, for every one workaholic there _____ at least

one hundred lazy and incompetent *workers*.   (was)

20. Most *people* in the work force, however, _____ somewhere

between the two extremes.   (fell)

Verbals Like verbs, verbals express action, occurrence, or a state of being. And they have endings—*ing, ed,* and *en*—that are the same endings verbs may have. Here, for example, are four verbal forms for the verb *take:*

> *taking, taken, having taken, to take*

(Notice that *taking* and *taken,* when accompanied by helping verbs, are true verbs: *are taking* and *have taken,* for example.)

Finally, like verbs, verbals are often followed by words that complete their meaning.

> *Taking* my **time,** I found just the job I wanted.   [Taking what? *Time* completes the meaning of the verbal.]
> *Having taken* a vocational aptitude **test,** I was better able *to plan* a **career.**   [Having taken what? *Test* completes the meaning of the first verbal. To plan what? *Career* completes the meaning of the second verbal.]

But in spite of its similarities to a true verb, a verbal cannot serve as the verb of a sentence. Consider, for example, this sentence with its verb *have taken.*

> We have taken our time.

Notice that when a verbal replaces the verb, the word group is no longer a sentence. (See also **2a.**)

> we *taking* our time
> we *having taken* our time
> we *to take* our time

Thus whenever there is a verbal (or verbals) in a sentence, there must also be a main, or true, verb.

> *Taking* our time, we filled out the application carefully.

> *Having taken* our time, we answered each question completely.

> *To take* our time we carried our applications home *to fill out.*

Recognizing Verbs and Verbals   Exercise 1–6

NAME _____ SCORE _____

DIRECTIONS   Here are ten famous quotations about work. The verbals have been printed in italics. Find the true verbs and underline them twice. In the first blank, write the verbal or verbals; in the second, write the verb or verbs.

EXAMPLE
I go on *working* for the same reason that a hen goes on *laying* eggs.

—H. L. MENCKEN

working, laying   *go on, goes on*

1. *Working* with people is difficult, but not impossible.   —PETER DRUCKER

   _____   _____

2. We work *to become*, not *to acquire*.   —ELBERT HUBBARD

   _____   _____

3. Work expands so as *to fill* the time available for its completion.

   —NORTHCOTE PARKINSON

   _____   _____

4. Anyone can do any amount of work *provided* it isn't the work he is

   supposed *to be doing* at that moment.   —ROBERT BENCHLEY

   _____   _____

5. No man is obliged *to do* as much as he can do; a man is *to have* part of his

   life to himself. —SAMUEL JOHNSON

   _____   _____

6. Many men are hard workers: they're [they are] always looking around *to*

   find something for others *to do.* —EVAN ESAR

   _____   _____

7. Next to *doing* a good job yourself the greatest joy is in *having* someone else

   do a first-class job under your direction. —WILLIAM FEATHER

   _____   _____

8. All the best work is done the way ants do things—by tiny but *untiring* and

   regular additions. —LAFCADIO HEARN

   _____   _____

9. A great many people have . . . asked how I manage *to get* so much work

   done and still keep *looking* so *dissipated.* —ROBERT BENCHLEY

   _____   _____

10. If there is one thing better than the thrill of *looking* forward, it is the ex-

    hilaration that follows the *finishing* of a long and *exacting* piece of

    work. —ALEC WAUGH

    _____   _____

1b Learn to recognize subjects and objects of verbs.

1b(1) Learn to recognize subjects of verbs.

A sentence that has a verb but no stated subject is a command. In a command the subject is understood to be *you*, though it is not actually written down.

[You] <u>Fill out</u> the application form and <u>return</u> it to the personnel director.

In all other kinds of sentences, the subject is written down, even in the shortest of sentences.

<u>I quit!</u>

Function   The subject is what (or whom) the sentence is about. Once you have located the verb in a sentence, all you need to do then is to ask who or what is *doing, occurring,* or *being*. Your answer will be the complete subject. To find the simple subject, ask specifically who or what the verb is talking about.

Many important <u>values</u> <u>are derived</u> from work.   [What are derived? Many impor-

tant values. What specifically are derived? Not "many important" but *values.*]

<u>One</u> of my friends <u>desires</u> a high income more than anything else.   [Who de-

sires? One of my friends. Who specifically desires? Not "of my friends," but *one.*]

It is important to be able to find the simple subject in a sentence so that you can make the number of the verb and the subject the same. If you mistake "friends" as the subject of the last example above, you will probably make the verb plural—"desire"—and thus make an error in agreement because the simple subject is *one* and the verb must be singular (*desires*) to agree with it in number. (See also Section **6.**)

Compound Subjects   Like the verb, the subject of a sentence may be compound. The parts of the compound subject are connected by a word like *and, but, or,* or *nor* (printed in boldface below).

Income, recognition, **and** *adventure* are three goals sought by workers.
Not *income* **but** *adventure* is my main concern now.

Noun Subjects   A majority of simple subjects are nouns, words that name persons, places, things, and ideas. Since people first appeared on the earth, they have been interested in nouns. We are told that the first job Adam had was to name the things he saw in the Garden of Eden: *sky, bird, flower, tree, apple, snake.* (Adam's name, of course, was a noun, too, as was the name of Eve.)

Modern people are still giving names to things. As soon as something new comes along, we rush to give it a name: *Skylab, astronaut, détente, rock and roll, Amtrak.*

Types of Nouns   Proper nouns begin with capital letters and name particular people, places, things, and ideas: *Columbus, New World, Mayflower, Thanksgiving, Declaration of Independence.* Common nouns are not capitalized; they are everyday names for general classes of people, places, things, and ideas: *explorer, continent, ship, holiday, capitalism.* Both common and proper nouns are often made up of more than one word: *home town, mother-in-law, oil well, Holy City, Bill of Rights.*

Many nouns name things that can be touched; these are called concrete nouns; *contract, report, insurance, corporation.* Other nouns refer to matters that cannot be touched; these are called abstract nouns: *praise, safety, satisfaction, plan, hostility.*

As you can see, we need nouns to say almost anything, even to speak a nonsense sentence like "*Peter Piper* picked a *peck* of pickled *peppers.*"

Noun Signals   Certain words signal that a noun is coming. Articles (*a, an, the*) and possessive pronouns (*my, your, his, her, its, our,* and *their*) are followed by nouns.

The *supervisor* gave us **a** *copy* of **our** latest *reports.*

Form   Nouns change their endings to show two things: plural number and possession. When we name more than one of anything, we usually add an *s* or *es* to show that the noun is plural. (Remember that verbs act in just the opposite way: an *s* or *es* ending means that the verb is singular.)

I wrote one report; Ethan wrote two report*s.*
I read one memo; Ethan read two memo*s.*
I hired one woman; Ethan hired two wom*en.*
I have one brother-in-law; Ethan has two brother*s*-in-law.   [Note that the chief word, *brother*, shows the sign of the plural.]

The dictionary shows you the plural for all nouns that form their plurals in some way other than the addition of *s* (for example, *man* → *men.*)

Singular nouns add an apostrophe and an *s* ('*s*) to show possession, or ownership: *Ethan's job* or *Ethan's house* (we do not write *Ethan house* or *Ethan job*). The possessive noun is placed in front of the person, place, thing, or idea possessed.

If the possessive noun is plural, we usually add only the apostrophe:

jobs' requirements	teachers' salaries	guests' arrival
potatoes' roots	cities' problems	wolves' howling

But if the plural of the noun does not end in *s* (*women, children,* and *alumni,* for example), we add '*s* to form the plural possessive:

women's rights	children's absences	alumni's contributions

When a compound noun is made possessive, the last word shows the sign of the possessive case:

sons-in-law's jobs   the King of England's biography

Note: When we give a noun the possessive form, whether singular or plural, we change it to a modifier, a descriptive or qualifying word. (You will study modifiers in **1d.**)

Recognizing Nouns

NAME _____ SCORE _____

DIRECTIONS   Use *a*, *an*, and *the* to decide which of the following words are nouns: if a word sounds right with *a*, *an*, or *the* in front of it, write its plural form in the blank. If it does not, the word is not a noun; in that case, leave the blank empty. (If you are uncertain how to make the plural of the noun, consult your dictionary. When no plural form is given, the noun forms its plural in the usual way—by adding an *s* or *es*. See also **18f**.)

EXAMPLES
joke   *jokes*

upon   _____

1. boy   _____
2. happy   _____
3. on   _____
4. book   _____
5. light   _____
6. time   _____
7. with   _____
8. slowly   _____
9. reason   _____
10. hobby   _____
11. some   _____
12. object   _____
13. man   _____

14. tomato   _____
15. dollar   _____
16. believe   _____
17. belief   _____
18. territory   _____
19. rank   _____
20. such   _____
21. loss   _____
22. sister-
     in-law   _____
23. shelf   _____
24. cupful   _____
25. big   _____

DIRECTIONS Use a possessive pronoun—*our*, for example—to decide which of the following words are nouns. If a word sounds right with *our* in front of it, write its plural in the blank. If it does not sound right with *our* in front of it, leave the blank empty because the word is not a noun. Use your dictionary to help you form the plurals of nouns that do not follow the usual pattern of adding *s* or *es*.

1. radio _____

2. receive _____

3. porch _____

4. crisis _____

5. industry _____

6. fulfill _____

7. bus _____

8. carefully _____

9. mosquito _____

10. ox _____

11. cloth _____

12. artist-in-

 residence _____

13. separate _____

14. strategy _____

15. until _____

16. them _____

17. mother-

 in-law _____

18. tendency _____

19. cargo _____

20. valley _____

21. decide _____

22. church _____

23. monkey _____

24. excellent _____

25. joy _____

Making Nouns Possessive

NAME _____   SCORE _____

DIRECTIONS   Rewrite each of the following word groups so that the second noun is placed in front of the first one. Give the possessive form to the noun you placed first. (Remember that by making the noun possessive, you change it to a modifier.)

EXAMPLES
goals of a person   _*a person's goals*_

benefits of jobs   _*jobs' benefits*_

1. the complaint of a customer   _____

2. interests of an applicant   _____

3. reports of experts   _____

4. stock owned by investors   _____

5. location of a company   _____

6. training of the workers   _____

7. addresses of employers   _____

8. locations of the cities   _____

9. office of the personnel director   _____

10. demands of the labor union   _____

11. opinions held by people   _____

12. experiment of the scientist   _____

13. choices made by the employer   _____

14. facilities belonging to IBM   _____

15. raise given to the employee   _____

16. word processor of the writer   _____

17. results of the market survey   _____

18. work of the cooks   _____

19. concern of laboratory

    technologists   _____

20. evaluation of the committee   _____

21. plan of the developer   _____

22. reports of the agriculture

    commissioner   _____

23. discussions of the employees   _____

24. jobs of the sons-in-law   _____

25. merger of the two firms   _____

Recognizing Simple Subjects

NAME _____ SCORE _____

DIRECTIONS   The complete subject in each of the following sentences is italicized. Find the simple subject that tells specifically who or what the verb (underlined twice) is speaking about. Underline the simple subject with one line and write it in the blank. (Remember that a simple subject may be compound.)

EXAMPLES

A *scowling applicant* slouched into the office.   *applicant*

The applicant's résumé, with its many typographical

errors, was difficult to read.   *résumé*

1. *The applicant's faded jeans* were not appropriate

   dress for an interview.   _____

2. *Neither the application nor the résumé* was neat.   _____

3. *The applicant's lack of preparation for the inter-*

   view did not favorably impress the personnel di-

   rector.   _____

4. *The job applicant's answers to the questions asked*

   by the personnel director were vague and halting.   _____

5. *The main requirements for the job that the appli-*

   cant sought were neatness and self-confidence.   _____

6. *The interview with the personnel director* did not

   last long.   _____

7. Needless to say, *this inappropriately dressed and*

   poorly prepared applicant did not get the job.   _____

8. *The decision about who is hired for a given job*

   often depends on small details.   _____

9. *Many well-qualified people* <u>may apply</u> for a job. _____

10. *The person who really wants a job* <u>must prepare</u> carefully for the interview. _____

11. *Various procedures for preparing for an interview* <u>may be</u> helpful. _____

12. *One thing that the applicant might do* <u>is</u> to write out an autobiography. _____

13. *The details recorded in the autobiography* usually <u>furnish</u> answers to questions one may be asked. _____

14. *The interests and abilities of the applicant* <u>come out</u> in the autobiography. _____

15. *These two important areas* <u>are</u> usually <u>covered</u> during an interview. _____

16. *Another way to prepare for an interview* <u>is</u> to make a list of questions the interviewer might ask. _____

17. *The time spent in thinking through answers to these questions* <u>is</u> always worthwhile. _____

18. *Some especially well-prepared applicants* <u>have</u> actually <u>staged</u> mock interviews. _____

19. *The self-confidence and fluency gained by careful preparation* <u>help</u> any applicant. _____

20. *A neatly filled-out application, a carefully typed résumé, and a businesslike appearance* <u>are</u> three decided assets for any job applicant. _____

Mastering Noun Subjects and Verbs　　　Exercise 1–10

NAME _____　SCORE _____

DIRECTIONS　Rewrite the subject and verb parts of the following sentences, changing the simple subjects and verbs from singular to plural. Underline the plural subjects with one line and the plural verbs with two lines.

EXAMPLE

A person trains for a job in various ways.

People (or Persons) train for

1. A student learns skills (for example, typing and bookkeeping) through high-school and college courses.

2. A course sometimes requires outside work in the field of the student's intended occupation.

3. For example, a would-be teacher does student teaching during the last year of college.

4. A prospective air-conditioning mechanic also serves an apprenticeship.

5. The experience in the field helps the trainee to understand the occupation.

6. Sometimes a trainee decides to change careers on the basis of experience in the field.

7. But often an apprenticeship persuades a trainee to continue with his or her chosen career.

8. A summer job gives the student further training in a specialized occupation.

9. A summer position often pays little or nothing at all, but gives valuable experience.

10. Hence the trainee is rewarded in many ways.

Pronoun Subjects   The other common type of simple subject besides the noun is the pronoun. The use of pronouns avoids the unpleasant repetition of nouns and adds variety to your sentences. Pronouns help you avoid repetitious sentences such as

> The *manager* reads *reports.*
> The *manager* evaluates the information the *reports* provide.
> The *manager* bases the *manager's* decisions on the *report's* recommendations.

Clearly, our discussion of decision making would have been much improved if we had used pronouns—words that substitute for nouns.

> The *manager* reads *reports.*
> *She* evaluates information *they* provide.
> *She* bases *her* decisions on *their* recommendations.

Function   Pronouns take the place of nouns. The meaning of a pronoun is clear only when the reader is sure what noun is being referred to.

> NOUNS   All graduating *seniors* must take a one-hour *course* in "How to Get a Job."
>
> PRONOUNS   *They* must take *it* so that *they* will be prepared for job interviews.   [*They* refers to *seniors; it* refers to *course.*]

Types of Pronouns   Unlike the almost limitless number of nouns, there are only a certain number of pronouns. The most frequently used ones are called personal pronouns: *I, me, you, he, him, she, her, it, we, us, they,* and *them.* As their name indicates, these pronouns refer to people or to living things.

Other pronouns refer only to things: *something, nothing, everything,* and *which,* for example. A few pronouns can refer to either persons or to things: *one, each, most, some, many, all, both,* and *that.*

A few important pronouns that you will study in depth later—*who, whom, which, that, what, whose, whoever,* and *whomever*—help to expand sentences. These pronouns sometimes serve as the subjects of their own word clusters; and they, too, take their meaning from the nouns that they refer to.

> The students *who* take this course are well prepared for their job interviews.   [*Who* is the subject of the verb *take;* it refers to the noun *students.*]
> This course, *which* is offered several times a semester, is invaluable to students. [*Which* is the subject of the verb *is offered;* it refers to the noun *course.*]

These same pronouns may be used to ask questions—and are called interrogative pronouns when they are so used (in which case they need not always refer to particular nouns).

> *Who* is your supervisor?
> *What* is your job?

Form   Unlike nouns, pronouns do not form their plural by adding *s* or *es.* Instead, *I* becomes *we; he, she,* and *it* become *they.* One personal pro-

33

noun—*you*—does not change form at all to show plural number. Other pronouns can only be singular: for example, *each* and *one;* still others can only be plural: for example, *both* and *many.*

A few pronouns, like nouns, form their possessive by adding an 's: someone's hat, everyone's concern, anyone's hope. All personal pronouns, however, have a distinct form for the possessive case: *my, mine; your, yours; his; her, hers; its; our, ours;* and *their, theirs.* And personal pronouns, unlike nouns, change their form to show whether they are being used as subjects or as objects of verbs (receivers of the action of the verb).

SUBJECT   *He* lent James five dollars for lunch.

OBJECT   James gave *him* his money back the next day.

Pronouns as Replacements for Nouns   Exercise 1–11

NAME _____ SCORE _____

DIRECTIONS   The following paragraph, adapted from Studs Terkel's *Working*, shows how repetitious our writing would be without pronouns. Above each underlined noun subject (which is sometimes accompanied by a modifier) write a pronoun that fits smoothly into the sentence.

As a child Vincent Maher dreamed of being a policeman. Vincent Maher

tried other jobs, but other jobs did not satisfy him. Vincent Maher was cut out

to be a policeman, and Vincent Maher finally became one. Police work totally

satisfied him. Police work made him feel necessary to people even though

people often ridiculed him. People called him a bigot and a hypocrite, but

Maher saw himself only as a human being with a job to do. Vincent Maher

tried not to judge people as superficially as people judged him. Maher preferred

to work in poor neighborhoods because the people there especially needed him.

In white middle-class neighborhoods Maher was expected to write parking

tickets and scold people when their dogs defecated on the grass. Maher did not

become a policeman to do this kind of work. All his life Maher worked com-

pulsively, both during and after hours, to become a detective. But being a

detective was a goal he never achieved.

Recognizing Pronoun Subjects

NAME _____ SCORE _____

DIRECTIONS   The verbs in the following sentences have been underlined twice. Underline all subjects with one line, and write the pronoun subjects in the blanks. Most sentences have more than one subject.

EXAMPLE
The jobs that require writing skills are many.   *that*

1. Who needs writing skills?   _____

2. Virtually everyone must do some writing.   _____

3. You and I will probably have desk jobs.   _____

4. That means writing reports, letters, and memos.   _____

5. Some careers that are very different from so-called desk

   jobs also require writing skills.   _____

6. An electrician, who may spend the night working on

   power lines broken during a storm, must fill out a re-

   port at the end of the job.   _____

7. Hardly anyone today escapes the job of writing.   _____

8. My friend, who is a park ranger, has published more

   books than I have as a textbook author.   _____

9. As often as not, the writing skills determine who gets a

   particular job.   _____

10. On the job, someone is often promoted on the basis of

    ability to handle paperwork effectively.   _____

Mastering Subjects: A Review   Exercise 1–13

NAME _____ SCORE _____

DIRECTIONS   All verbs in the following sentences are underlined twice. You are to underline once the noun or pronoun subjects that tell who or what is doing, occurring, or being. Then write the subject in the first blank and the verb in the second blank. (Remember that a sentence may have a compound subject and/or verb.)

EXAMPLE
Studs Terkel's *Working* was a best seller in the early 1970s.

_____*Working*_____   _____*was*_____

1. Terkel's book gives us a different way of looking at life in the twentieth

century.   _____   _____

2. This book shows people's attitudes toward their jobs.

_____   _____

3. The people interviewed by Terkel speak honestly and straightforwardly

about their jobs. _____   _____

4. Everyone interviewed by Terkel has strong feelings about his or her work.

_____   _____

5. Some of the workers feel fulfillment in their jobs.

_____   _____

6. Others simply endure their jobs in order to live.

_____   _____

7. Terkel interviewed all kinds of people.

_____   _____

8. Both blue-collar and white-collar workers speak out in Terkel's book.

_____   _____

9. Even a prostitute <u>has</u> her say in *Working*.

   _____   _____

10. Terkel's interviewees <u>are</u> all <u>searching</u> for meaning in life.

    _____   _____

11. They <u>want</u> to be remembered for something.

    _____   _____

12. Some <u>find</u> a kind of immortality through their work.

    _____   _____

13. Many, though, simply <u>survive</u> their workdays.

    _____   _____

14. There <u>are</u> more unhappy workers than happy workers.

    _____   _____

15. <u>Does</u> this fact <u>surprise</u> you?

    _____   _____

16. Or <u>are</u> you also pessimistic about satisfaction being provided by work?

    _____   _____

17. The unhappy workers in Terkel's book <u>view</u> themselves as machines or ob-

    jects.   _____   _____

18. Usually <u>included</u> in their descriptions of their roles <u>is</u> the word *robot*.

    _____   _____

19. A few of the workers <u>take</u> pride in their jobs.

    _____   _____

20. A bookbinder and a fireman both <u>speak</u> of the satisfaction of saving some-

    thing.   _____   _____

Mastering Subjects and Verbs: A Review   Exercise 1–14

NAME _____ SCORE _____

DIRECTIONS   Underline the verbs with two lines, the noun or pronoun subjects with one line. (Remember to look first for the verbs in the sentences.) Then write the subject in the first blank and the verb in the second.

EXAMPLE
Our country is supposedly built on the work ethic.

_____*country*_____   _____*is built*_____

1. Even children in grade school learn the value of competition.

_____   _____

2. Their teachers often reward good behavior with candy or other treats.

_____   _____

3. We have rarely questioned the ideal of hard work.

_____   _____

4. Today, however, some people are questioning the importance of work.

_____   _____

5. Is it impossible for a person to find fulfillment outside of work?

_____   _____

6. Workers express dissatisfaction with their jobs in many ways.

_____   _____

7. Putting little care into the product is one way to show dissatisfaction.

_____   _____

8. Another is to make fun of workers' pride in their craftsmanship.

_____   _____

9. Soon quantity becomes more important to workers than quality.

_____   _____

10. Not all symptoms of workers' dissatisfaction show up in the products themselves. _____   _____

11. Excessive absenteeism and tension often result from workers' unhappiness with their jobs. _____   _____

12. Managers, too, are evaluating their jobs and are finding them unrewarding. _____   _____

13. But is it necessary for people to dislike their jobs?

    _____   _____

14. Perhaps this problem helps to illustrate the difference between a *job* and a *career*. _____   _____

15. A *job* would be something merely to put money in the bank.

    _____   _____

16. A *career* can, on the other hand, become a part of a person's main interest in life. _____   _____

17. Should American workers rededicate themselves to finding satisfaction in their work? _____   _____

18. No one can answer these important questions for someone else.

    _____   _____

19. However, there are good reasons for thinking about these issues.

    _____   _____

20. Knowing why we work may help us to improve the working environment.

    _____   _____

To find the object or objects of verbs, use the subject and verb in a question end-ing with *whom* or *what*.

1b(2) Ask the subject and verb "who?" "whom?" or "what?" to find the objects of a sentence.

If a sentence provides an answer when you follow the subject and verb with *whom* or *what*, the sentence has an object or objects.

NO OBJECT   Our workday ends at 4:30. [Workday ends whom or what? There is

no answer in the sentence. The words that follow the verb answer a dif-

ferent question—"when?"]

OBJECT   Our schedule gives us a head start on the afternoon traffic. [Our

schedule gives whom? *Us.* Gives us what? A *head start.*]

Objects   Transitive verbs transfer or pass their action along to an object or objects. Some verbs such as *give, buy, send, call, consider,* or *find* may have a direct or an indirect object.

OBJECT   My supervisor, Mr. Tom McMahon, manages twenty employees in our

laboratory. [The object, *employees*, shows whom the verb, *manages*, is

acting upon. It is called the direct object.]

OBJECTS   He gives us careful instructions for each experiment. [The first object,

us, is the indirect object. The second object, *instructions*, is the direct ob-

ject. An indirect object shows *to* or *for* whom (or what) the action is done.]

Often you must be able to pick out the exact object or objects in the sentence to avoid mistakes in the form of the pronoun or the modifier. (See also Sections **4** and **5.**)

Basic Formula   Now you have the basic formula for a sentence:

SUBJECT–VERB–(and usually) OBJECT(s).

A sentence that has only these three parts, and usually a modifier or two, is short and direct. Often it has no punctuation marks other than the final end mark (period, question mark, or exclamation point), which indicates that the sentence is finished. In technical and business writing many of your sentences will include no more than the basic formula and a modifier or two because you will be more interested in making your writing clear to your reader than in anything else.

1c Learn to recognize the parts of speech.

Now that you have learned about the basic structure of a sentence, you are ready to begin working with all of the elements that combine to give a sentence its meaning. The following chart lists the various functions words can perform in a sentence and the types of words that perform each function.

Function	Kinds of Words
Naming	Nouns and Pronouns
Predicating (stating or asserting)	Verbs
Modifying	Adjectives and Adverbs
Connecting	Prepositions and Conjunctions

The next chart summarizes the parts of speech that you will study in detail in the rest of this section (except for interjections).

Part of Speech	Uses in Sentences	Examples
1. Verbs	Indicators of action, occurrence, or state of being	Tom *wrote* the report. Mary *evaluated* the stocks. They *are* executives.
2. Nouns	Subjects and objects	*Kay* gave *Ron* the *list* of *clients*.
3. Pronouns	Substitutes for nouns	*He* will return *it* to *her* later.
4. Adjectives	Modifiers of nouns and pronouns	The *detailed* prospectus is the *convincing* one.
5. Adverbs	Modifiers of verbs, adjectives, other adverbs, or whole clauses	presented *clearly* a *very* interesting study *entirely* too long *Indeed*, we are ready.

Parts of Speech	Uses in Sentences	Examples
6. Prepositions	Words used before nouns and pronouns to relate them to other words in the sentence	*in* a hurry *with* no thought *to* them
7. Conjunctions	Connectors of words, phrases, or clauses; may be either coordinating or subordinating	reinvest *or* sell before the meeting *and* after it *since* the sale of the stock
8. Interjections	Expressions of emotion (unrelated grammatically to the rest of the sentence)	*Good grief!* *Ouch!* *Well,* we tried.

1d Learn to recognize phrases and subordinate clauses.

You are already familiar with a group of words that may function as the verb of a sentence—the verb phrase (*will be writing*) and the verb with a particle (*put up with*). Other word groups may function as the subject or object (**1d(1)** below) or as modifiers (**1d(2)**).

1d(1) Learn to recognize phrases and subordinate clauses used as subjects and objects.

SUBJECT *Keeping a careful record of expenses* was a part of our job.

OBJECT We decided *to keep a log of our daily expenditures.*

SUBJECT AND *Whoever examined our log* could find *what we had spent our money*
OBJECT *for each day.*

The main types of word groups that function as subjects and as objects are verbal phrases and noun clauses.

Verbal Phrases   A phrase is a series of related words (words grouped together) that lacks either a subject or a verb or both. The verbal phrase is the kind that most frequently functions as a subject or object. The main part of the verbal phrase is the verbal itself—a word that shows action, occurrence, or a state of being as a verb does but that cannot function as the verb of a sentence (see page 17). You may remember from your study of verbs and verbals in

1b(1) that verbals usually end in *ing, ed, en,* or are preceded by *to.* The verbal, along with the other words in the phrase, can function as a subject or an object, just as an individual noun or pronoun can.

NOUN   *Machines* have eliminated many jobs.   [subject]

VERBAL PHRASE   *Using machines in the place of workers* has eliminated many jobs.   [subject]

NOUN   Machinery has increased the *efficiency* of many jobs.   [direct object]

VERBAL PHRASE   Machinery helps *to increase the efficiency of many jobs.*   [direct object]

Noun Clauses   A clause is a series of related words (words grouped together) that has both a subject and a verb. One kind of clause, referred to as a main clause or independent clause, can stand alone as a sentence. The other, called a subordinate clause or dependent clause, may function as a noun—either a subject or object—or as a modifier in a sentence. (**1d(2)** discusses the use of phrases and subordinate clauses as modifiers. In fact, they are more commonly used as modifiers than as subjects or objects.) As nouns, subordinate clauses usually are introduced by one of these words: *who, whom, whose, which, that, whoever, whomever, what, whether, how, why,* or *where.* These introductory words are clause markers; they are printed in boldface in the following examples.

NOUN   An *applicant* must fill out an application.   [subject]

NOUN CLAUSE   ***Whoever** wants a job* must fill out an application.   [subject]

NOUN   Applicants' responses to the questions often show their *skills* as writers.   [direct object]

NOUN CLAUSE   Applicants' responses to the questions often show ***whether** they can write well or not.*   [direct object]

                        OR

                        Applicants' responses to the questions often show *how well they can write.*   [direct object]

**Recognizing Phrases and Clauses
Used as Subjects and Objects** Exercise 1–17

NAME _____ SCORE _____

DIRECTIONS In the first of each of the following pairs of sentences, the complete subject is underlined once or the complete object is underlined three times. In the second sentence of each pair, underline once the clause or phrase that functions as the subject or underline three times the clause or phrase that functions as the object. Then in the blank identify the phrase or clause with a **P** or **C.**

EXAMPLE

Future growth is important when one plans a career.

Knowing future growth possibilities is important when one plans a career.

P

1. For the next decade, some corporations project fewer employees.

   For the next decade, some corporations project that they will employ fewer people. _____

2. An exact forecast for a specific occupation is difficult.

   Forecasting exactly the employment opportunities for a specific occupation is difficult. _____

3. Changes in national policy determine the future growth of certain areas of employment.

   Changes in national policy determine whether certain areas of employment will grow. _____

4. For example, the government might decide that a new area of scientific research should be sponsored.

   For example, the government might decide to sponsor a new area of scientific research. _____

5. The new government-sponsored program would increase the demand for scientists and laboratory personnel.

   The government's sponsoring of a new program of research would increase the demand for scientists and laboratory personnel. _____

6. Predictions about employment are based on certain assumptions.

   Predicting employment is based on certain assumptions. _____

7. We must assume a peacetime economy.

   We must assume that the country will not be involved in a major war. _____

8. The changes caused by a war no one could accurately predict.

   What would happen as a result of war no one could accurately predict.

   _____

9. Stability in other respects is also a basic assumption.

   That the economy will remain stable in other respects is also a basic assumption. _____

10. People's basic attitudes toward work, education, income, and leisure must remain unchanged.

    That people's attitudes toward work, education, income, and leisure will not change is another basic assumption. _____

1d(2) Learn to recognize words, phrases, and subordinate clauses used as modifiers.

A modifier is a word or word group that describes, limits, or qualifies another, thus expanding the meaning of the sentence. A sentence made up only of the two main parts (the basic pattern of subject + predicate) is always short and direct, but it may lack the information necessary to be entirely clear, as the following sentence illustrates:

The applicant had qualifications.

Almost any reader would want to know what applicant and qualifications for what. The basic formula is not very satisfying in this example. The addition of modifiers makes the sentence more exact in meaning.

The applicant *from Calabash, Michigan,* had the *best* qualifications *for the job.*

The first addition (*from Calabash, Michigan,*) makes the subject (*applicant*) more exact; the second and third additions (*best* and *for the job*) make the direct object (*qualifications*) more exact.

Modifiers added to the basic formula may be words, phrases, or clauses. Often you can combine two choppy sentences into a single, more effective sentence by making the essential information in one an added modifier in the other.

TWO SENTENCES | The report was poorly written. It was rejected by the manager.

COMBINED | The *poorly written* report was rejected by the manager.

TWO SENTENCES | The report contained several noticeable errors in grammar and spelling. It probably had not been proofread carefully by the writer.

COMBINED | *Since it contained several errors in grammar and spelling,* the report probably had not been proofread by the writer.

THREE SENTENCES | The manager examined the first page of the report. He did not bother to read any further. The report did not represent careful work on the part of the writer.

COMBINED | *After the manager had examined the first page of the report,* he did not bother to read any further *because it did not represent careful work on the part of the writer.*

Single Words as Modifiers Nearly all sentences have one or more articles—*a, an,* and *the*—which modify nouns or elements functioning as nouns. In addition to *a, an,* and *the,* most sentences contain other words that modify various elements.

A *large* increase in employment is expected in the field of landscape architecture. [*Large* modifies *increase.*]

The increase is *largely* due to the *continued* interest in *city* and *regional environ-mental* planning. [*Largely* modifies *due; continued* modifies *interest; city, regional,* and *environmental* modify *planning.*]

Punctuation   Single-word modifiers are punctuated only if they are placed in an unusual position in the sentence or if they modify the whole sentence.

Attractive, the grounds for the building contribute to a happy work environment. [usual position; *the attractive grounds*]
Surprisingly, no employee objects to the long walk through the trees to enter the building. [*Surprisingly* modifies the whole sentence.]

Two modifiers in succession are usually punctuated when there is no *and* between them if *and* is understood. Where no *and* would fit, no comma is used.

The *large, well-landscaped* grounds surrounding the building make the work environment pleasant. [You could say "large and well-landscaped grounds."]
Beautiful flower gardens are also nearby. [You would not say "beautiful and flower gardens"; *beautiful* modifies *flower gardens,* not just *gardens.*]
Both large and *small* plants line the street curving up to the building. [You would not say "both and large plants."]

(See also **12c.**)

Using Word Modifiers Exercise 1–18

NAME _____ SCORE _____

DIRECTIONS   In each blank write the required modifier or modifiers that fit smoothly into the sentence. Punctuate with commas where necessary. After each sentence explain the reason for punctuating or not punctuating each modifier you have added.

EXAMPLE
A modifier describing the physical condition of the boy

Exhausted _____, the boy collapsed into a chair in the living room.

Reason: _Modifier is out of its usual position—"the exhausted boy."_

1. Two modifiers describing *day*

   The _____ _____ first day on the job was

   ended. Reason:

2. A modifier of the entire sentence

   _____ he looked forward to the next day. Reason:

3. Two modifiers describing *work*

   The work _____ and _____ was never-

   theless interesting. Reason:

4. A modifier describing *day*

   And this _____ day had shown him a great deal about

   himself. Reason:

5. Two modifiers describing *person*

   He was not a _____ _____ person. Reason:

6. Two modifiers describing *body*

   And his body _____ and _____ proved his

   lack of conditioning. Reason:

7. A modifier of the entire sentence

   _____ he needed to begin a daily exercise program.

   Reason:

8. A modifier of *hours*

   His body would require _____ hours of sleep each night.

   Reason:

9. A modifier of *needed* and a modifier of *breakfast*

   He also _____ needed to eat a _____

   breakfast each morning. Reason:

10. A modifier of the entire sentence and a modifier of *shoes*

    _____ he would have to buy a pair of _____

    shoes. Reason:

Phrases as Modifiers Three types of phrases are commonly added as modifiers: appositives, prepositional phrases, and verbal phrases.

Appositives An appositive is a word or phrase that identifies or explains in some way the noun or pronoun it is placed next to. Usually the appositive follows the noun or pronoun it identifies or explains. Appositives are set off by commas—or sometimes by dashes or a colon (see Section **17**)—except on the few occasions when they are essential to the meaning of the noun or pronoun they refer to (see **12d**).

> *Working, a book by Studs Terkel,* was on the *New York Times* best-seller list for many weeks.   [The appositive explains what *Working* is.]
>
> Mr. Jones, *the career counselor,* urges students to read *Working* before they choose their career.   [The appositive explains who Mr. Jones is.]

The appositive allows the writer to combine ideas that would otherwise be stated in two sentences.

TWO SENTENCES   *Working* is a book by Studs Terkel. It was on the best-seller list for many weeks.

APPOSITIVE ADDITION   *Working, a book by Studs Terkel,* was on the best-seller list for many weeks.

Prepositional Phrases The prepositional phrase is the most frequent type of phrase modifier added to the sentence. It begins with a preposition—a word like *in, on, between,* or *to*—and ends with a noun, a pronoun, or an *ing* verbal: *in* the report, *on* the desk, *between* the machines, *to* everyone, *without* our knowing.

A prepositional phrase used to modify one word within a sentence is usually not punctuated. But a prepositional phrase that modifies the entire sentence is usually set off by a comma or commas (the comma may be omitted after a prepositional phrase that begins a sentence if no misreading would result).

MODIFIER OF NOUN   We examined the manual *of operation.*

MODIFIER OF VERB   We studied the manual *for several minutes.*

MODIFIER OF SENTENCE   We studied, *in fact,* every instruction and drawing carefully.

MODIFIER OF SENTENCE   The illustrations, *in addition to the words,* are important in a manual of operation.

MODIFIER OF SENTENCE   *In an operation manual* the main sections always have headings.   [Introductory prepositional phrase; no possible misreading.]

Verbal Phrases   A verbal phrase includes a verbal (see page 17) and the other words related to it—usually a modifier or modifiers and an object.

> *Applauding the speaker enthusiastically*, the audience rose to their feet.   [The verbal, *applauding*, is followed by an object, *speaker*, and a modifier, *enthusiastically*.]

> *To show their appreciation*, the audience remained standing until the speaker had left the platform.   [The verbal, *to show*, is followed by an object, *appreciation*, and a modifer, *their*].

Adding a verbal phrase allows the writer to combine ideas that would otherwise be stated in two separate sentences.

TWO SENTENCES   The audience applauded the speaker enthusiastically. They rose to their feet.

VERBAL PHRASE ADDITION   *Applauding the speaker enthusiastically*, the audience rose to their feet.

Punctuation   Verbal phrases used as modifiers are usually punctuated by commas, whether they appear at the beginning, in the middle, or at the end of sentences.

BEGINNING   *Having limited herself to five main points,* the speaker finished her presentation in fifteen minutes.

MIDDLE   The speaker, *having limited herself to five main points,* finished her presentation in fifteen minutes.

END   The speaker finished her presentation in fifteen minutes, *having limited herself to five main points.*

Placement   Verbal phrases used as modifiers must be placed so that they clearly modify one word in the sentence, usually the subject. If the writer puts a verbal phrase in the wrong place or includes no word for the phrase to modify, the verbal phrase is called a dangling modifier (see also Section **25**). A dangling modifier is sometimes laughable and is always confusing.

DANGLING MODIFIER   *Having always enjoyed books,* the library was where Dean chose to work.   [*Dean,* not *the library,* enjoyed books.]

CLEAR MODIFIER   *Having always enjoyed books,* Dean chose to work in the library.

DANGLING MODIFIER   *While flying over Washington, D.C.,* the government buildings were an amazing sight.   [There is no word for the verbal phrase to modify.]

CLEAR MODIFIER   *While flying over Washington, D.C.*, I found the government buildings an amazing sight.   [The verbal phrase now has a word to modify—*I*.]

Note: The verbal phrase can also function as an appositive.

EXAMPLE   His goal, *to start his own business*, is still a long way off.

Using Appositives

NAME _____ SCORE _____

DIRECTIONS   Combine each of the following pairs of sentences by making the essential information in one an appositive in the other. Place the appositive next to the noun it identifies or explains, and punctuate the appositive with commas (**Note:** Sometimes the appositive may precede the noun it identifies.)

> EXAMPLE
> The nurse practitioner is a relative newcomer to the field of the health sciences. The
>
> nurse practitioner can relieve the physician of many duties.
>
> *The nurse practitioner, a relative newcomer to the field of the health sciences, can relieve the physician of many duties.*

1. The nurse practitioner is usually a graduate of an advanced nursing program. The nurse practitioner is involved in both preventive medicine and treatment of minor or chronic disorders.

2. The nurse practitioner is an important aid to the physician. The nurse practitioner can given physical examinations, record medical histories, and order laboratory tests.

3. Rapport is necessary for a successful joint practice. Rapport is a smooth working relationship between the physician and the nurse practitioner.

4. The employment of nurse practitioners in Shimshon has allowed doctors to spend more time with their patients. Shimshon is a town near Jerusalem.

5. The Shimshon Center was one of the first medical centers to make extensive use of nurse practitioners. The center found that nurse practitioners could handle 67 percent of the center's patients without a physician's direct aid.

Using Appositives

DIRECTIONS   The appositive often says as much as a longer construction does. Reduce the number of words in each of the following sentences by making the *who* or the *which* clause into an appositive. Below the sentence, write the appositive that results from your revision.

EXAMPLE

Of the many areas open in nursing, one of the newest is that of the nurse practitioner, ~~who is~~ a professional trained to perform many of the duties of a physician.

a professional trained to perform many of the duties of a physician

1. Nursing as a career has come a long way since the days of Florence Nightingale, who was the founder of modern nursing.

2. The Nightingale Home for Nurses, which was the school Florence Nightingale founded in London in 1860, trained many nurses from all parts of the world.

3. Boston General Hospital and Bellevue Hospital in New York, which were the first educational centers for nursing in the United States, began their training programs in 1873.

4. The American Nurses Association, Inc., which was the first professional organization of registered nurses, was founded in 1896.

5. During the nineteenth and twentieth centuries there have been many famous nurses, such as Clara Barton, who was the founder of the American Red Cross.

Using Prepositional Phrases

NAME _____ SCORE _____

DIRECTIONS   In the blanks on the left, indicate whether the italicized prepositional phrase in each of the following sentences modifies a sentence part (P) or modifies the entire sentence (S). Punctuate with commas those prepositional phrases that modify entire sentences. In the blanks on the right, write the italicized prepositional phrases and include the punctuation marks that you have added for the phrases that modify entire sentences.

EXAMPLES
The area *of health care delivery* is not as limited as many people believe.

_____*P*_____ _____*of health care delivery*_____

In fact more and more people enter branches of this field every year.

_____*S*_____ _____*In fact,*_____

1. A student *with an Associate's degree* can enter the health care delivery field.

_____ _____

2. College programs *in dental hygiene or respiratory therapy* often include on-the-job training.

_____ _____

3. People studying *for these careers* receive valuable training as they work with patients.

_____ _____

4. *Besides reading about how things should be done* students see how treatment is delivered by experienced teaching staff.

_____ _____

5. People *in these lines of work* express a high level of satisfaction with their jobs.

   _____ _____

6. Other types *of medical practitioners* will also be needed in increasing numbers during the coming decade.

   _____ _____

7. Many Americans have grown more conscious *of maintaining their good health.*

   _____ _____

8. Some people think of the 1980s *as the Physical Fitness Decade.*

   _____ _____

9. Concern about fitness is growing *among both young and old people.*

   _____ _____

10. Moreover *as the baby boom generation ages and requires additional health care* more and more jobs will open up in the health care professions.

   _____ _____

Using Verbal Phrases

NAME _____ SCORE _____

DIRECTIONS   Each of the following sentences has a verbal phrase written after it. Rewrite the sentence using the verbal phrase as a clear modifier. Be sure to include the punctuation needed. (Often, verbal phrases may be inserted in more than one place in their sentences.)

EXAMPLE
The labor force is involved in two kinds of industries.   considered very broadly

Considered very broadly, the labor force is involved in two kinds of industries.

1. One kind of industry is involved with the production of goods.   expected to increase slowly during the coming decade

2. Industries that provide services are expected to increase more rapidly than those that provide goods.   currently employing more than one-half of all workers

3. Some industries produce both goods and services.   not so easily categorized

4. Service-producing industries include such divisions as government, transportation, public utilities, finance, insurance, and real estate.   requiring more and more college graduates

5. Citizens of the United States demand more service industries than ever before.   to keep up their standard of living

6. Government at the state and local levels has shown the largest growth of all service-producing industries.   having increased by about 90 percent in the last twenty years

7. State and local government is expected to need more and more college-trained employees.   to meet the public's demand for education, health, and protective services

8. Employment at the federal level of government will not be so readily available during the coming decade.   increasing by only a small percentage in the last twenty years

9. You can determine the service areas that hold the most promise for future employment.   studying graphs that show projected rates of growth

10. Health services are expected to expand more rapidly than any others.   to satisfy the public's demand for more and better health care

Subordinate Clauses as Modifiers   In **1d(1)** you studied one kind of subordinate clause—the noun clause, which can function as a subject or object. (As you may remember, a subordinate clause contains both a subject and a verb, but, unlike a main clause, cannot stand by itself as a sentence because of the subordinator that introduces it.) Other kinds of subordinate clauses—the adjective clause and the adverb clause—act as modifiers.

Adjective Clauses   Adjective clauses are introduced by a subordinator such as *who, whom, that, which,* or *whose*—often referred to as *relative pronouns.* A relative pronoun relates the rest of the words in its clause to a word in the main clause, and, as a pronoun, also serves some noun function in its own clause, often as the subject. (Remember that a clause, unlike a phrase, has both a subject and a verb.)

> Another field *that interests students* is health science.   [The relative pronoun *that* relates the subordinate clause to the main clause, *field,* and also serves as the subject of the verb, *interests,* in its own clause.]

An adjective clause follows the noun or pronoun that it modifies. It cannot be moved elsewhere without confusing either the meaning or the structure of the sentence.

> CORRECT PLACEMENT   The best-paying occupations, *which students are most likely to want,* are listed in various directories.
>
> INCORRECT PLACEMENT   The best-paying occupations are listed in various directories *which students are most likely to want.*
>
> CONFUSING STRUCTURE   *Which students are most likely to want,* the best-paying occupations are listed in various directories.

Sometimes the relative pronoun is omitted when the clause is short and no misreading could result.

> WITH RELATIVE   Zoo management is a career *that* few students have considered.
> PRONOUN
>
> WITHOUT RELATIVE   Zoo management is a career few students have considered.
> PRONOUN

An adjective clause may be either restrictive or nonrestrictive. A restrictive (defining) clause is not punctuated because it limits the meaning of the words it follows and is, consequently, essential to the meaning of the sentence. A nonrestrictive (nondefining) subordinate clause, on the other hand, is punctuated, usually with commas, because it is not essential to the meaning of the sentence. When used as a relative pronoun, the word *that* usually introduces a restrictive (defining) subordinate clause.

RESTRICTIVE CLAUSE   The person *who decides to be a farmer* faces many hardships.   [The clause defines or identifies the kind of person who faces many hardships.]

NONRESTRICTIVE CLAUSE   My nearest neighbor, *who is a farmer,* faces many hardships.   [The word *neighbor* is identified or defined by the modifier *nearest.*]

RESTRICTIVE CLAUSE   My neighbor is not discouraged by the hardships *that he endures.*   [The word *that* introduces a restrictive clause.]

Adverb Clauses   An adverb clause is introduced by a subordinator such as *since, when, if, because, although,* or *so that* (see the Appendix for a list of the most commonly used subordinators). Like the adjective clause, the adverb clause adds another subject and verb (and sometimes other elements) to the sentence. But unlike the relative pronoun that introduces the adjective clause, the subordinator of an adverb clause does not function as a main part of its own clause. The adverb clause usually modifies the verb of the main clause, but it may also modify an adjective or adverb in the main clause.

> *If economists could only capture the economy in a bottle,* they could explain it more accurately.   [The subordinator, *If,* introduces the adverb clause, which modifies the verb *could explain.*]

> Economists are seldom as confident *as they appear.*   [The subordinator, *as,* introduces the adverb clause, which modifies the adjective *confident.*]

> Nevertheless, economists can predict changes in the economy better *than anyone else can predict them.*   [The subordinator, *then,* introduces the adverb clause, which modifies the adverb *better.*]

Placement and Punctuation   Adverb clauses may be added to a sentence at various places. When an adverb clause is added in front of a main clause, it is followed by a comma; when it is added in the middle of a main clause, it is usually set off by commas (a comma at the beginning and end of the clause); when it is added after a main clause, it it usually unpunctuated.

BEGINNING   *When our country was first settled,* almost every worker was a farmer.

MIDDLE   Almost every worker, *when our country was first settled,* was a farmer.

END   Almost every worker was a farmer *when our country was first settled.*

In general, subordinate clauses introduced by clause markers like *which, that, who, whom,* and *whose* may be added to sentences only after the words they modify; otherwise, the clauses are misplaced modifiers.

Using Subordinate Clauses

NAME _____ SCORE _____

DIRECTIONS   After each of the following main clauses (sentences) is a subordinate clause. Combine the subordinate clause with the main clause, using commas whenever necessary. If the subordinate clause may be added at more than one place, write a check mark (✔) at the right.

EXAMPLES

c̶College graduates will face stiff competition in most occupations.

I̶f present trends continue,

_____✓_____

Many students train for their professions in two-year colleges. who

do not want a B.S. or B.A. degree

_____

1. The number of students entering junior and community col-

   leges is increasing rapidly. because these colleges can suc-

   cessfully train students for many occupations in two years or

   less

   _____

2. The outlook for jobs during the 1980s varies according to the

   occupation. although there is a general shortage of openings

   for graduates of both four-year and two-year colleges

   _____

3. A need for graduates in most engineering fields is expected. if

   past trends continue

   _____

4. On the other hand, there is a surplus of graduates. who are

   trained in teaching and biological sciences

   _____

5. Obviously, students must be increasingly aware of the job

 market. if they are to find suitable work after graduation   _____

6. Today's students must think of marketing their skills. who

 want jobs   _____

7. Careful planning must be a part of a student's education.

 which considers the skills needed by the job market   _____

8. Thus students must choose their subjects carefully. when they

 are scheduling their classes for the semester or quarter   _____

9. Certain subjects, like composition and basic arithmetic, are

 needed. since the skills taught relate to success in most oc-

 cupations   _____

10. In the 1980s there are jobs for all graduates. who have

 trained themselves for the openings available   _____

1e Learn to use main clauses and subordinate clauses in various types of sentences.

Sometimes a writer has two or more related ideas to set forth. Depending on the relationship of the ideas and on the desired emphasis, the writer may choose to express the ideas in separate sentences or to combine them in one of several ways.

Types of Sentences   There are four types of sentences: *simple, compound, complex,* and *compound-complex.* Which of these types a given sentence is depends on the number of main and subordinate clauses it includes.

Simple Sentences   The simple sentence consists of only one main clause and no subordinate clauses. A simple sentence is often short, but not always, since one or more of the basic sentence parts—the subject, verb, or objects—may be compound and since many single-word and phrase modifiers may be attached to the main clause.

SIMPLE   Computers handle many routine office chores.

SIMPLE   **Once used only by scientists,** computers now help *to reduce the amount of repetitious work in the modern office.*   [The main clause, or basic formula, *Computers help reduce work,* has been expanded by the addition of one adjective (underlined), one verbal phrase (in boldface) and three prepositional phrases (in italics).]

SIMPLE   In the modern office, complicated word processing, routine accounting work, and complex data processing all are done with a computer.   [The subject is compound; single-word modifiers and prepositional phrases also expand the main clause.]

Compound Sentences   A compound sentence consists of two or more main clauses (but no subordinate clauses) connected by a coordinating conjunction (*and, but, or, for, nor, so, yet*) or by a conjunctive adverb (such as *thus* or *therefore*) or other transitional expressions (such as *as a matter of fact*). In a compound sentence the connecting word (in boldface below) acts like a fulcrum on a seesaw, balancing grammatically equivalent structures.

COMPOUND   Computer experience will help a person get a clerical position, **but**

some people still refuse to learn this skill.   [The first main clause is

balanced by the grammatically equivalent second main clause. The

clauses are connected by the coordinate conjunction *but*.]

COMPOUND   Most businesses still keep records; **however,** employees must now use

computers to handle many filing jobs.   [The conjunctive adverb,

however, balances the first main clause against the grammatically

equivalent second main clause.]

Caution: If you overdo the joining of main clauses with *and*, your style will be childish. Save the *and*'s for ideas that should be stressed equally. Use a subordinate clause and main clause when one idea is dependent upon another. Or use two separate sentences when there is no strong relationship between the two ideas.

CHILDISH   I went to college so that I could get a good job, and I wanted to find work writing for a large corporation. I thought I would like the challenge of preparing reports, and I knew I could communicate ideas clearly. I learned about technical writing in an English course, and I took advanced classes to gain the skills I needed to be a technical writer.

BETTER   I went to college so that I could get a good job. I wanted to find work writing for a large corporation. I thought I would like the challenge of preparing reports, and I knew that I could communicate ideas clearly. After I learned about technical writing in an English course, I took advanced classes to gain the skills I needed to be a technical writer.

You will notice that the better paragraph has only one sentence in which two main clauses are joined by *and*, whereas the childish paragraph has three such sentences.

Punctuation   Either a comma or a semicolon shows the reader that one main clause has ended and another is about to be added. The punctuation mark is written after the first main clause, just *before* the joining word. When two main clauses are joined by a coordinating conjunction (a word such as *and* or *but*), a comma is used. When the two main clauses are joined by a conjunctive adverb (a word such as *however*) or other transitional expressions (a phrase such as *for instance*), a semicolon is used. A comma normally follows the conjunctive adverb or other transitional expression. (However, this comma is sometimes omitted when it is not needed to prevent misreading.)

Finally, when no conjunction joins two main clauses, a semicolon is used.

AND   The opportunities for receptionists are expected to increase during the late 1980s, and this occupation, unlike file clerking, should not be affected by automation.

HOWEVER   Thousands of job openings are expected for cashiers during the next few years; however, future growth may slow because of the widespread use of automated check-out systems.

NO JOINING WORD   Some clerical occupations depend on people more than on machinery; job openings in these areas will be increasing rapidly during the 1980s.

Complex Sentences   A complex sentence consists of one main clause and one or more subordinate clauses. The subordinate clause in a complex sentence may function as the subject, an object, or a modifier. Like the compound sentence, the complex sentence contains more than one subject and more than one verb; however, at least one of the subject–verb pairs is introduced by a subordinator such as *what, whoever, who, when, or if* (in boldface below) which makes its clause dependent on the main clause.

COMPLEX   **Whoever has visited Epcot Center in Florida** has had a glimpse into the future. [The subordinate clause functions as the subject of the sentence.]

COMPLEX   **When we stop to think about it**, even the eighties resemble a "science fiction" world. [The subordinate clause functions as a modifier—as an adverb clause.]

Compound-Complex Sentences   A compound-complex sentence consists of two or more main clauses and at least one subordinate clause. Thus it has three or more separate sets of subjects, verbs, and sometimes objects.

COMPOUND-COMPLEX   No one can predict what the machines of the future will do,

but it is safe to say that businesses of the future will undoubt-

edly rely heavily on the new machine technology.

Combining Main Clauses

NAME _____ SCORE _____

DIRECTIONS\ Using the joining punctuation and word indicated, combine the second main clause with the first one. (In some cases you will be asked to use no conjunction, only a semicolon.) Cross out the period and insert the correct punctuation mark at the end of the first main clause. In the blank write the joining word and punctuation you have used. If you used no joining word, simply list the punctuation mark.

EXAMPLE
for example

People who enjoy sales work can choose from a variety

; for example,

of occupations/They can become insurance agents, real

estate brokers, or retail trade salesworkers.   *; for example,*

1. *and*

   Each year thousands of positions open up in real

   estate sales. Many beginners will have to transfer

   to other occupations because of the competitive

   nature of the occupation.   _____

2. *however*

   During the last half of the 1980s modeling agen-

   cies should offer over eight hundred openings a

   year. The glamour of this occupation will attract

   many more than eight hundred applicants.   _____

3. *nevertheless*

Self-service gasoline stations have eliminated the
need for many attendants. Service stations still
place ads for service station attendants. _____

4. *for example*

Projections indicate that some businesses will still
have openings for large numbers of salespeople.
The demand for computer salespeople will increase greatly because of the growing popularity
of home and business computers. _____

5. *use no conjunction*

Employment for route drivers will probably not
increase during the coming decade. Neither will
openings for manufacturers' salesworkers. _____

Combining Main Clauses Exercise 1–23 (continued)

6. *use no conjunction*

   Sales work provides opportunities for high school

   as well as college graduates. People who want to

   work for someone else as well as those who want

   to run their own businesses should consider this

   line of work. _____

7. *consequently*

   Salespersons must enjoy meeting people. Someone

   who feels uncomfortable around strangers or who

   does not understand the needs of others should not

   consider sales as a potential career. _____

8. *use no conjunction*

   Sales work probably requires more exceptional

   character traits than any other occupation. A

   good salesperson is imaginative, self-confident,

   ambitious, and energetic. _____

9. *but*

   Good salespersons understand people. They also
   understand the business community and good
   business practice.   _____

10. *in fact*

    Many people in sales must be willing to travel.
    Some salespeople spend as much as four or five
    months of the year on the road.   _____

Building Sentences Exercise 1–24

NAME _____ SCORE _____

DIRECTIONS   From each of the following sets of phrases and/or clauses write a sentence (or sentences) of the specified type in the space provided. Where indicated, use the connecting word given in italics. Be sure to punctuate correctly the segments you join together.

EXAMPLE

COMPOUND

about combining them into one career

they do not know where to look for advice

many people have several interests

but

Many people have several interests, but they do not know where to look for advice about combining them into one career.

1. SIMPLE

this office can help a person investigate potential careers

students often neglect to consult their school's placement bureau

2. COMPLEX

while students are in their first years of college

placement counselors can help them evaluate their goals

3. COMPOUND-COMPLEX

there are tests that students can take

the placement office may also provide information

to identify their real interests

about internship opportunities

however

4. COMPLEX

   especially if a person wants
   summer jobs and internships are worth investigating
   to explore a new career possibility

5. COMPOUND

   others only employ summer interns
   on a year-round basis
   many companies hire interns

6. COMPOUND-COMPLEX

   to earn money
   interests some students
   to continue their education
   the co-op program that large companies offer
   it enables them

7. COMPOUND

   this training supplements the theoretical courses
   co-op students work at a full-time job
   that they have taken in school
   and

8. COMPLEX

   with schools offering technical degrees
   although not all colleges and universities have co-op programs
   most large corporations participate in this type of arrangement

9. SIMPLE

   to hire permanent employees
   many companies like
   from among their former co-op students

2

Write complete sentences.

A sentence fragment is a nonsentence beginning with a capital letter and ending with a period. A sentence fragment is usually a phrase (a group of related words that lacks a subject and/or a verb) or a subordinate clause (a group of related words that has both a subject and a verb but that is introduced by a clause marker—a word like *who, which, that, if, since,* or *because*).

PHRASE	needing to prepare a report for your employer
SUBORDINATE CLAUSE	when you need to prepare a report for your employer
SENTENCE	You need to prepare a report for your employer.

Few people write isolated fragments; rather they write fragments as parts of a paragraph. They separate what should be sentence additions from the main clauses they belong with. Notice that the writer of the following has mistakenly separated what should be sentence additions from the main clause they belong with.

> *When you need to prepare a report for your employer.* You may panic at the assignment. *Realizing that your writing skills as well as your knowledge of your field will be examined carefully.*

When the italicized words are treated as additions to the main clause, and are punctuated with commas, the fragments are avoided.

> *When you need to prepare a report for your employer,* you may panic at the assignment, *realizing that your writing skills as well as your knowledge of your field will be examined carefully.*

Of course, the fragments may also be avoided by making the italicized words into main clauses themselves, but the writing that results sounds childish.

> You need to prepare a report for your employer. You may panic at the assignment. You realize that your writing skills as well as your knowledge of your field will be examined carefully.

Usually, then, the best correction for a sentence fragment is to connect it with the main clause it has been separated from. The exercises in this section will provide you with experience in making fragments into additions to main clauses and in correctly punctuating these additions.

Avoiding Phrase Fragments   Exercise 2–1

NAME _Justin McCarthy_ _____ SCORE _____

2a To avoid fragments, connect verbal phrases, prepositional phrases, and appositives to the independent clauses with which they belong.

DIRECTIONS   Join the sentence fragment to the main or independent clause it has been separated from. Use a comma either before or after the fragment. (You will need to change the capitalization of one of the word groups.) In the blank write either *a* or *b* to show which word group is the fragment.

EXAMPLES
ᵃAn important part of many jobs, ᵇThe business report is usually

presented in written form.   _a_

ᵃMost reports are quite simple, ᵇRequiring no more than one page of

composition.   _b_

1. ᵃMost reports follow a general-to-specific format, ᵇThe main

   point of the report being presented first and the supporting

   facts following.   _a_

2. ᵃReports may sometimes end with the main point, ᵇUnlike

   business letters, which nearly always state the main point

   first.   _B_

3. ᵃIn a report that ends with recommendations, ᵇThe facts or

   supporting points of proof are listed first to help persuade the

   reader.   _a_

4. ᵃThe reader may be ready to accept the recommendation,

   ᵇHaving been prepared for it by the writer's presentation.   _b_

5. [a]Many formal reports are written by professional technical writers within the corporation or by outside consulting firms; [b]Often for presentation to corporate executives, clients, or stockholders.

6. [a]Unlike complicated formal reports, [b]Short informal reports are usually written by ordinary workers.

7. [a]To help an individual or a group of individuals make a decision, [b]Many short reports present the facts needed to support a recommendation or a conclusion.

8. [a]Business reports help their readers make any number of decisions, [b]Such as whether a procedure is practical or the project is feasible.

9. [a]Often a permanent record to be kept on file, [b]A report may help a writer to prepare a future report of a similar nature.

10. [a]Before preparing any report, [b]The writer should be clear about the purpose of the report.

Avoiding Phrase Fragments—Continued   Exercise 2-2

NAME _Justus M. McCarthy_   SCORE _____

To avoid fragments, connect a list of items or the second part of a compound verb or compound direct object to the main clause it belongs with.

DIRECTIONS   Join a list of items or the second part of the compound verb or compound direct object to the main clause it belongs with. Use no comma before the second part of the compound verb or compound direct object. Use a comma or a colon before a list that you attach to the main clause: use a comma if the list is introduced by a phrase like *such as;* use a colon if there is no introductory phrase. (You will need to change the capitalization of each word group that you join to the main clause.) In the blank write *compound* if the fragment that you join to the main clause is the second part of the verb or direct object; write *list* if the fragment is a series of items.

EXAMPLES

Sources of information for reports can include data ob-

tained firsthand, *or* material obtained through gath-

ering and assembling the research done by others.   _compound_

Information from primary sources is obtained in sev-

eral ways: *Q*uestionnaires, experiments, and surveys.   _list_

1. Information from primary sources is obtained

   firsthand. And has not been analyzed by someone

   else.   _Compound_

2. Gathering information from primary sources

   takes more time. And costs more than consulting

   secondary sources.   _Compound_

3. Thus, when writing a report, you should consult

   secondary sources first, And should use them to

   avoid duplicating someone else's work.   _List_

4. Secondary sources are found in three places, Libraries, research departments in some companies, and occasionally, data-gathering firms.

    List

5. There are many kinds of libraries available, Such as school, college, and municipal.

    List

6. Information may be copied word for word from books or articles, Or may be summarized.

    List

7. You may obtain information about office equipment and supplies from several primary sources, By studying manufacturers' brochures, by observing other offices, and by attending sales and professional conventions.

    List

8. As you collect your information, you will need to organize your findings. And to evaluate them.

    Compound

9. If you do your research carefully, you may have more information than you need, Or more than your supervisor will care to read about.

    Compound

10. Before writing a report you must decide on a final plan for presentation. As well as eliminate all the information that does not suit your plan.

    Compound

Avoiding Subordinate Clause Fragments   Exercise 2-3

NAME _Justin M⁰Carthy_ _____   SCORE _____

2b To avoid fragments, connect subordinate clauses to the main clauses they belong with.

DIRECTIONS Join the subordinate clause to the main clause it has been separated from. Use a comma after the subordinate clause if it comes before the main clause; use no comma if the subordinate clause follows the main clause unless it is introduced by the clause marker *although*. (You will need to change the capitalization of one of the clauses.) In the blank write either *a* or b to show which word group is the fragment.

EXAMPLES

ᵃBefore a report is requested, ᵇIts probable usefulness to the com-

pany should be considered.   _a_

ᵃUnnecessary reports should be eliminated, ᵇBecause they are expen-

sive and time-consuming to produce and distribute.   _b_

1. ᵃBecause routine reports are written frequently, ᵇPrepared

   forms are often used.   _a_

2. ᵃIf a company receives frequent inquiries about its products,

   ᵇA prepared form providing the information requested saves

   both time and energy.   _a_

3. ᵃPrepared forms are used in most medical fields, ᵇSince

   definite information must be presented.   _b_

4. ᵃWhen patients report for dental or medical checkups, ᵇThey

   are usually asked to respond to a definite set of questions. _a_

5. ᵃPatients' answers may become the basis for longer, formal

   reports, ᵇWhenever the dental or medical firm must supply

   insurance companies with details concerning claims.   _b_

6. ᵃWhereas formal reports often require a long time to prepare, ᵇShort routine reports usually can be handled in minutes.   *a*

7. ᵃWhile the forms of reports vary, ᵇNo report is useful unless the information included is accurate, objective, and carefully organized.   *a*

8. ᵃA writer must first determine the audience for the report, ᵇBecause who will read the report and what purpose it will serve determine the report's structure.   *b*

9. ᵃIf similar reports have been completed in the past, ᵇThe writer should read them carefully before preparing the new report.   *a*

10. ᵃA past report can keep the writer from wasting a great deal of time. ᵇAlthough, unfortunately, previous reports are often unavailable because they have been lost in someone's files.   *b*

Avoiding Subordinate Clause Fragments   Exercise 2–4

NAME _____ SCORE _____

DIRECTIONS   For the following pairs of clauses, write *a* or *b* in the first blank to show which group is the dependent clause. Join that subordinate clause to the main clause it has been separated from. If the subordinate clause defines or limits in some way the meaning of the term it refers to, use no comma before it. If the subordinate clause simply adds useful but not necessary information about the term it refers to, use a comma before the clause marker. No comma should be used before the clause marker *that*. (See **1d** on restrictive and nonrestrictive clauses) (You will need to change the capitalization in each subordinate clause.) In the second blank write the clause marker, if one is included, that signals the beginning of the subordinate clause fragment. (**Note:** Sometimes *that* is omitted when the subordinate clause is joined to the main clause.)

EXAMPLES
ᵃAs an employee of any business, you may be asked to write reports, ᵇThat must be

prepared according to certain specifications.

_____*b*_____   _____*that*_____

ᵃIf the request comes to you in written form, carefully note the authoriza-

tion, ᵇWhich should make clear the exact nature of the report you are to

prepare.   _____*b*_____   _____*which*_____

1. ᵃAfter underlining all the major points in the authorization, make a list of

   any questions. ᵇThat you have about the nature of the report.

   _____   _____

2. ᵃIf you do have questions, you may either call or write the person. ᵇWho re-

   quested the report.   _____   _____

3. ᵃIf you call the person, you may want to follow up the telephone conversa-

   tion with a memo. ᵇThat spells out the understandings you and the person

   have reached about the report.   _____   _____

4. [a]Let us assume that Mr. Brooks has written to you requesting a report. [b]Which should list the new equipment and supplies needed by your office for the next financial year. _____ _____

5. [a]After reading the request carefully, you find that you have several questions about the exact information wanted by Mr. Brooks. [b]Who is your immediate supervisor and also the manager of the company.

   _____ _____

6. [a]You first make a list of the questions. [b]That you want Mr. Brooks to answer. _____ _____

7. [a]Perhaps your questions concern the meaning of "new" supplies and equipment and the amount of detail to be supplied about each item. [b]That you plan to list. _____ _____

8. [a]You should consult any previous reports. [b]Your predecessors have prepared. _____ _____

9. [a]Afterward you call Mr. Brooks. [b]Who is happy to respond to any questions left unanswered by your reading of previous reports.

   _____ _____

10. [a]Your next problem is to collect the information. [b]That you will need to prepare the report. _____ _____

Avoiding Sentence Fragments: A Review Exercise 2–5

NAME _____ SCORE _____

DIRECTIONS   Each sentence or fragment in the following paragraphs is numbered. Circle the numbers of the ten fragments. Then connect the fragments to the main clauses they belong with. (In a few cases a fragment can be joined to either of two main clauses. Also, a few fragments occur in succession.) Change the capitalization and include commas and colons as needed.

¹Your final written report will probably fall into one of three categories. ²The memorandum, the letter, or the short informal report. ³The memorandum and letter forms are alike. ⁴Except that the letter is slightly more formal. ⁵And will probably be read by people outside the company. ⁶Most likely, though, the information you have gathered will be presented in the form of the short informal report. ⁷Which is usually no longer than ten pages. ⁸If, for example, your subject is limited to the acquisition of new office equipment and supplies. ⁹You should have little trouble with the final organization. ¹⁰Since the various kinds of equipment and supplies can serve as the basis for your paragraphing.

¹¹Your report probably should include several sections. ¹²The title page should be followed by the letter or memorandum requesting or authorizing the report. ¹³Or by a statement indicating who requested or authorized it. ¹⁴Part one of the body of the report clearly and concisely states the purpose of the report. ¹⁵The next section should give a summary of your findings. ¹⁶Including a description of the method or sources used to arrive at the conclusions. ¹⁷Such as surveys, questionnaires, direct observations, and research. ¹⁸Finally, you should present your recommendations. ¹⁹Which will include the list of supplies and equipment you feel should be purchased, together with information about

the best products available, their particular features, and the prices of those products that you recommend. [20]Headings should be used within the body of the report to identify its three main divisions: purpose, findings, and recommendations.

3

Avoid comma splices and fused sentences.

In **1g** you learned that when one main clause is added to another, either a comma or a semicolon is used between the main clauses whenever the main clauses are connected by a coordinating conjunction: *and, but, or, nor, so, for,* or *yet*.

> Most people think of a report as a written document, *but*, in reality, employees present almost as many oral reports as written ones.

To use a comma between main clauses not connected by a coordinating conjunction is to make a comma splice error (also called a comma fault). To use no punctuation mark at all is to write a fused sentence (also called a run-on sentence.)

> COMMA SPLICE   Most people think of a report as a written document, in reality, employees present almost as many oral reports as written ones.
>
> FUSED SENTENCE   Most people think of a report as a written document in reality employees present almost as many oral reports as written ones.

If the coordinating conjunction is omitted between main clauses, then a semicolon is placed between the main clauses; if a colon is used, sometimes the second clause explains the first one.

> Most people think of a report as a written document; in reality, employees present almost as many oral reports as written ones.
>
> Employees may present oral reports to a variety of people: they may be called on for oral presentations by their immediate supervisors, by the upper management of their companies, and even, on occasion, by the general public. [Here the second main clause does not present a related point but rather explains the idea of the first main clause.]

If the coordinating conjunction is replaced by another type of connecting word—a conjunctive adverb (*thus, then, therefore, however*) or a transitional expression (*on the other hand, in fact, for example, to sum up*)—the standard mark of punctuation between the main clauses is still the semicolon.

> Most people think of a report as a written document; *however*, in reality, employees present as many oral reports as written ones.

Note: Remember that a conjunctive adverb or a transitional expression may be used as an added modifier in a main clause rather than as a connector between main clauses. In this case the conjunctive adverb or transitional expression is normally set off by commas: "Few employees, however, escape the task of preparing some written reports."

In addition to the use of the semicolon, there are two other ways to correct a comma splice or fused sentence: write two separate sentences, or make one of the main clauses into a subordinate clause.

TWO SENTENCES   Most people think of a report as a written document. In reality, employees present almost as many oral reports as written ones.

SUBORDINATION   Although most people think of a report as a written document, in reality, employees present almost as many oral reports as written ones.

The exercises in this section will give you experience in correcting comma splices and fused sentences in all three ways: by using a semicolon or colon, by writing two separate sentences, and by subordinating one idea to another.

**Avoiding Comma Splices and
Fused Sentences**

Exercise 3-1

NAME _Justin McCarthy_ SCORE _____

3a Use a comma between main clauses only when connecting them with a coordinating conjunction (*and, but, or, nor, for, so* or *yet*). If no coordinating conjunction is used, do one of the following: (1) use a semicolon (but only if the statements made by the two main clauses are closely related); (2) use a colon (but only if the second main clause explains the first); (3) make the two main clauses separate sentences, each beginning with a capital letter and ending with a period; (4) rewrite one of the main clauses to make it a subordinate clause addition to the other main clause.

Note: Be especially careful to avoid fused sentences and comma splices when dividing a quotation.

> "Prepare an oral report as carefully as you would a written one," my technical writing instructor advised. [Do not use a comma here.] "Be especially conscious of your audience in preparing an oral report."

DIRECTIONS   In the following fused and comma-spliced sentences, insert an inverted caret (**V**) where two main clauses come together. Then correct the error in the way you think best. Write **;** in the blank if you use a semicolon to make the correction, **:** if you use a colon, **.** if you use two sentences, and *sub* if you make one of the clauses subordinate.

EXAMPLE
According to one survey, preparation of oral reports takes up 25.4%

of a worker's time, preparation of written reports occupies 24.5%. _____;_____

1. Technicians write many descriptive reports, they may also

   write one or more long analytical reports each year. _____;_____

2. For example, a telephone technician working away from the

   plant usually submits a report on the work completed during

   a given shift, the report describes all breakdowns in tele-

   phone service and the steps taken to restore service. _____;_____

3. Technicians frequently write descriptive reports about

   changes in product specifications, these reports are as essential

   to the company as the products themselves. _____. _____

4. Smaller companies depend on technicians to write most of the descriptive literature about their products, technicians may also write the instructions that appear on labels and in user's manuals. _____

5. The second major kind of report is the analytical one, it summarizes and evaluates tests performed by the company. _____

6. Computerized record keeping has not eliminated the need to write analytical reports in small companies; technicians tabulate and report test results. _____

7. Readers of technical reports want to see the facts stated clearly, you must be precise and choose your words carefully. _____

8. Supervisors are often shocked by the poor spelling of their employees, many comment that their employees' spelling ranges from "poor" to "atrocious." _____

9. A report that has misspelled words in it is not well received the misspelled words imply carelessness and cast doubt on the report's accuracy. _____

10. "Companies will not tolerate technicians who cannot spell correctly," one company president remarked, "if a technician misspells a common word in the description of a product, the customer does not trust the product." _____

Avoiding Comma Splices and
Fused Sentences

Exercise 3–2

NAME _____ SCORE _____

3b Use a semicolon between two main clauses joined by a word like *however* or *therefore* or a transitional expression like *for example* or *on the other hand*.

DIRECTIONS   In the following fused and comma-spliced sentences, insert an inverted caret (**V**) where the two main clauses come together. Then add a semicolon if no mark of punctuation is there; if a comma is there, cross it out and insert a semicolon. In the blank write the semicolon and the word or phrase that follows it, as well as any punctuation that follows the word or phrase.

EXAMPLE

The memo is the shortest, most direct form of business

communication; therefore it is the form most fre-

quently used within companies.   ; therefore

1. In a memo the main point usually comes first,

   however, the sequence of points depends on the

   writer's purpose.   ; however

2. The memo next briefly supplies important details

   about the conclusion, then it offers further

   assistance or information.   _____

3. A memo is generally short in fact, it should seldom

   run more than two pages.   ; in fact

4. A memo primarily supplies information, therefore

   it does not have to present recommendations.   ; therefore

5. Memos should be dated and should include

   headings for instance, *To, From, Subject* (rather

   than *Re*), and *Date* usually introduce a memo.   ; for instance

6. Information can, of course, be communicated orally, however, a memo provides a lasting record.

; however

7. A spoken message may be ignored or forgotten, on the other hand, a memo demands attention and can be referred to again.

; on the other

8. A report in letter form often supplies the same information that a memo would however, the more formal letter-report generally goes to readers outside the company.

; however

9. A letter-report often omits some of the parts of the usual business letter for example, it may leave out the inside address, the salutation, and the complimentary close.

; for

10. For ease of reading, the letter-report contains headings and subheadings in addition, it may include tables or other illustrations.

; in addition

**Avoiding Comma Splices and
Fused Sentences: A Review**

Exercise 3–3

NAME _____ SCORE _____

DIRECTIONS   In the following paragraphs insert an inverted caret (**V**) where two main clauses are incorrectly joined. Then correct the fused and comma-spliced sentences by writing in semicolons or colons, by adding a period and a capital letter to make two separate sentences, or by rewriting one of the sentences as a subordinate clause.

[1]A report writer must observe certain conventions of style. [2]First, and most important, a simple, straightforward presentation is essential poetic words and roundabout phrasing have no place in reports. [3]The main purpose of a report is to communicate information clearly; therefore anything that interferes with clarity should be avoided. [4]Sentences in memos and reports are usually much shorter and less complex in structure than are those in other types of writing again clarity, not variety, is the primary aim of a report writer.

[5]Report writers should avoid the personal or subjective approach. [6]Try not to use personal pronouns, especially the first person *I* or *we*, the first person pronoun makes the report seem to be the opinion of the writer rather than an objective presentation of information. [7]For example, it is weak to say "We found errors" however, you could say that "The investigators found errors." [8]"Furthermore, vague evaluations like *expensive* and *superior* should be avoided. [9]The writer must give concrete details, and the reader will make judgments

based on the facts the report presents. [10]"This product is the most *exciting* thing our company has ever manufactured," one enthusiastic technician wrote, "it is a *must* for every household." [11]Needless to say, the supervisor reading the technician's report was not impressed with these subjective opinions, furthermore, the technician's failure to give an unbiased description of the product's operation annoyed the supervisor.

[12]Finally, a report writer, like any other writer, must give credit for all facts and ideas gained through the research of others, otherwise, the writer is guilty of plagiarism, as serious an offense in business and industry as it is in college. [13]Footnotes or source identifications, which are enclosed in parentheses within the body of the report, are needed to acknowledge sources used in the preparation of the report, of course, note pages and, usually, a bibliography appear at the end of the report.

4

Use adjectives and adverbs correctly.

In **1d** you learned how a modifier can make a word in the basic formula more exact in meaning.

> Writing a *good business* letter is *not* the *extraordinarily difficult* task *most* people feel that it is.

Without the modifiers—not to mention the articles—this sentence would not even have the same meaning, as is clearly shown when the sentence is written without any modifiers.

> Writing a letter is the task people think that it is.

The modifiers (*good, business,* and *most*) of the subjects (*letter* and *people*), the modifier (*not*) of the verb (*is*), the modifier (*difficult*) of the complement (*task*), and the modifier (*extraordinarily*) of another modifier (*difficult*) are all necessary to make the meaning of the sentence clear.

Adjectives   Modifiers of nouns and pronouns are called adjectives.

> Of all the types of *business* letters the *most difficult* one for *most* people to write is
>
> the letter of introduction.

Note: The pronouns *everyone* and *everybody* are often modified by adverbs rather than adjectives because they are compound words made up of a pronoun (*one* and *body*) and an adjective (*every*): "*Almost* everyone can learn to write an effective business letter to a friend as well as to a stranger."

An adjective may also be used either as a *subject complement* or as an *object complement*.

Subject Complements   Adjectives used as subject complements follow linking verbs—mainly forms of *be* (*am, is, are, was, were, has been, have been, will be,* and so on) and verbs like *appear, seem, look, feel,* and *taste*—and describe or show something about the subject of the sentence. (Because they appear as part of the predicate, they are also called predicate adjectives.)

> SUBJECT COMPLEMENT   She is strict but considerate.   [*Strict* and *considerate* describe the subject, *She*.]

Note: Some subject complements are nouns: She is the *boss*.

Object Complements   Adjectives used as object complements are also found in the predicate, but they describe or refer to the direct object of the verb.

OBJECT COMPLEMENT   Our boss finds competition healthy.   [The object comple-

ment, *healthy*, modifies the direct object, *competition*.]

Note: Some objective complements are nouns: Our boss considers us a *team*.

Adverbs   Adverbs modify verbs or modify other modifiers.

> A business letter to a friend or an acquaintance is *quite often highly* informal.   [*Often* modifies the verb *is; quite* modifies the adverb *often; and highly* modifies the adjective *informal*.]

Writers often have special difficulty with sentences that include linking verbs and their modifiers and other verbs that function as linking verbs.

In sentences with linking verbs (*be, seem,* and so forth), or verbs sometimes used as linking verbs (for instance, *feel* or *look*), it is especially important to determine whether a modifier refers to the verb or to the subject. If it refers to the verb, an adverb must be used; if it refers to a subject, an adjective must be used.

When the modifier refers to a verb like *be, seem, feel,* or *look* rather than to the subject, an adverb, not an adjective, is used.

> The sales manager looked *eagerly* through the pile of papers on his desk.   [*Eagerly*, an adverb, modifies the verb, *looked*.]
> The sales manager looked *eager* as he searched through the pile of papers on his desk.   [*Eager*, an adjective, modifies the subject, *sales manager*.]
> She was *certain*.   [*Certain*, an adjective (subjective complement) modifies the subject, *she*.]
> She *certainly* was.   [*Certainly*, an adverb, modifies the verb, *was*.]

Form   Both adjectives and adverbs change their form when two or more things are being compared. An *er* on the end of a modifier or a *less* or *more* in front of it indicates that two things or groups of things are being compared (the comparative degree); an *est* on the end of a modifier or a *least* or *most* in front of it indicates that three or more things or groups of things are being compared (the superlative degree). Some desk dictionaries show the *er* and *est* ending for those adjectives and adverbs that form their comparative and superlative degrees in this way (for example—old, old*er*, old*est*). Most dictionaries show the changes for highly irregular modifiers (for example—good, *better, best*). As a rule of thumb, most one-syllable adjectives and most two-syllable adjectives ending in a vowel sound (*tidy, narrow*) form the comparative with *er* and the superlative with *est*. Most adjectives of two or more syllables and most adverbs form the comparative by adding the word *more* and the superlative by adding the word *most*.

COMPARATIVE DEGREE   A business letter to a friend is no *more dificult* to write than a personal letter is.

SUPERLATIVE DEGREE   The *most difficult* letter to write is the one to a prospective employer.

Caution: Many dictionaries do not list the *er* or *est* endings. Double-check if you are uncertain.

Note: For many adjectives the choice of *er* and *est* or *more* and *most* is optional.

The answer seems *more and more* clear every day.

OR

The answer seems *clearer and clearer* every day.

**Distinguishing Between Adjective
and Adverb Modifiers**

Exercise 4–1

NAME _____ SCORE _____

4a Use adverbs to modify verbs, adjectives, and other adverbs.

4b Use adjectives as subject or object complements.

DIRECTIONS   In each of the following sentences, choose the form of the word that would be considered appropriate in business and professional correspondence and reports. Cross out the incorrect choice; write the correct one in the blank. To help you decide which choice is correct, the word or words modified are underlined. (If you are uncertain about the part of speech of the underlined word or of the modifiers, consult your dictionary.)

EXAMPLE
(Almost, ~~Most~~) every employee must write many

business letters each year.   *almost*

1. Writing one's first business letter can be an

   (awful, awfully) frustrating experience.   _____

2. Most people feel (reluctant, reluctantly) to write

   business letters.   _____

3. Putting off writing a letter makes the task more

   (difficult, difficulty).   _____

4. Write your letters when the topic is (current, cur-

   rently).   _____

5. Good letter writers (usual, usually) try to jot down

   ideas about what they want to say.   _____

6. A letter that is (real, really) clearly written prob-

   ably means its writer took the time to revise.   _____

7. A courteous businessperson <u>will</u> (careful, carefully) <u>plan</u> exactly what to say before writing. _____

8. Letters from customers (most, mostly) <u>often</u> request answers to their questions. _____

9. Any unnecessary <u>delay</u> in answering an important letter can prove (disastrous, disastrously). _____

10. You are judged by employers as well as by customers on how (quick, quickly) you <u>respond</u> to their requests. _____

**Using Comparative and
Superlative Modifiers**   Exercise 4-2

NAME _____ SCORE _____

**4c Modifiers usually are changed to their comparative form (comparing two
things) either by the addition of *er* to the end of the modifier or by the addition of
more in front of it. Modifiers usually are changed to their superlative form (comparing three or more things) by the addition of *est* to the end of the modifier or by
the addition of *most* in front of it. (See also 18d(3).)**

DIRECTIONS   In each of the following sentences cross out the incorrect form or forms of
the modifier within parentheses and write the correct form in the blank. The word the
modifier refers to is underlined. (If you do not know how to form the comparative or
superlative form of the modifier, consult your dictionary.)

EXAMPLE
You <u>will write</u> letters (~~frequentlier,~~ more frequently)

than reports.   *more frequently*

1. Convincing customers that they matter is one of
   the (expensivest, most expensive) <u>goals</u> a business
   has.   _____

2. These days many businesses "talk" to (fewer, more
   few) <u>customers</u> in person than in letters.   _____

3. For that reason <u>it</u> has become (importanter, more
   important) than ever to write good letters.   _____

4. Although the telephone call can replace some letters, many people still <u>feel</u> (better, more better)
   seeing things set down in writing.   _____

5. A letter provides the reader with a clearer, (ex-
   acter, more exact) <u>record</u> of what the company
   has agreed to do.   _____

6. If legal questions arise later, a letter <u>will show</u> the
   judge (clearlier, more clearly) what exactly went
   on.   _____

7. For this reason, the writer must use the (clearest, most clear) possible <u>words</u> to avoid misunderstandings later. _____

8. Most good writers think of clarity and conciseness as the two (more essential, essentialest, most essential) <u>qualities</u> of good business letters. _____

9. The three (more important, most important) <u>things</u> a business letter does are get the reader to do what you want, give the reader information, and build goodwill. _____

10. Business <u>writers</u> who accomplish these goals can expect to be (successfuller, more successful) than writers who forget about their readers. _____

Mastering Adjective and
Adverb Modifiers: A Review

Exercise 4–3

NAME _____ SCORE _____

DIRECTIONS   In each of the following sentences cross out the inappropriate modifier within parentheses and write the correct modifier in the blank. Then underline the word or words modified. (If you are uncertain about the part of speech of the word or words you underline or about the proper form of the modifier, consult your dictionary.)

EXAMPLE
This letter is the most (~~careful,~~ carefully) written piece

of correspondence I have seen.   *carefully*

1. (Nearly, Near) all good business letters follow the

   same general pattern.   _____

2. Without being unpleasantly abrupt, the opening

   makes clear the purpose of the letter as (quick,

   quickly) as possible.   _____

3. The body of the letter then develops (fuller, more

   fully) what has been said in the opening.   _____

4. Finally, the closing emphasizes a point that the

   sender considers the (more, most) important one

   in the letter.   _____

5. The closing also says goodbye as (courteous,

   courteously) as possible.   _____

6. There is only one (noticeable, noticeably) excep-

   tion to this pattern.   _____

7. The so-called "bad-news letter" opens (different,

   differently).   _____

8. Bad news is (easier, more easier) to bear if the

   writer begins the letter on a positive note.   _____

9. For example, instead of opening with "We refuse

   to fix your toaster," begin (pleasanter, more

   pleasantly) with "Thank you for writing to us

   about your toaster."   _____

10. In other words, the writer of the bad-news letter must be (real, really) careful to maintain the receiver's goodwill by being as helpful as possible. _____

5

Use the correct form of the pronoun to show its function.

As you learned in Section **1**, a noun or pronoun may change form to indicate the way it works in a clause. The form of the noun or pronoun, referred to as its *case*, may be *subjective* (if it functions as a subject), *objective* (if it functions as an object), or *possessive* (if it shows ownership or possession). Nouns change their form for only one case—the possessive. (See also Section **15**.)

Certain pronouns change their form for each case, and you must be aware of the various forms in order to make the function of these pronouns clear in your writing.

Subjective	*Objective*	*Possessive*
I	me	mine
we	us	our, ours
he, she	him, her	his, her, hers
they	them	their, theirs
who, whoever	whom, whomever	whose

Subjective Case   The subjective case is used for subjects and for subject complements.

> *She* answers all letters of complaint.   [subject]
> The best writer in the firm is *she*.   [subject complement]

Note: You may sometimes find it more comfortable to avoid using the pronoun as a complement: "*She* is the best writer in the firm." OR "The best writer in the firm is *Mary*."

Objective Case   The objective case is used for both direct and indirect objects, for objects of prepositions, and for both subjects and objects of infinitives.

> The customer called *me* about his problem with our product.   [direct object]
> He gave *me* his opinion about what should be done to improve the product.   [indirect object]
> He sent the unused portion of the product to *me*.   [object of preposition]
> He asked *me* to refund his money.   [subject of infinitive *to refund*]
> He wanted to tell *me* about his difficulty in using the product.   [object of infinitive *to tell*]

Possessive Case   The possessive case is generally used before a gerund—a verbal that ends in *ing*—and acts as a noun. But a participle also sometimes has an *ing* ending. The possessive case is used before a gerund, which acts as a noun, but not before a participle, which acts as an adjective.

GERUND   I got tired of *his* criticizing my company's product.   [*Criticizing* acts as a noun, the object of the preposition *of*.]

PARTICIPLE   I found *him* unrelenting in his attack on our product.   [*Unrelenting* acts as an adjective, modifying *him*.]

Case Forms of Pronouns   Exercise 5–1

NAME _____ SCORE _____

The subjective case (*I, we, he, she, they, who, whoever*) is used for subjects and subject complements; the objective case (*me, us, him, her, them, whom, whomever*) is used for objects of verbs and verbals, for objects of prepositions, and for both subjects and objects of infinitives (for example, *to go, to be*); the possessive case (*my, our, his, her, their, whose*) is generally used to modify a gerund.

      SUBJECTIVE   OBJECTIVE   OBJECTIVE
      He expected *us* to hire *him*.

      SUBJECTIVE   POSSESSIVE   OBJECTIVE
      He heard about *their* criticizing the product from *me*.

      OBJECTIVE POSSESSIVE   POSSESSIVE
      We regret *his* not being able to attend *your* meeting.

DIRECTIONS   In the following sentences cross out the incorrect case form or forms within parentheses and write the correct form in the blank. List your reason for your choice in the space provided after the sentence. (After your answers have been checked, you may find it helpful to read them aloud several times to accustom your ear to the sound of the correct case forms.)

    EXAMPLE

    She told (~~he,~~ him) that the product had passed many demanding

    tests.   *him*

    Reason: *object of verb*

1. No one but (she, her) is qualified to answer the letters.   _____
   Reason:

2. Only (she, her) knows the history of the product.   _____
   Reason:

3. One customer told about (him, his) trying to make the product burn.

Reason:
_____

4. She sent (he, him) a report about the flammability studies that had been conducted on the product.

Reason:
_____

5. It was (she, her) who defended the product's safety record.

Reason:
_____

6. Her letter was convincing enough to make (he, him) withdraw his complaint.

Reason:
_____

7. It was necessary for (she, her) to follow up this first response with additional correspondence.

Reason:
_____

8. Her letters impressed all of (we, us) who read them.

Reason:
_____

9. After observing (she, her) for one day, we realized how much time an employee spends answering letters.

Reason:
_____

10. (We, Us) now believe that a business writing class for employees is a good investment.

Reason:
_____

Pronouns in Compounds
and as Appositives

Exercise 5–2

NAME _____ SCORE _____

5a A pronoun has the same case form in a compound or an appositive construction as it would if it were used alone.

COMPOUND CONSTRUCTIONS	Mel and *I* took business writing courses taught by Mr. Brabstock and *her*. [Compare with "I took courses taught by *her*."]
APPOSITIVE CONSTRUCTIONS	*She*, the director of product information for a local firm, taught *us* students what we needed to know about business correspondence. [Compare with "*She* taught *us* what we needed to know about business correspondence."]

DIRECTIONS   In the following sentences cross out the incorrect case form within parentheses and write the correct form in the blank. (To decide which case form is correct, say aloud each part of the compound construction separately or say aloud the pronoun without the appositive that follows it, as illustrated in the examples.)

EXAMPLES

(We, ~~Us~~) students took business writing. [*We took business writing.*] .... _____*We*_____

The best writers in the class were (she and he, ~~her and him~~). [*The best writer in the class was she; the best writer in the class was he.*] .... _*she and he*_

1. Our teacher made (we, us) students write many business letters. _____

2. (We, Us) students learned a lot from sample letters. _____

3. The samples helped make the format of a business letter clear to (the rest of the class and I, the rest of the class and me). _____

4. Because we had taken the business writing class, (my classmates and I, my classmates and me) felt we could write well. _____

5. Both (Peggy and he, Peggy and him) knew how to write a courteous refusal letter. _____

6. Writing a sales letter to a prospective client was also easy for (Tim and she, Tim and her). _____

7. (She, as well as he; Her, as well as him,) had had experience placing and responding to orders for various items. _____

8. Furthermore, the business writing course taught (Tim and she, Tim and her) how to write requests for information or assistance. _____

9. Finally, (Peggy and he, Peggy and him) learned how to write and answer a claim or a complaint letter. _____

10. Because of their classroom experience, the best writers that the company hired were (she and he, her and him). _____

**Pronouns in Subordinate Clauses
and with *Self* Added**   Exercise 5–3

NAME _____ SCORE _____

5b The case of a pronoun depends on its use in its *own* clause.

I think I know *who* should be chosen.   [Although *who* begins the clause that is the object of *I know*, in its own clause *who* is the subject of the verb *should be chosen*.]

It is she *whom* we should choose.   [In its own clause, *whom* is the object of the verb *should choose*.]

Self is added to a pronoun only when a reflexive or an intensive pronoun is needed.

I *myself* will answer the letter.   [intensive pronoun: intensifies *I*]
I wrote a letter to *myself*.   [reflexive pronoun: reflects back to *I*]
He wrote a letter to *me*.   [NOT *myself*; neither intensive nor reflexive]

Note: *Hisself, theirselves, it self,* and *its self* are nonstandard forms of *himself, themselves,* and *itself.*

DIRECTIONS   In the following sentences cross out the incorrect case form or forms within parentheses and write the correct form in the blank.

EXAMPLE
She was the personnel director (who, ~~whom~~) everyone

thought gave the best presentation.   *who*

1. The students wanted to know (who, whom) they should write to about job opportunities within her company.   _____

2. The personnel director said they should first write to (her, herself) for information and for application blanks.   _____

3. The completed application (it self, itself) and the request for an interview would be forwarded to the appropriate department head.   _____

4. Most students find these letters difficult because they must write about (them, themselves, theirselves).   _____

5. The students (who, whom) had studied business writing were obviously the best prepared for job hunting. _____

6. It was their instructor in business writing (who, whom), they remembered, had said that writing skills were important in acquiring a first job. _____

7. When they were told the number of people in the company (who, whom) might read their letters, they realized how much their writing would represent them. _____

8. The practice letters they had written proved extremely valuable to (them, themselves, theirselves). _____

9. Well-written letters make (whoever, whomever) reads them think of the writer as being professional and businesslike. _____

10. A correctly organized letter shows (whoever, whomever) reads it that the writer understands correct business form and style. _____

Mastering Case: A Review   Exercise 5-4

NAME _____   SCORE _____

DIRECTIONS   In the following sentences cross out the incorrect case form or forms within parentheses and write the correct form in the blank. Determine the use of the pronoun in its own clause before you choose the case form.

EXAMPLE

The personnel director is the employee within the com-

pany (who, ~~whom~~) usually answers letters from job

applicants.   ___who___

1. Most companies have form letters to send to (whoever, whomever) they would like to interview for a job.   _____

2. The personnel director adds specific information for individual applicants to tell them briefly what they need to know about the interview: (who, whom) they are to see; when and where the interview is to take place; and what positions they are being considered for.   _____

3. It is important, of course, that applicants know (who, whom) they will be interviewed by.   _____

4. Furthermore, an applicant should know what (she, her) should bring to the interview.   _____

5. Finally, the letter tells applicants about any tests that will be given to (they, them, themselves) at the time of the interview.   _____

6. (They, Their, Them) knowing what to expect will make the interview productive.   _____

7. Applicants (who, whom) the company does not wish to interview should receive a polite letter of rejection.   _____

8. A good letter of rejection first thanks the applicant for his interest shown in the company and then explains that there is no immediate opening for (he, him, himself). _____

9. The finalists for a position may receive an invitation for a second visit: "(We, Us) at XYZ Corporation would like to invite you to tour our plant." _____

10. Even though a rejection letter will always be disappointing, the writer must still try to retain the goodwill of the applicant (who, whom) is being turned down. _____

6

Make a verb agree in number with its subject; make a pronoun agree in number with its antecedent.

In **1b(1)** you learned about the importance of making subjects and verbs agree in number; a singular subject requires a singular verb, and a plural subject requires a plural verb. (Remember that an *s* ending shows plural number for the subject but singular number for the verb.)

SINGULAR   A good business <u>letter</u> <u>makes</u> clear the response that is expected from the

recipient of the letter.

PLURAL   Good business <u>letters</u> <u>make</u> clear the responses that are expected from the

recipients of the letters.

In the same way, a pronoun agrees in number with the noun (or the other pronoun) it refers to, its *antecedent*.

SINGULAR   A good business *letter* makes *its* purpose clear.

PLURAL   Good business *letters* make *their* purpose clear.

Mastering agreement requires that you be able to do three things: (1) match up the simple subject or subjects with the verb or verbs; (2) know which nouns and pronouns are traditionally singular and which are traditionally plural; and (3) identify the antecedent of a pronoun (the noun the pronoun refers to) so that you can determine the number of the antecedent.

6a Make a verb agree in number with its subject.

Simple Subjects   To make the subject and verb agree in number, you must be able to recognize the simple subject of a sentence as well as the verb. You may remember from your study of **1b(1)** that the simple subject is often surrounded by other words that are a part of the complete subject and that can easily be mistaken for the exact word or words that should agree in number with the verb.

SINGULAR   A <u>device</u> that encourages quick responses from recipients of request let-

ters <u>is</u> the stamped, addressed return envelope.   [The complete subject contains several plural nouns—*responses, recipients,* and *letters*—that must not be mistaken for the simple subject, which is singular.]

PLURAL   <u>Devices</u> that encourage a quick response from the recipient of a request letter <u>include</u> the stamped, addressed return envelope, a reply card with answers to check, and free prizes or other rewards for a prompt response. [The complete subject contains several singular nouns *response, recipient,* and *letter*—that must not be mistaken for the simple subject, which is plural.]

Be careful about the subject–verb agreement in the following situations:

when the subject or the verb ends in *t* or *k:*

<u>Scientists</u> <u>study</u> the results.

The <u>manager</u> <u>asks</u> for daily progress reports.

when the subject is followed by a prepositional phrase or a subordinate clause:

The <u>purpose</u> *of the reports* <u>is</u> clear.

The <u>purpose,</u> *which was stated in all the reports,* <u>is</u> clear.

when the subject follows the verb:

There <u>are</u> many daily <u>reports</u> from agencies of the government.

when the subject and subject complement do not have the same number (Usually you should rewrite the sentence, without using a form of *be,* to avoid the conflict in number.):

AWKWARD   <u>Reports</u> <u>are</u> one <u>way</u> to monitor progress within a company.

BETTER   <u>Reports</u> <u>serve</u> as one monitor of progress within a company.

Singular and Plural Nouns and Pronouns   Some noun subjects are traditionally singular, while others are traditionally plural. Those subjects that are traditionally singular include

(1)₀ singular subjects joined by *or* and *nor* and subjects introduced by *many a:*

Neither the letters [note plural] *nor* the advertisement gets good results.

Many a letter goes unnoticed.

(2)₀ collective nouns regarded as a unit:

The *number* of request letters amazes me.

The *committee* has made its recommendation.

(3)₀ nouns that are plural in form but singular in meaning:

The news depresses me.

Two thousand dollars buys little today.

(4)₀ titles of works or words referred to as words:

Sixty Minutes features some of the best interviews on television.

Employee benefits is a term we prefer to *fringe benefits.*

Those subjects that are traditionally plural include

(1)₀ subjects joined by *and:*

A memo *and* a report have many similarities.

(2)₀ a plural subject following *or* or *nor:*

Neither the manager *nor* his employees neglect correspondence. [The verb agrees

with *employees,* the part of the subject it is nearer to.]

(3) collective nouns that do not act as a unit:

A number of organizations contribute to that charity.

Certain nouns and pronouns are sometimes singular and sometimes plural, depending on their contexts in their sentences.

SINGULAR   A group of request letters has been examined by management. [Here

group is considered a unit.]

PLURAL   A group of employees are taking various business writing courses offered by their company. [Here *group* refers to many individuals, not to a unit.]

SINGULAR Some of this report is extremely well written.

PLURAL Some of those reports are extremely well written.

Pronouns such as *each, everyone, someone,* and *anyone* are traditionally singular; pronouns such as *both, few, several,* and *many* are traditionally plural.

SINGULAR Each of the letters we send out is direct but courteous.

PLURAL Many of the letters request payment of delinquent accounts.

6b Make pronouns agree in number with their antecedents.

A pronoun must agree in number with the noun (or the other pronoun) it refers to—that is, with its antecedent.

SINGULAR A clearly stated *request* is the *one* most likely to get action.

PLURAL Clearly stated *requests* are the *ones* most likely to get action.

A pronoun agrees in number with its antecedent even when the antecedent is in a different clause. (Remember, however, that the *case* of a pronoun is determined entirely by its function in its own clause; see **5b.**)

SINGULAR A good business letter makes clear the *response that* is expected from the recipient of the letter. [Notice that the verb *is expected* is singular because the antecedent of *that, response,* is singular.]

PLURAL Good business letters make clear the *responses that* are expected from the recipients of the letters. [Notice that the verb *are expected* is plural because the antecedent of *that, responses,* is plural.]

SINGULAR A *request that* is clearly stated is usually answered. [*Request,* the antecedent of *that,* is singular; therefore *that* is also singular.]

PLURAL *Requests that* are clearly stated are usually answered. [*Requests,* the antecedent of *that,* is plural; therefore *that* is also plural.]

Singular and Plural Antecedents Some pronouns (like some nouns) are traditionally considered singular, whereas others are considered plural.

Pronouns such as *each person, one person, everybody, anyone, either, neither, sort,* and *kind* are traditionally considered singular.

We try to give *each* of our products the promotion *it* deserves.

Naturally, *everyone* expects *his* own favorite to be the most popular. [CONTRAST:

Many expect *their* own favorites to be the most popular.]

Each of the one hundred women chosen for the survey was asked to send *her* reply

promptly.

Note: Today most writers, and especially business writers, try to avoid sexism in the use of personal pronouns. Whereas most writers once wrote, "*Each* of us should do *his* best," they now try to avoid using the masculine pronoun to refer to both men and women. To avoid sexism, some writers give both masculine and feminine pronoun references.

Each of us did *his or her* best.
Each of us did *his/her* best.

Other writers prefer to use *one's* in the place of *his or her.*

One should do *one's* best.

Perhaps the easiest way to avoid sexism is to use plural pronouns and antecedents unless a feminine or a masculine pronoun is clearly called for, as *his* would be in reference to a male employee or *her* in reference to a female employee.

All of *them* did *their* best.
All of *us* did *our* best.

Pronouns such as *both, several, many,* and *few* are considered plural.

Few of the people surveyed said that *they* disliked the product.

Pronouns such as *all, any, half, most, none,* and *some* may be singular or plural, depending on their context (that is, depending on the rest of the sentence or paragraph in which they appear).

PLURAL   *All* of the people surveyed *have sent their* replies.

SINGULAR   *All* of the information *has served its* purpose.

Similarly, a collective noun, such as *staff, committee,* or *board,* may call for either a singular or plural pronoun, depending on whether—in its context—it signifies a unit or individual members.

SINGULAR   The *committee has completed its* report.

PLURAL   The *committee have gone* back to *their* various departments.

Caution: Avoid confusing or awkward shifts between singular and plural pronouns that refer to the same collective noun.

CONFUSING   The *committee has completed its* report and gone back to *their* various

departments.

CORRECTED   The *committee has completed its* report, and the *members have gone*

back to *their* various departments.

Subject and Verb Agreement

Exercise 6-1

NAME _____ SCORE _____

DIRECTIONS In each of the following sentences underline the subject with one line (remember that a verbal may act as a subject); then match it with one of the verbs in parentheses. Cross out the verb that does not agree with the subject, and write in the blank the verb that does agree. (When all of your answers have been checked, read aloud each sentence, emphasizing the subject and verb.)

EXAMPLE
The purpose of persuasive letters (is, ~~are~~) to sell a prod-

uct, an idea, or a service. *is*

1. Persuasive writing (~~try~~, tries) to win over a reader. *tries*

2. The reader (~~expect~~, expects) to be convinced by facts, figures, and logic. *expects*

3. Another way to sway readers (is, ~~are~~) to touch on their emotions. *is*

4. A persuasive letter, like a persuasive essay, (~~use~~, uses) emotional appeals. *uses*

5. The writer's tactics (~~is~~, are) not obvious. *are*

6. An exaggerated emotional appeal, however, sometimes (~~make~~, makes) the reader grow irritated with the writer. *makes*

7. The successful writer generally (~~match~~, matches) the emotional appeal to the special interests of the audience. *matches*

8. The writer of persuasive letters (has, ~~have~~) to remember that uninvited mail can annoy people. *has*

9. The biggest job a writer therefore has (is, ~~are~~) making the reader want to keep reading. *is*

10. Once the reader loses interest, the letter (is, ~~are~~) quickly thrown away. *is*

Subject and Verb Agreement

Exercise 6–2

NAME _____   SCORE _____

DIRECTIONS   Rewrite the following sentences, replacing the plural subjects and verbs with singular ones and the singular subjects and verbs with plural ones. Underline the subject with one line, the verb with two lines. You will also need to change the articles (*a*, *an*, and *the*) to make the sentences sound right.

EXAMPLES
Persuasive <u>letters</u> usually <u><u>arrive</u></u> uninvited.

A persuasive <u>letter</u> usually <u><u>arrives</u></u> uninvited.

The <u>reader</u> <u><u>has</u></u> not requested such a letter.

<u>Readers</u> <u><u>have</u></u> not <u><u>requested</u></u> such a letter.

1. The <u>writer</u> of persuasive letters <u><u>convinces</u></u> readers to look beyond the first few lines.

2. The opening <u>lines</u> of a persuasive letter <u><u>are</u></u> extremely important.

3. There <u><u>is</u></u> a definite <u>way</u> to gain the readers' attention.

4. The <u>opening</u> of persuasive letters <u><u>appeals</u></u> to the readers' self-interest.

5. The <u>opening</u> <u>promises</u> certain rewards to the readers, like health, popularity, success, or some other personal benefit.

6. A successful <u>advertisement</u> <u>suggests</u> effective ways to open a persuasive letter.

7. The <u>headlines</u> of advertisements <u>serve</u> much the same purpose as the opening sentence of a persuasive letter.

8. The <u>headline</u> <u>gets</u> the audience to pay attention to the rest of the advertisement.

9. The <u>benefit</u> promised the audience <u>is</u> specific in successful advertisements and in persuasive letters.

10. The <u>reward</u> offered by Dale Carnegie's *How to Win Friends and Influence People* <u>is</u> clearly stated.

Singular and Plural Noun Subjects

Exercise 6-3

NAME _Justin McCarthy_   SCORE _____

DIRECTIONS   In each of the following sentences underline the subject (or subjects, if compound) with one line and match it (or them) with one of the verbs in parentheses. Circle any key word or words that affect the number of the subject. Then cross out the verb that does not agree with the subject and, in the blank, write the verb that does agree.

EXAMPLE

(A) number of appeals (~~is~~, are) available to the persuasive

writer.   _are_

1. News that benefits the reader (~~aim,~~ aims) at taking

   advantage of the reader's secret wishes.   _aims_

2. "How will this product make my life better?" (is, ~~are~~)

   the reader's main question.   _is_

3. Either health or comfort (~~provide~~, provides) an answer.   _provides_

4. Education and popularity (~~is,~~ are) two other appeals.   _are_

5. A promise of something good or tips about finances

   favorably (~~impress~~, impresses) many readers.   _impresses_

6. Promises and tips, of course, (~~get,~~ gets) the reader's

   attention.   _gets_

7. A number of other tactics (~~is,~~ are) used to gain the

   reader's attention.   _are_

8. New information and satisfaction of curiosity (~~is,~~ are)

   frequently promised by persuasive letters.   _are_

9. "Completely new!" or "You've been selected!" (~~arouse~~,

   arouses) the reader's curiosity.   _arouses_

10. The group of attention-getting words writers typically
    use (is, are) surprisingly small.   ~~are~~ is

**Singular and Plural Noun
and Pronoun Subjects**

Exercise 6-4

NAME _____ SCORE _____

DIRECTIONS   In the following sentences cross out the verb in parentheses that does not agree with its subject. Then enter the correct verb in the blank.

EXAMPLE

One of the most important things to do in persuasive

letters (~~are,~~ is) to involve the reader quickly.   *is*

1. Most of us (wants, want) to receive the benefits promised by the opening line of a persuasive letter.   _____

2. Few of us (reads, read) far if we do not see the value of the product or service for ourselves.   _____

3. One who (writes, write) successful persuasive letters will generally introduce the word *you* in the first few sentences.   _____

4. A number of different persuasive strategies (is, are) commonly employed to make readers imagine the benefits they will enjoy.   _____

5. "Is this the day you do something about your weight?" is an opening line that immediately (puts, put) us into the picture.   _____

6. Since most of us (is, are) at least a little overweight, we are sure to read further.   _____

7. Then follows a chart that (shows, show) desirable weights for men and women.   _____

8. Almost everyone (checks, check) to see how his or her weight compares with the ideal weight.   _____

9. Neither the male nor the female reader (wants, want) to be overweight in today's weight-conscious society.

_____

10. Finally, then, the letter (suggest, suggests) that the product advertised will reduce one's weight to the ideal level shown on the chart.

_____

Pronoun and Antecedent Agreement

Exercise 6–5

NAME _____ SCORE _____

DIRECTIONS   In each of the following sentences select the pronoun that agrees in number with its antecedent (***Note:*** sometimes the antecedent comes *after* the pronoun that refers to it); cross out the incorrect pronoun, and write in the blank whether the pronoun is singular or plural. Finally, underline the noun (or nouns) functioning as the antecedent (or antecedents) of the pronoun you selected.

EXAMPLE

The writer and the designer of an advertisement work

together to plan (~~their~~, its) contents.   *singular*

1. These advertising specialists decide on the funda-

    mental persuasive strategy (~~he,~~ they) will use.   P

2. The pictures in an advertisement are very impor-

    tant; (it, they) will catch a reader's eye.   P

3. Even if the reader is not aware of (its, their) ef-

    fect, big, flashy lettering can draw attention to

    an advertisement.   S

4. Because the visual components attract the most

    attention, the writer and designer plan (it, them)

    very carefully.   _____

5. The most important part of the advertisement

    should be placed where readers will notice (it,

    them).   _____

6. Generally, an <u>advertisement</u> will devote more space to pictures than to words in order to make (its, their) point.

_____

7. The pictures in an <u>advertisement</u> should not, however, distract the reader from (its, their) text.

_____S_____

8. If a writer needs to include the <u>product's cost</u>, (he, they, it) will usually appear in small print near the end of the advertisement.

_____

9. Of course, if the <u>price</u> of a company's products is a selling point, then a writer will emphasize (them, it).

_____

10. Good letter writers wishing to sell products may use the same strategy—emphasize <u>price</u> if (it, they) will help them sell the product.

_____

Mastering Agreement: A Review　　　　　　　Exercise 6–6

NAME _____ SCORE _____

DIRECTIONS　In the following sentences underline the subject; then cross out the verb or pronoun in parentheses that does not agree with its subject or antecedent. Write the correct pronoun or verb in the blank.

EXAMPLE

Most successful <u>advertisements</u> (~~appeals~~, appeal) to both

　　our minds and our emotions.　　　　　　　　*appeal*

1. Details (convinces, convince) our minds to buy what our hearts desire.　　　　　　　　　　_____

2. Everyone (tries, try) to rationalize his or her desires.　　　　　　　　　　　　　　　　　_____

3. The details presented in the persuasive letter (provides, provide) the needed rationalization.　_____

4. If someone (wants, want) to buy a new car, that person must be convinced that the car is really necessary.　　　　　　　　　　　　　　　_____

5. The facts the advertisement lists (gives, give) the reader proof that that particular car is "the one."　_____

6. Effective kinds of information (includes, include) physical features of the product, the reputation of the company, and test and performance data.　_____

7. Another source of persuasion (is, are) the testimonial of a satisfied customer.　　　　　_____

8. Many popular advertisements for health and diet products demonstrate still another strategy: showing (it, them) in action.　　　　　　　　　_____

9. Many an out-of-shape person buys an exercise bike hoping to see (himself or herself, themselves) transformed into a slender, fit person like the one in the advertisement.　　　　　　　　　_____

10. Of course, the claims a writer makes must be (one, ones) the writer believes to be true.

    _____

11. But there (is, are) usually many legitimate claims that can be made about a product or service if a writer knows the facts.

    _____

12. As a persuasive writer, you must emphasize the facts about your product that give it an edge over (your, their) competitor's.

    _____

13. A successful persuasive letter usually (asks, ask) the reader to do something.

    _____

14. The closing of the letter (suggests, suggest) that the reader send for more information or fill out a questionnaire or an application form.

    _____

15. Writers of persuasive letters must make clear exactly what action (he expects, they expect) from the reader.

    _____

16. Most persuasive letters (follows, follow) a set pattern: they capture their readers' attention; they interest the readers in a product or service; they call for some response.

    _____

17. Sentences and paragraphs in an effective persuasive letter are relatively short; (its, their) vocabulary is simple but mature.

    _____

18. The company or firm the writer represents must also never seem to be talking down to (its, their) potential clients.

    _____

19. Neither sarcasm nor a condescending tone (wins, win) customers.

    _____

20. As in any other kind of business letter, one of the main purposes of a persuasive letter (is, are) to build goodwill for the company or business.

    _____

7

Master verb forms.

Learn the main tenses of verbs.

Regular Verbs   Most verbs are called regular verbs; that is, the changes they undergo to show tense (or time) are predictable; *d* or *ed* is added to the end of the present tense to form the past tense and the past participle. From the three principal parts of the verb—present, past, and past participle—together with auxiliary (helping) verbs, such as *will* and *have,* all the tenses of verbs are formed. There are different ways of classifying the number of tenses in English, but the usual practice is to distinguish six tenses.

PRESENT   I prepare the report.   [denotes action (or occurrence) at the present time]

PROGRESSIVE   I am preparing . . .   [denotes action in progress at the present time]

PAST   I prepared the report yesterday.   [denotes action in the past]

PROGRESSIVE   I was preparing . . .   [denotes action in progress at a past time]

FUTURE   I will prepare the report tomorrow.   [denotes action in the future]

PROGRESSIVE   I will be preparing . . .   [denotes action in progress at a future time]

PRESENT PERFECT   I have prepared the report many times.   [emphasizes completion in the present of action previously begun]

PROGRESSIVE   I have been preparing . . .   [emphasizes progress to the present of action previously begun]

PAST PERFECT   I <u>had prepared</u> the report before the manager requested it.

[emphasizes completion at a past time of action previously begun]

PROGRESSIVE   I had been preparing . . . [emphasizes progress until some past

time of action previously begun]

FUTURE PERFECT   I <u>will have prepared</u> the report before the manager requests

it. [emphasizes completion of an action by some future time]

PROGRESSIVE   I <u>will have been preparing</u> . . . [emphasizes progress of an ac-

tion continuing until some future time]

Note: You may have noticed that other words besides the main verb and its auxiliaries can express time—for example, *yesterday, tomorrow,* and *before.* The future is frequently expressed by a form of the present tense plus a word like *tomorrow* and/or an infinitive.

I <u>*am preparing*</u> the report *tomorrow.*

I <u>*am going*</u> *to prepare* the report *tomorrow.*

Irregular Verbs   Irregular verbs do not form the past and past participle in the usual way; instead, they undergo various kinds of changes or, in a few cases, no change at all. (See the chart of frequently used irregular verbs in the Appendix.)

> *run, ran, run, running*
> *choose, chose, chosen, choosing*
> *burst, burst, burst, bursting*

The dictionary lists all four parts of irregular verbs, usually at the beginning of the entry. The dictionary also lists all forms of regular verbs that undergo a change in spelling for the past, the past participle, or the present participle. This change in spelling is most frequently the substitution of *i* for *y*, the doubling of the last letter, or changing *y* to *id*.

> tr*y*, tri*ed*, tri*ed*, tr*y*ing
> occur, occu*rr*ed, occu*rr*ed, occu*rr*ing
> pa*y*, pa*id*, pa*id*, pa*y*ing

Do and Did

Do   The auxiliary verb *do* (OR *does*) is used with the present tense form of a verb to express questions, for the negative, and for special emphasis.

Does she *prepare* reports well?   [a question]

She *does* not (OR *doesn't*) *prepare* reports well.   [a negative]

She *does prepare* reports well.   [special emphasis]

Did   When the past-tense form of *do* is used as an auxiliary with a main verb, the writer emphasizes past time, even though the main verb remains in the present-tense form. This *did* form is used mainly for questions, for the negative, and for special emphasis.

Did she *prepare* the report yesterday?   [a question]

She *did* not (OR *didn't*) *prepare* the report yesterday.   [a negative]

She *did prepare* the report yesterday.   [special emphasis]

Learn the uses of the passive voice.

In most sentences, the verb is in the active voice; that is, the verb expresses an action carried out by the subject. Sometimes, however, this pattern is reversed and the subject does not act but is acted upon; in this case the verb is in the passive voice.

Form the passive voice by placing a form of the verb *be* in front of the past participle form of the verb (for example—*is prepared, was prepared, has been prepared, will be prepared*).

ACTIVE VOICE   The executives often prepare reports.

PASSIVE VOICE   Reports are often prepared by the executives.

As you probably noticed from the above examples, the object of a sentence with an active verb can become the subject of a sentence with a passive verb. The actual doer of the action of the passive verb is sometimes expressed after the preposition *by* (as in the first example of the passive voice) and is sometimes left unstated (as in the second example of the passive voice).

The passive voice is used when you do not know the doer of the action ("Mr. McDowell's store was robbed last night") or when you want to emphasize the verb or the receiver of the action of the verb ("A report is sometimes rewritten three times before it is submitted to upper management"). The passive voice is sparingly used because it sounds highly impersonal and sometimes deprives writing of emphasis (see also Section **29**).

Note: The passive voice is most useful in business writing when you do not want to hurt the reader's feelings ("The motor was left on" instead of "You left the motor on") OR when you do not wish to use the first person pronoun in formal report writing ("The cost was estimated to be $10,000" rather than "I estimated the cost to be $10,000").

Regular and Irregular Verbs

Exercise 7-1

NAME _____ SCORE _____

DIRECTIONS   Mastering verb forms, especially irregular verb forms, requires memorizing them (just as you would memorize multiplication tables or chemical formulas) and accustoming your ear to the correct forms. The best way to learn verb forms, then, is through written and oral drill of five forms of those verbs that cause difficulty: present, past, present or past perfect (both formed from the past participle), progressive, and the form with *did* as an auxiliary.

Following the models given for the example, make up your own short sentences for the verbs and objects or modifiers listed. Use either *he* or *she* for your subject. (See your dictionary if you are unsure of the way to form any of the tenses.)

After you have written the sentences and your verbs have been checked, read the sentences aloud, emphasizing the verbs. If you stumble over a verb or if a verb form sounds strange to you, then you have probably discovered one that gives you trouble in speaking and writing.

EXAMPLE
draw/illustration
PRESENT
She draws an illustration.
PAST
She drew an illustration.
PRESENT PERFECT
She has drawn an illustration!
PROGRESSIVE PRESENT
She is drawing an illustration.
did FORM OF PAST AS A QUESTION
Did she draw an illustration?

1. collect/vouchers
   PRESENT

   PAST

   PRESENT PERFECT

   PROGRESSIVE PRESENT

   did FORM OF PAST AS A QUESTION

2. sit/on the bench
   PRESENT

   PAST

   PRESENT PERFECT

   PROGRESSIVE PRESENT

   did FORM OF PAST AS A QUESTION

3. bring/the blueprints
   PRESENT

   PAST

   PRESENT PERFECT

   PROGRESSIVE PRESENT

   did FORM OF PAST AS A QUESTION

4. break/the rules
   PRESENT

   PAST

   PRESENT PERFECT

   PROGRESSIVE PRESENT

   did FORM OF PAST AS A QUESTION

Regular and Irregular Verbs   Exercise 7–1 (continued)

5. take/vacation
   PRESENT

   PAST

   PRESENT PERFECT

   PROGRESSIVE PRESENT

   did FORM OF PAST IN THE NEGATIVE

6. choose/a career
   PRESENT

   PAST

   PRESENT PERFECT

   PROGRESSIVE PRESENT

   did FORM OF PAST IN THE NEGATIVE

7. begin/to understand
   PRESENT

   PAST

   PRESENT PERFECT

   PROGRESSIVE PRESENT

   did FORM OF PAST IN THE NEGATIVE

8. speak/to clients
   PRESENT

   PAST

   PRESENT PERFECT

   PROGRESSIVE PRESENT

   did FORM OF PAST IN THE NEGATIVE

9. go/to a meeting
   PRESENT

   PAST

   PRESENT PERFECT

   PROGRESSIVE PRESENT

   did FORM OF PAST FOR EMPHASIS

10. write/reports
    PRESENT

    PAST

    PRESENT PERFECT

    PROGRESSIVE PRESENT

    did FORM OF PAST FOR EMPHASIS

Using Irregular Verbs   Exercise 7–2

NAME _____ SCORE _____

DIRECTIONS   The questions below use either *past tense or future tense* verbs with the auxiliaries *did* and *will* (the verbs are underlined twice). Answer those questions having past tense verbs with statements that use the past tense form of the verb without an auxiliary. Answer those questions that have future tense verbs with statements that use the present perfect tense with *already*. Consult your dictionary for the various forms of all verbs that you are unsure of.

EXAMPLES

PAST TENSE   Did he fly to Boston?

Yes, he flew to Boston.

FUTURE TENSE   Will you see the clients?

I have already seen the clients.

1. Did Dr. Jones know the answers?

2. Will you speak to the reporter?

3. Did the project begin on schedule?

4. Will the steam rise from that chimney?

5. Did the explosion shake the building?

6. Will the customer really want to buy that car?

7. Will this client pay the fee?

8. Did the experiment support your hypothesis?

9. Did the worker finally take a break?

10. Will the pressure burst the valve?

Verbs That Cause Difficulties

Exercise 7-3

NAME _____ SCORE _____

There are four main points to be aware of when you write the tense of a verb.

(1) Be sure to put *ed* on the end of all past tense regular verbs (unless they end in *e*—in which case, simply add *d*), being especially careful with those verbs that you tend not to pronounce distinctly.

When the company developed problems, a trouble-shooter was requested.

(2) Be sure not to confuse the past tense with the past participle form.

The trouble-shooter was carefully chosen [NOT *chose*].

The trouble-shooter began [NOT *begun*] his investigation.

(3) Be sure not to give an irregular verb the *ed* ending.

The whistle blew [NOT *blowed*] loudly at noon.

The employees knew [NOT *knowed*] what the whistle meant.

(4) Be especially careful with troublesome verbs like *lie* and *lay*, *sit* and *set*, and *rise* and *raise*.

Notice that *lie* and *sit* are alike: they signify a *state* of resting and do not take objects. Notice also that *lay* and *set* are alike: they signify the *action* of placing, and they do take objects.

He lay [NOT *laid*] down on a couch in his office.

He had sat [NOT *had set*] too long on a hard chair.

Notice finally that *rise* does not take an object; *raise*, on the other hand, does take an object.

Stock prices rose [NOT *raised*] during the last month.

DIRECTIONS   After each of the following sentences the present form of a verb is given. In the blank within the sentence and also in the blank at the right, write the tense called for by the meaning of the sentence. Consult your dictionary if you are uncertain about the other forms of a verb.

EXAMPLE
Managers are frequently ___*asked*___ to

describe the qualities of a good report.   (ask)   ___*asked*___

1. Before a report or letter is _____,

   you should consider your audience.   (begin)   _____

2. Words for any piece of technical writing should be

   _____ carefully.   (choose)   _____

3. Successful vocabulary in technical writing does

   not _____ in choosing difficult

   words.   (lie)   _____

4. When you _____ down to write a

   report, choose words that the reader is likely to

   know.   (sit)   _____

5. A report that is _____ with much

   jargon will make a poor impression.   (write)   _____

6. A great deal of research has been _____

   to determine what makes writing clear.   (do)   _____

7. The conclusion that short words and sentences

   communicate most easily is _____

   from this research.   (draw)   _____

8. Whatever has _____ should be

   reported simply and concisely.   (occur)   _____

9. No writer should use fifteen words when only ten

   are _____ to communicate the

   idea.   (require)   _____

Special Problems with Verbs Exercise 7–4

NAME _____ SCORE _____

Make the tense of a verb in a subordinate clause or of a verbal relate logically to the tense of the verb in the main clause.

She rested for a few minutes after she *had finished* the year-end report. [The

action of the subordinate verb, *had finished*, occurred before the action of the

main verb, *rested.*]

Having finished the year-end report, she was able to begin other projects. [The

perfect form of the verbal, *having finished*, shows action completed before the

action of the main verb, *was.*]

She would have liked *to rest* for an hour or two. [Use the present infinitive after

a verb in the perfect tense.]

She would like *to have* rested for an hour or two. [The perfect infinitive may be

used after a verb that is not in the perfect tense.]

Caution: Avoid switching tenses needlessly in a sentence. (See also **27a.**)

Use the subjunctive mood to express a condition contrary to *fact* (often intro-duced by *if*); to state a wish; and to express a demand, a recommendation, or a re-quest in a *that* clause.

If I *were given* forty-eight hours in a day, I might finish this report on time.

I wish I *were* capable of writing faster.

My supervisor insisted that I *be given* this assignment.

Use the present tense to state facts or ideas that are generally regarded as being true.

A well-developed outline helps one write an organized rough draft.

Haste makes waste.

DIRECTIONS   In the following sentences cross out the incorrect form of the subordinate verb or verbal in parentheses and write the correct form in the blank.

EXAMPLE

After Mario (~~studied,~~ had studied) his first draft, he found many words that he could omit.   *had studied*

1. Mario wanted (to write, to have written) as clearly and concisely as possible.

    _____

2. When he finished his report, he found that he (used, had used) many unnecessary words.

    _____

3. Remembering to eliminate useless words, Mario (crosses, crossed) out "in regard to" and wrote "regarding."

    _____

4. He ought (to use, to have used) "since" instead of "in view of the fact that."

    _____

5. "If I (was, were) receiving this report," Mario thought, "I would not want my time wasted with meaningless words."

    _____

6. After he (examines, had examined) his first draft even more carefully, he found too many weak "there is" and "there are" sentences.

    _____

7. He noticed that he (wrote, had written), "There is a product available," when he should have said, "A product is available."

    _____

8. "This report requires that my words (are, be) carefully chosen," Mario reminded himself.

    _____

9. He realized that it is generally wise (to choose, to have chosen) the shortest wording possible.

    _____

10. (Working, Having worked) hard to eliminate wordiness, Mario found the final draft easy to write.

    _____

Mastering Verbs: A Review
Exercise 7–5

NAME _____ SCORE _____

DIRECTIONS In the following sentences cross out the incorrect form of the verb in parentheses and write the correct form in the blank.

EXAMPLE

To make the point clearly, the writers have (~~chose~~,

chosen) their verbs with care.   *chosen*

1. One place many writers (get, have got) into trouble is with word choice, especially verbs.   _____

2. Like spelling errors, verb errors (will rise, will
   raise) doubts about a writer's accuracy.   _____

3. One piece of advice my teacher (give, gave) me
   was to proofread carefully to make sure all the
   verb tenses were correct.   _____

4. I was also (advise, advised) to be concise, even
   with verbs.   _____

5. When I began writing business reports, I (use,
   used) to like long sentences.   _____

6. I had (suppose, supposed) they made me sound in-
   telligent, but they only made my writing wordy.   _____

7. One type of wordiness is (cause, caused) by the use
   of long verbal phrases.   _____

8. Some writers are (tempt, tempted) to use wordy
   verbal phrases such as *be in receipt of* instead of
   the less-stuffy *received*.   _____

9. When you have the choice, the simpler, clearer
   verbs should be (select, selected).   _____

10. Many reports have been (wrote, written) that
    could have communicated the same point with
    fewer words.   _____

11. The use of long verbal phrases has often (lead, led) to confusion for the reader.

   _____

12. The verbs *get* and *make* are sometimes (use, used) too frequently by poor writers.

   _____

13. Many managers have (shook, shaken) their heads at the number of *gets* found in a report.

   _____

14. One such report (began, begun): "After we get through an investigation of all products now available, we will get a look at those being developed."

   _____

15. Because active verbs result in more concise, informative sentences, report writers have generally (choose, chosen) them over passive verbs.

   _____

16. A passive verb is "slow" because it always (require, requires) an additional verb, a form of *be*, and often a *by* phrase.

   _____

17. No definite rules can be (sat, set) for when it is appropriate to use the passive voice.

   _____

18. However, a formula can be (lay, laid, lain) out: passive verbs can be used when the doer of the action is not known.

   _____

19. If the doer of the action is not (saw, seen) as more important than the receiver of the action, then a passive verb is appropriate.

   _____

20. *The store gave each customer a ten percent discount* emphasizes the store's action, whereas *Each customer was (gave, given) a ten percent discount* emphasizes the customer.

   _____

MANUSCRIPT FORM   ms 8

8

Follow acceptable form in writing your paper. (See also Section **35.**)

Business letters, memorandums, and reports have definite formats, which are illustrated in Section **35.** The format for an essay written in college varies according to the length of the paper. A research paper, for example, may require a title page, an outline, the text, an endnote page or pages, and a bibliography. But the average college writing assignment usually includes no more than the essay itself and sometimes an outline and a title page.

Whether you are writing for college or a career, the most important advice to remember about format is to follow the directions given by your instructor or your supervisor. Many instructors and supervisors refuse to read papers that do not follow the guidelines for preparation that they have indicated.

Usually a college instructor's guidelines for manuscript preparation include the points discussed in this section.

8a Use proper materials.

If you handwrite your papers, use wide-lined, $8\frac{1}{2}$ x 11-inch theme paper (not torn from a spiral notebook). Write in blue or black ink on one side of the paper only.

If you type your themes, use regular white $8\frac{1}{2}$ x 11-inch typing paper (not onion skin). Use a black ribbon, double space between lines, and type on one side of the paper only.

8b Arrange your writing in clear and orderly fashion on the page.

Margins   Theme paper usually has the margins already marked. With unlined paper, be sure to leave about $1\frac{1}{2}$ inches at the left and at the top of each page after the first one; leave 1 inch at the right and at the bottom of each page.

Indentions   Indent the first lines of paragraphs uniformly: about an inch in handwritten copy and five spaces on the typewriter. Leave no long gap at the end of any line except the last one in a paragraph.

Paging   Use Arabic numerals (1, 2, and so forth)—without parentheses or periods—in the upper right-hand corner to mark all pages.

Identification   Instructors vary in what information they require and where they want this information placed. Usually papers carry the name of the student, the course title and number, the instructor's name, and the date. Often the number of the assignment is also included.

Title   On the first page, center your title about 1½ inches from the top or on the first ruled line. Use neither quotation marks nor underlining with your title. Capitalize the first word of the title and all other words except articles, coordinating conjunctions, prepositions, and the *to* in infinitives. Leave one blank line between the title and the first paragraph. (Your instructor may ask you to make a title page. If so, you need not rewrite the title on the first page of the paper unless your instructor asks you to do so.)

Punctuation   Never begin a line of your paper with a comma, a colon, a semicolon, a dash, or an end mark of punctuation; never end a line with the first of a pair of brackets, parentheses, or quotations marks.

8c Write or type your manuscript so that it can be read easily and accurately.

Avoid fancy handwriting flourishes or crowded lines. If your instructor allows you to cross out mistakes, do so neatly. If such corrections become so numerous that the page looks messy or is difficult to read, recopy it. You may prefer to use correction fluid or eraseable ink to fix mistakes so that your finished product will create a good impression. If you type, be sure that your ribbon is reasonably fresh and that the type is clean. If you make errors, correct them neatly with correction tape or fluid. Whether writing or typing, do not use erasable bond paper; it smears and looks messy. If you produce your manuscript on a word processor, be sure to ask your instructor if the typeface is acceptable.

8d Whenever possible, avoid dividing a word at the end of a line. If you must, make such divisions only between syllables and according to standard practice.

The best way to determine where to divide a word that comes at the end of a line is to check a dictionary for the syllable markings (usually indicated by dots). In general, though, remember these guidelines: never divide a single-syllable word; do not carry over to the next line one letter of a word or a syllable like *ed;* divide a hyphenated word only at the hyphen. Keep in mind that an uneven right-hand margin is to be expected and that too many divisions at the ends of lines make a paper difficult to read.

8e Proofread your papers with care.

Always leave a few minutes at the end of an in-class writing assignment for proofreading. Few people write good papers without revising their first drafts. When you need to make a change, draw a straight horizontal line through the part to be deleted and insert a caret (∧) at the point where the addition is to be made above the line. When writing out-of-class papers, try to set your first draft aside for several hours or even for a day so that you can proofread it with a fresh mind.

9

Learn to capitalize in accordance with current practices. Avoid unnecessary capitals.

In general, capital letters are used for first words (the first word of a sentence, including a quoted sentence, a line of poetry, the salutation and complimentary close of a letter, and an item in an outline) and for names of specific persons, places, and things (in other words, proper nouns). A recently published dictionary is your best guide to current standards for capitalization and for the use of italics, abbreviations, and numbers.

The most important rules for capitalization are listed below, but you may find the style sheet on the next page as helpful as the rules.

9a Capitalize words referring to persons, places, things, times, organizations, races, and religions, but not words that refer to classes of persons, places, or things. Capitalize geographic locations only when they refer to specific areas of the country (*the West Coast*) or the world (*the Near East*).

> Most of the doctors in the East attended the medical convention held in Atlanta, Georgia, last August.
> We are taking Business English 201 and also a course in report writing at the University of North Carolina.

9b In general, capitalize a title that immediately precedes (but not one that follows) the name of a person. Capitalize nouns that indicate family relationships when they are used as names or titles or are written in combination with names (*Uncle Ben*).

> My mother and her sister, my Aunt Nancy, met Professor Joseph Tate of the English Department and also the heads of several departments of Northern State College.

Note: Usage varies with regard to capitalization of titles of high rank and titles of family members.

> Lamar Alexander is governor (OR Governor) of Tennessee.

9c Capitalize the first word and the last word of a title, and all other key words (not *a, an,* or *the,* prepositions, coordinating conjunctions, or the *to* in infinitives).

> I think that *How to Write for the World of Work* is an excellent reference book for all occupational writers.

Note: When only a part of a sentence is quoted, the first word is not capitalized.

Most experts agree that workers in the twenty-first century will demand "a bigger voice in decisions that affect their job performance."

9d Capitalize the pronoun *I*, the interjection *O*, most nouns referring to the deity (*the Almighty*), and words that express personification (*the Four Horsemen of the Apocalypse*).

9e Capitalize the first word of each sentence (including a quoted sentence).

I told my boss, "The report will be in the mail tomorrow."

Style sheet for capitalization

SPECIFIC PERSONS   Shakespeare, Buddha, Mr. Keogh, Mayor Koenig

SPECIFIC PLACES   Puerto Rico; Atlanta, Georgia; Western Avenue; the West (BUT "he lives west of here"); Broughton High School

SPECIFIC THINGS   the Statue of Liberty, the Bible, History 304 (BUT history class), the First World War, Parkinson's disease, Sanka coffee

SPECIFIC TIMES AND EVENTS   Wednesday, July (BUT winter, spring, summer, fall, autumn), Thanksgiving, the Age of Enlightenment, the Great Depression (BUT the twentieth century)

SPECIFIC ORGANIZATIONS   the Peace Corps, the Rotary Club, Phi Kappa Phi

SPECIFIC POLITICAL AND MILITARY BODIES   State Department, the United States Senate, Republican Party, United States Army (BUT the army)

RELIGIONS AND BELIEFS   Judaism, Methodists, Marxism (BUT capitalism, communism)

WORDS DERIVED FROM PROPER NAMES   Swedish, New Yorker, Oriental rugs, Labrador retriever

ESSENTIAL PARTS OF PROPER NAMES   the Bill of Rights, the Battle of the Bulge, the New Deal

PARTS OF A LETTER   Dear Mr. Jacobs, Very truly yours

ITEMS IN AN OUTLINE   I. Parts of a letter
        A. Date
        B. Inside address

Capitalization   Exercise 9–1

NAME _____ SCORE _____

DIRECTIONS   Words in one of each of the following groups should be capitalized. Identify the group that needs capitalization by writing either *a* or *b* in the blank. Then make
the necessary revision for the appropriate group of words.

EXAMPLE
(a) a class in economics at our college

(b) *G*eology 201 at *P*urdue *U*niversity   *b*

1. (a) the gods of the ancient romans

   (b) the god of the sun   _____

2. (a) the mountains of our area

   (b) the blue ridge mountains   _____

3. (a) bought a computer for the office

   (b) bought an apple computer   _____

4. (a) chicken pox

   (b) parkinson's disease   _____

5. (a) the age of reason

   (b) the eighteenth century   _____

6. (a) reading an interesting economic study

   (b) reading *megatrends*   _____

7. (a) representative quillen speaking during assembly

   (b) the representative from our district   _____

8. (a) a course in business law

   (b) a course in spanish   _____

9. (a) modern architecture

(b) gothic architecture   _____

10. (a) president Lee Iacocca of chrysler corporation

(b) the president of our company   _____

11. (a) a branch office in the east

(b) flying east to visit a new plant   _____

12. (a) an army during a war

(b) the british army during world war II   _____

13. (a) an article in a popular magazine about psychology

(b) "what you really want from your job" in *psychology to-day*   _____

14. (a) wrote that you have the contract

(b) wrote, "you have the contract."   _____

15. (a) drove north during the holiday

(b) drove to alaska during christmas season   _____

Capitalization   Exercise 9–2

NAME _____ SCORE _____

DIRECTIONS   Each of the following sentences contains words and word groups that require capitalization. First, underline three times the letters that should be capitalized (a
proofreader's symbol for capitalization); then rewrite the sentences with the appropriate
words and word groups capitalized.

EXAMPLE

A friend of mine from south america is studying geology at columbia university this

summer.

A friend of mine from South America is studying
geology at Columbia University this summer.

1. The professor in our business economics class said, "i hope you finish your

   term project during christmas break."

2. The president of our college and professor george gaston of the marketing

   department attended the annual convention of the american association of

   university professors.

3. Many companies, like the burroughs corporation, have corporate head-

   quarters in detroit, michigan.

4. The moslems who work for our corporation were given tuesday off in observance of a religious holiday.

5. This spring we hope to see the statue of liberty and the empire state building while we are vacationing in the east.

6. vice president james williams said that the review committee would arrive on thursday, july 26.

7. ROLM corporation, a telecommunications-equipment company in santa clara, california, provides a full recreational center for its employees.

8. *The wall street journal* ran an interesting series several years ago entitled "the american workplace."

10

Underline words that should be printed in italics.

To show which words should be printed in italics, use underlining. If your composition is set in type by a printer, the words that you have underlined will then appear in italic type.

Since some of the rules for the use of quotation marks and italics overlap, you may want to study Section **16** together with this section. In general, italics are used for works that are contained under one cover, while quotation marks are used for works that are parts of longer words.

> The article "Importing a Recession" appeared in the July 1, 1985, issue of *Newsweek*.
> Flannery O'Connor's short story "The Life You Save May Be Your Own" is a part of the collection *A Good Man Is Hard to Find*.
> "The Imperial March" is from *The Empire Strikes Back*.

10a Italicize (underline) the titles of books, films, long plays (three or more acts), long poems (several pages), record albums, and titles of magazines, journals, and newspapers.

> *Dangerous Words: A Guide to the Law of Libel* can help you understand the power of the written word.
> *Nine to Five* was a popular movie of 1981 that called attention to some of the problems faced by secretaries.
> Archibald MacLeish wrote his play *J.B.* in verse.

Note: Italicize legal citations.

> In 1973 the Supreme Court ruled in the case of *San Antonio Independent School District v. Rodriguez* that property taxes could be used to finance public education.

10b Italicize (underline) foreign words and phrases that are not a part of the English vocabulary.

> Most people would not think wearing jeans, a sweatshirt, and tennis shoes to a job interview to be *très chic*. [In general, it is best to avoid a foreign term when an English equivalent is available.]

Note: Many words that were italicized as foreign—like *coup d'état* and *détente*—are now so frequently used that the italics have been dropped.

10c Italicize (underline) the names of specific ships, airplanes, satellites, and spacecraft as well as works of art.

Russian cosmonauts spent 185 days in orbit aboard the space station *Salyut 6.*
The *Mona Lisa* is housed at the Louvre in Paris.

10d Italicize (underline) words, letters, and figures spoken of as such.

Remember that *misspelled* has two *s*'s and two *l*'s.
The word *petroleum* comes from two Latin words—*petra,* which means "rock," and
oleum, which means "oil."

Italics   Exercise 10–1

NAME _____   SCORE _____

DIRECTIONS   In the following sentences underline the words or word groups that should
be printed in italics.

EXAMPLE
In Florence, Italy, stands the original of Michelangelo's David.

1. Communication and Organizational Behavior is a very interesting book
   about how offices operate.

2. The word interview comes from the Middle French word entrevue, which
   means "to see one another."

3. A popular rock 'n' roll song of the 1950s, Get a Job, talked about an out-of-
   work teenager.

4. Surprisingly, Herman Melville's novel Moby Dick used the slang expression "cool" made popular in the 1970s by the television character "The Fonz"
   of Happy Days.

5. Many people forget that the possessive pronoun has no apostrophe, and so
   they write it's when they mean its.

6. The Smithsonian Air and Space Museum in Washington has the original
   airplane flown by the Wright brothers in 1903 as well as Charles Lind-
   bergh's Spirit of St. Louis.

7. I used to forget that in receive the second e comes before the i.

8. The first American space shuttle was called the Columbia.

9. Some people would argue that the Pilgrims' Mayflower was the first
   "company car."

10. The term ergonomics, which means "fitting the work to the worker," has
    an ics on the end, as do many of the names of other applied sciences.

11. The Atlanta Journal-Atlanta Constitution ran an interesting series during
    August 1978 entitled "Working in the Year 2000."

12. Arthur Miller's play, Death of a Salesman, portrays a "little man" ground
    down by the system.

13. Probably the most famous single ruling of the Supreme Court was handed down in 1954 in Brown v. Board of Education of Topeka, which made segregation in the public schools unconstitutional.

14. My English class is reading The Jungle, Upton Sinclair's exposé of the meat packing industry.

15. We went to see Norma Rae, a film based on the life of a real factory worker.

11

Follow current practices in the use of abbreviations, acronyms, and numbers.

Abbreviations are more common in business and technical writing than in other kinds of composition, but even there writers should take note of the following. First, a writer should only use those abbreviations that the reader is sure to understand. Second, a letter, memo, or report should never look as though it is overflowing with abbreviations. Finally, once an abbreviation has been introduced, the writer should use it consistently throughout the document.

Acronyms abound in almost any field; an acronym is a word made up of the first letters in a compound phrase—for instance, NASA, which stands for National Aeronautics and Space Administration. Few things are as annoying to a reader as an avalanche of these "invented" words. When you use an acronym, always write out the complete phrase or title the first time unless it is one all your readers will understand.

Figures are commonly used in occupational writing except when a number is the first word in a sentence or when the number to be used is ten or under. In other kinds of writing, figures are used only when the numbers could not be written out in one or two words (for example, 150; 2,300; $250.00) or when a series of numbers is being reported.

11a Certain abbreviations are commonly used even for first references.

TITLES Dr., Mr., Mrs., Ms., Jr.

Note: Do not use redundant titles: Dr. H. U. Farr OR H. U. Farr, Ph.D. [NOT Dr. H. U. Farr, Ph.D.]

TIMES A.M. (OR a.m.), P.M. (OR p.m.), B.C., A.D., E.S.T.

DEGREES B.S., M.A., Ph.D., C.P.A.

PLACES U.S.A., U.S.S.R.

ORGANIZATIONS TVA, UNICEF, HEW, FBI, NASA [Notice that the abbreviations for organizations require no periods.]

LATIN TERMS etc. (and so forth), i.e. (that is), e.g. (for example), cf. (compare), vs. (versus) [Do not interchange *i.e.* and *e.g.*]

Note: Today the English forms (enclosed in parentheses) are generally preferred over their Latin equivalents.

11b Spell out the names of states, countries, continents, months, days of the week, and units of measurement.

> *Great Britain* (NOT *G.B.*), *New York* (NOT *N.Y.*) [except for long names, like
>   *U.S.S.R.* for Union of Soviet Socialist Republics or *D.C.* for District of Columbia]
> *January* (NOT *Jan.*)
> *Wednesday* (NOT *Wed.*)
> nine *pounds* (NOT *nine lbs.*)
> *Washington* (NOT *WA* or *Wash.*)   [It is appropriate to use the two-letter Post Office
>   abbreviations for states on envelopes and in the heading and return address sec-
>   tions of business letters.]
> *and* (NOT *&*)

Note: Do not use & (the ampersand) except in copying official titles or names
of firms: AT&T.

11c Spell out *Street, Avenue, Road, Park, Mount, River, Company,* and other similar words used as a part of a proper name.

11d Spell out the words *volume, chapter,* and *page* and the names of courses of study.

> *chapter* 9 (NOT *ch.* 9)
> *chemistry* (NOT *chem.*)

11e Spell out the meaning of any acronym your reader may not know when you first use it.

> The Read Only Memory (ROM) of the computer contains the routines that make it
>   run. The ROM cannot be altered.
>
>   OR
>
> The computer's ROM (Read Only Memory) is installed when it is manufactured.

11f Although usage varies, writers tend to spell out numbers that can be expressed in one or two words; they ordinarily use figures for other numbers.

> The *forty*-hour workweek may soon be changed to *thirty-five* hours.
> In 1976 our country was *200* years old; our state, *187;* and our county, *125.*

Note: Business and technical writers generally use figures for all numbers
above ten except when (1) a number occurs at the beginning of the sentence; (2)
a fraction is used alone; or (3) the exact amount or number is not known.

> The 40-hour workweek may soon be changed to 35 hours.
> *One hundred* years ago the average American worked about *fifty-five* hours a week,
>   or *one-third* of the *168* hours in a week.

11g In documentation for reports and charts, certain abbreviations are commonly used: *p.* (page), *pp.* (pages), *col.* (column), *cols.* (columns), *no.* (number), *nos.* (numbers).

11h In special circumstances—for instance, in tables or footnotes, where space is limited—any abbreviation listed in a standard dictionary is acceptable.

Abbreviations and Numbers

Exercise 11–1

NAME _____ SCORE _____

DIRECTIONS   Change any part of each of the following items to an abbreviation or a figure if the abbreviation or figure would be appropriate as a first reference in writing (not in tables or footnotes). Write your revision in the blank. If it would not be correct as a number or figure, rewrite the item as it stands.

EXAMPLES

nine o'clock in the morning

9 a.m. or A.M.

last Saturday afternoon

last Saturday afternoon

1. page twelve of part five

2. the governor of Oregon

3. fifteen hundred years before Christ

4. Alexis J. Powell, doctor of philosophy

5. Canyon Park on Lexington Avenue

6. eight hundred dollars

7. sixteen pounds, seven ounces

8. Captain Brewster

9. sixty-five percent

10. the introductory economics classes in Sanford Hall

DIRECTIONS   Rewrite the following sentences to correct any errors in the use of abbreviations, acronyms, or numbers. If the sentence is correct, rewrite it as it stands.

11. 100 people visited the exhibit in the first twenty minutes it was open.

12. The office is located at 25 Elm St. in Boone.

13. Their chief executive officer (CEO) is Dr. Theresa L. Braker, Ph.D.

14. We usually have staff meetings on Mon. and Wed. mornings.

15. She will have worked at IBM 25 years as of September 1, 1986.

16. A person can shelter income from taxes by opening an IRA (Individual Retirement Account).

17. She told us that the contract went to a firm in Calif.

18. Emory said he liked the advertisement & that he would buy the computer.

19. I believe he said Nov. is when General Williamson's report is due.

20. After looking for nearly seven hours, John found the figure twenty-six percent on page 1943 of the book.

Capitalization, Italics, Abbreviations, Acronyms, and Numbers: A Review

Exercise 11-2

NAME _____ SCORE _____

DIRECTIONS   The following passages have been altered to include errors. Revise them to reflect the correct use of capital letters, italics, abbreviations, acronyms, and numbers. (In the scoring, a word group counts as a single change.) Apply the principles in **11f.**

tests over the years show that the average sentence length in successful pulp magazines has been kept between 12 and 15 words. The Reader's Digest average is consistently between fourteen and seventeen, and that of *Time* seventeen to nineteen. Our count of three-syllable words shows the following averages for the same publications: *True Confessions*, 3 percent; reader's digest, eight to nine percent; Time, 9 to 10 percent.   —ROBERT GUNNING, *The Technique of Clear Writing*

Career decision-making, whether it involves choosing or changing one's job, is an important process. most people spend more than one hundred thousand hours—1/6 of their lives—at work. As Chas. F. Kettering, the inventor and engineer, once said, "the future is all we are interested in, because we are going to spend the rest of our lives there." obviously, anything that takes up so much of our lives should be carefully planned—to ensure a career directed by choice rather than chance.   —DEAN L. HUMMEL, "What Should I Be When I Grow Up?"

Rangely, Maine, is the home of TRANET, transnational network for appropriate alternative technologies. . . . Tranet's purpose is to link people, projects, and resources in the appropriate technical community. The network has five hundred members worldwide, publishes a quarterly newspaper, . . . maintains files on some fifteen hundred appropriate technology projects and ten thousand individuals, has an extensive library, & is able to arrange many successful linkages.   —JOHN NAISBITT, *Megatrends: Ten New Directions Transforming Our Lives*

THE COMMA

12 and 13

Let sentence structure guide you in the use of commas.

In speaking, you use pauses and changes in voice pitch to make your sentences easier to follow. In writing, you use punctuation marks in a similar way, especially as you make additions to the basic pattern of subject-verb-complement. Such additions may occur at the beginning, in the middle, or at the end of a sentence.

> *After studying the report,* the president of the company decided to go ahead with the project.
> The president of the company, *after studying the report,* decided to go ahead with the project.
> The president of the company decided, *after studying the report,* to go ahead with the project.
> The president of the company decided to go ahead with the project, *after studying the report.*

Five main rules govern the use of the comma. In the exercises that follow, each of these rules is explained and illustrated (**12a, 12b,** and so forth). Cautions against the corresponding misuses are also provided (**13a, 13b,** and so forth).

Commas and Coordinating
Conjunctions

Exercise 12/13-1

NAME *Justin McCarthy*   SCORE _____

12a A comma follows a main clause that is linked to another main clause by a coordinating conjunction—*and, but, or, nor, for, so, yet.*

> Proposals are written by businesses to gain new contracts, and they are usually assigned to experienced writers.

13a A comma is not used to separate a subject from its verb or a verb from its object.

13b A comma is not used *after* a coordinating conjunction, nor is it used *before* a coordinating conjunction when only words, phrases, or subordinate clauses (rather than main clauses) are being linked. (Throughout this section, a circled comma , indicates a misuse of the comma.)

> Business proposals are written for many purposes, and , they require different types of formats. [The comma comes *before*, but not *after*, the coordinating conjunction.]
> Proposals vary in both length , and format. [A comma is not used before a coordinating conjunction that links two words or phrases.]

DIRECTIONS   In the following sentences insert an inverted caret (**V**) before coordinating conjunctions that connect main clauses. Then insert a comma after the first main clause and write a comma in the blank. If a sentence without commas is correct as it stands, write *C* in the blank to show that no comma is needed. If a sentence contains a misused comma, circle the comma; then place a circled comma (,) in the blank.

EXAMPLES

People or companies submit written proposals showing what they

will do for someone and at what price.   *C*

Many times proposals total hundreds of pages, but short proposals

need to be thorough and specific too.   ,

1. A good proposal convinces the reader that its writer

   understands the company's needs, and it offers a practical

   solution to the problem.   ,

2. Many companies have specific guidelines for proposal

   writing, so your document should conform to their re-

   quirements.   ,

3. A proposal must make clear, what needs to be done and how it will be accomplished. ____(,)____

4. Details are important and your proposal should include specific time schedules and budgets. ____,____

5. But, such details should be selected and organized so that they do not overwhelm the reader. ____(,)____

6. Personal qualifications may be important so you may wish to include background about key personnel. ____,____

7. One problem a proposal writer faces is "overkill" but your proposal must include enough information to be convincing. ____,____

8. Sometimes you will be asked by a company or a client to investigate a problem and submit a proposal showing how your firm would solve it. ____,____

9. An *unsolicited* proposal must persuade a company that it has a problem and that you are the one to solve it. ____C____

10. An unsolicited proposal is more difficult to write for you must devise your own pattern of organization. _____

Commas and Introductory Additions   Exercise 12/13–2

NAME *Justin McCarthy*   SCORE _____

12b A comma usually follows adverb clauses that precede main clauses. A comma often follows introductory phrases (especially verbal phrases) and transitional expressions. A comma follows an introductory interjection (like *oh*) or an introductory *yes* or *no.*

> *When our company received a request for a proposal,* we asked our best writer to prepare it.   [introductory adverb clause (for a list of common adverb clause markers, see *Subordinators* in the Appendix)]
> *Following the guidelines suggested by the company,* the writer prepared an excellent proposal.   [introductory verbal phrase]

A comma is often omitted after introductory prepositional phrases when no misreading would result. When an adverb clause comes at the end of a sentence, it is not usually preceded by a comma unless the clause is introduced by *although.*

> *Not long after,* the company received a positive response from the company that solicited the proposal.   [The comma prevents misreading.]
> Our company was chosen ⊙ *because the writer of the proposal had prepared an excellent presentation.*   [concluding adverb clause]
> The writer of the proposal sold our company's product, *although more than twenty other companies also presented proposals.*   [concluding adverb clause introduced by *although*]

DIRECTIONS   After each introductory element in the sentences below, either write a *C* to indicate that the sentence is correct as it stands or insert a comma where one is needed. Then write the *C* or the comma in the blank.

EXAMPLES

When you write an unsolicited proposal, you generally may choose

your own format.   ___,___

Quite often *C* an unsolicited proposal is presented in the form of a

letter.   ___*C*___

1. Even when a writer drafts a letter proposal, captions or

headings still identify major sections.   ___,___

2. In section one the writer usually provides an abstract which

summarizes the contents of the proposal.   ___C___

3. By using the first section of the report to summarize or sketch the main points the writer tries to make the reader's job as easy as possible. _____

4. In just seconds the reader can decide which sections of the report to read. _____

5. Moreover keeping this abstract in mind can help the reader understand the details of the report. _____

6. Because one of your goals as a writer is to make your report easy to read you will want to use clear, helpful headings for all sections. _____

7. You can often build a good heading from the key words in the first sentence although you cannot always do so. _____

8. Accuracy in a proposal is extremely important because the proposal may be interpreted as a legal document. ___C___

9. Legally you can be held accountable for the contents of your proposal. _____

10. In court you would be judged responsible for making good your promises. _____

Commas and Items in a Series

NAME _____ SCORE _____

12c Commas are used to separate items in a series and to separate coordinate adjectives (in pairs or series).

A series is a succession of three or more parallel elements. Note the commas:

> *English, mathematics,* and *psychology* are all disciplines with important applications to nearly any career.
>
> The office is *pleasant to work in, easy to get to,* and *inexpensive to maintain.*

Adjectives are coordinate when they describe the same noun (or noun substitute) in a parallel fashion—so that they could logically be joined by *and* or *or* and so that their order could be reversed without loss of sense. *Pleasant, easy,* and *inexpensive* in the preceding example are coordinate adjectives. Coordinate adjectives are used not only in series but in pairs:

> They are *alert, energetic* employees.   [Note that the sequence could be reversed and the comma replaced by *and:* They are *energetic and alert* employees.]

Notice in all the preceding examples that the commas are used where the coordinating conjunction *and* would otherwise appear. (In a series, the last comma usually is accompanied by the coordinating conjunction rather than replacing it.)

> English *and* mathematics *and* psychology
> English, mathematics, and psychology
>
> pleasant to work in *and* easy to get to *and* inexpensive to maintain
> pleasant to work in, easy to get to, and inexpensive to maintain
>
> alert *and* energetic
> alert, energetic

13e Commas are not used between adjectives that are not coordinate (those that could not be linked by *and*), before the first item or after the last item in a series, or between *two* items linked by a coordinator.

> A modern ⊙ chrome ⊙ rocking chair stood in one corner.   [The adjectives are not coordinate: their sequence cannot be reversed, nor can they logically be joined by *and.*]
>
> The office did not lack such necessary equipment as ⊙ desk, file cabinets, and typewriters.   [No comma is used before the first item in the series.]
>
> Yesterday a supply center delivered a photocopy machine, a calculator, and a Dictaphone ⊙ to the office.   [No comma is used after the last item in the series.]
>
> Our office was now both attractive ⊙ and functional.   [No comma is used between *two* items that are linked by a coordinator.]

DIRECTIONS Identify each series (or pair) that needs commas by writing *1, 2* or *1, 2, and 3* above the items and also in the blanks. Insert commas where they belong in the sentence and also between the numbers in the blank to show the punctuation of the pattern. Write *C* after each sentence that has no items in a series that need punctuation.

EXAMPLES

Almost everyone has to present a formal oral report. _____**C**_____

Oral reports are used to explain policies and procedures, teach others what they need to know, and persuade others to accept the speaker's position. _____*1, 2 and 3*_____

1. You need to know how to prepare an oral report, how to make use of visual effects in the report, and how to deliver the report effectively. _____

2. Three of the main considerations in preparing oral reports are audience, occasion, and purpose. _____

3. You must consider whether the occasion for the report is business, social, or both. _____

4. A short report with touches of humor may be appropriate at a luncheon or dinner meeting. _____*C*_____

5. At a formal business meeting of the company, a formal detailed report would be called for. _____

6. In other words, the same speech may be a huge success at one time and a dismal failure at another, depending on the occasion and the audience. _____*C*_____

7. Another aspect of the occasion is the place itself: the size of the room the number of chairs and the time of day. _____

8. If you are to show slides a filmstrip or a movie, you must be sure that the room is equipped with the right kind of projector and screen. _____

9. A very effective oral presentation may be made to forty people in a room meant for thirty; but, in general, a report given to forty people in a room large enough to hold two hundred is destined for trouble. _____

10. A cold dimly lit room may also handicap a speaker. _____

Commas and Restrictive and Nonrestrictive
Additions

Exercise 12/13-4

NAME _____ SCORE _____

12d Commas are used to set off nonrestrictive clauses and phrases (those that are not essential or necessary to the meaning of the terms they refer to) and other parenthetical elements.

> The North Carolina Technical Writers' Workshop, *which was held in Raleigh during August,* attracted middle management personnel from all over the state. [The *which* clause is not needed to identify *Workshop.*]
> The organizer of the Workshop, *Leo Bernstein,* was pleased with the turnout. [An appositive is usually nonrestrictive.]
> The new managers, *not to mention the experienced ones,* learned a great deal from the seminars. [*Not to mention* introduces a parenthetical element.]

Caution: Avoid the serious error of using only one comma to set off a nonrestrictive phrase or clause. When the second comma is not used, the writer seems to be separating the subject from the verb or the verb from the complement. (Remember that commas do not separate the parts of the basic sentence—subject–verb–complement—but rather show where additions that require punctuation have been made.)

> WRONG The Workshop which met in August ⊙ led to an immediate improvement in the reports written by the managers.
>
> WRONG The Workshop ⊙ which met in August led to an immediate improvement in the reports written by managers.
>
> RIGHT The Workshop, *which met in August,* led to an immediate improvement in the reports written by the managers.

Remember, then, to use two commas when a nonrestrictive or other parenthetical element appears in the middle of a sentence.

> The managers, fortunately for all concerned, praised the Workshop's leaders.

When the explanatory phrase or clause begins a sentence, only the second comma is used.

> Fortunately for all concerned, the managers praised the Workshop's leaders.

When the explanatory phrase or clause ends a sentence, the second comma is replaced by the period.

> The managers praised the Workshop's leaders, *I might add.*

When two sentences are joined, however, one of the two commas setting off a parenthetical element may be replaced by a semicolon.

> We were pleased with the training sessions; *I might add,* the managers praised the Workshop's leaders.

13d Restrictive phrases and clauses (those that give information essential to the meaning of the terms they refer to are not set off with commas. The circled commas in the following examples are incorrect.

> The seminar ⊙ in technical writing ⊙ attracted students from all over the country.   [The phrase identifies *seminar*.]
>
> The professor ⊙ *who planned the seminar* ⊙ was surprised by the number of applications received.   [The *who* clause identifies *professor*.]
>
> Much of the writing *that was done as a result of the seminar* was published.   [*That* introduces a restrictive clause, essential to identify *writing*.]

DIRECTIONS   Set off with commas all nonrestrictive and parenthetical additions in the sentences below. Then in the blanks place (1) a dash followed by a comma (—,) if the nonrestrictive or parenthetical addition begins the sentence, (2) a comma followed by a dash (,—) if the nonrestrictive addition ends the sentence, or a dash enclosed within commas (,—,) if the nonrestrictive addition comes within the sentence. Write *C* if there is no nonrestrictive or parenthetical addition to set off.

EXAMPLE

Public speaking, like any skill, requires practice.   ,—,

1. If you forget a word or phrase a memorized speech can fail.   _____

2. Generally, only people like guides and tour leaders make use of memorized speeches.   _____

3. Written speeches, on the other hand, are used in many different business situations.   ,—,

4. Listening to someone read a speech, especially a long one, can put people to sleep.   ,—,

5. A written speech requires a well-lighted room a condition that the speaker cannot count on.   _____

6. Most speakers, even in formal business settings, prefer to deliver an extemporaneous speech.   _____

7. Just like other types of speeches an extemporaneous speech demands skill and preparation.   _____

8. Although it is not memorized, a successful extemporaneous speech as a rule has been carefully planned.   _____

9. The speech that demands the least preparation is the impromptu speech.   C

10. The unskilled speaker who makes no advanced preparation at all will, much to everyone's dismay, make many mistakes.   _____

Conventional Uses of Commas   Exercise 12/13–5

NAME _____ SCORE _____

12e Commas are conventionally used to set off a variety of constructions: (1) negative or contrasted elements, (2) words in direct address, (3) words that explain who is speaking in a direct quotation, (4) items in dates, addresses, and geographic locations, and (5) complimentary closes of letters (see Section **35**).

> The most common kind of speech is extemporaneous, *not written or memorized.* [A contrasted element is commonly introduced by *not.*]
>
> "*Harold,* would you plan a presentation for the board of directors next Friday," *the sales manager asked,* "to explain our new marketing program?" [A comma is used after the name of someone addressed directly; commas set off expressions like *he said* or *she asked* (unless a question mark or exclamation point is called for). See also Section **16** for the placement of other punctuation in relationship to quotation marks.]
>
> The annual convention of the Junior Chamber of Commerce will be held at *Laguna Beach, California,* on *March 16, 1986.*

Sometimes dates are arranged differently in official documents and reports, and the punctuation then varies from the usual practice: *14 August 1986.* The usual form in letters would be *August 14, 1986.*

Note: If only the month and the year are given, no comma is necessary: *August 1986.*

Caution: No comma is used before the zip code in a postal address: *New York, NY 10017.*

DIRECTIONS   Insert commas as they are needed in each of the following sentences. In the blank write the number that represents the reason you inserted the comma or commas: *1* for negative or contrasted elements, *2* for words in direct address, *3* for words that explain who is speaking, and *4* for items in dates, addresses, or geographic locations. Some sentences require more than one comma.

EXAMPLE

"Sara, could you come to our Chicago office for an interview?" the

personnel director asked.   *2*

1. The company wanted Sara to see the plant, not just look at

   pictures.   _____

2. Since July 1, 1985, the company asked job finalists to give brief

   presentations to a small group of supervisors.   _____

3. The personnel director told Sara to give an extemporaneous

   speech, not a formal written one.   _____

4. "Just tell us about your training as a technical writer," the personnel director told Sara. _____

5. "My business writing class showed me," Sara said, "how to organize this kind of talk." _____

6. She continued, "I think I will describe the types of reports I know how to write." _____

7. Sara would also mention her writing internship at IBM in Atlanta, Georgia, from January to May 1985. _____

8. "And, Sara, could you please bring samples of your written work?" the personnel director asked. _____

9. "I had planned to bring copies of ads I wrote at IBM," Sara told the personnel director. _____

10. On Wednesday, August 8, 1985, Sara flew from Greensboro, North Carolina, to Chicago, confident that her presentation would go well. _____

Mastering Commas: A Review

Exercise 12/13–6

NAME _____ SCORE _____

DIRECTIONS Insert commas as they are needed in the following sentences. (Not all sentences require commas.) Then in the blanks write the number representing the reason for the comma or commas that you add to a sentence: *1* for main clauses linked by a coordinator, *2* for introductory elements, *3* for items in a series, *4* for nonrestrictive clauses and phrases and other parenthetical elements, and *5* for any other conventional uses. If you do not need to add a comma to a sentence, write *0* in the blank.

EXAMPLE

When you are asked to prepare a report, find out as much as you can

about your audience.   __2__

1. If your reading audience is composed of friends and colleagues your report can be less formal than if you are writing to strangers.   _____

2. At the same time, writing for a group of friends and/or co-workers can be difficult.   _____

3. An old saying states, "A prophet is not without honor save in his own country."   _____

4. To a certain extent, this maxim applies whenever you must write for an audience that is familiar with you.   _____

5. It is often more difficult to convince friends than strangers that you know what you are talking about.   _____

6. It often requires more evidence, not less, to convince an audience of friends and co-workers.   _____

7. Since these readers know you quite well, they may not take you seriously unless you support what you say with details.   _____

8. Of course, a reading audience that does not know you also presents difficulties.   _____

9. Such an audience may make harsh, unjustified judgments about you even before finishing your report.   _____

10. These readers may, for example, decide that you are too inexperienced to be an expert.   _____

11. When writing for an audience that does not know you, you should prepare a rather formal report. _____

12. It is important to know who makes up your audience, and it helps to know how much understanding the audience has of the field about which you will be speaking. _____

13. If the audience is unfamiliar with your subject you may need to give some background information. _____

14. It is wise to avoid technical vocabulary as much as possible whenever you are writing for a group of people who are un-familiar with your subject. _____

15. People in your own field, on the other hand, are able to follow a report that makes use of common technical words. _____

16. Professionals in your own field, who are likely to know the technical vocabulary associated with your subject, must be treated with respect. _____

17. You should not define simple technical terms, offer background information, or otherwise talk down to a reading audience that is already familiar with your subject. _____

18. You will be more likely to write an effective report if you know the kind of audience you are addressing, but sometimes it is not possible to analyze an audience carefully. _____

19. There are three suggestions, however, that can help you write to any audience. _____

20. You should be clear, argue logically, and support your claims with facts and details. _____

14

Use the semicolon between two related main clauses not joined by a coordinator, between two main clauses that are joined by a coordinator but which themselves contain commas, and between coordinate items to separate a series of items which themselves contain commas. Elements with semicolons between them should be of equal grammatical rank.

14a Use the semicolon between two main clauses not joined by a coordinator.

Often the semicolon between clauses is accompanied by a conjunctive adverb (such as *however*) or a transitional expression (such as *on the other hand*) that signals the exact relationship between the clauses. A semicolon can be used instead of a coordinating conjunction to join two main clauses if they are closely related. Usually, one of the clauses explains the other or stands in contrast to it.

> A formal speech is written down and memorized; an extemporaneous speech is planned but not written down.   [The content of the second main clause contrasts with the idea in the first clause; the semicolon acts as the balancing point between the first and the second clause.]

If the second clause explains the first clause, often a colon is more appropriate. (See **17d.**)

> An impromptu speech is just what the term suggests: it is an unplanned speech that is delivered on the spur of the moment.

Often the semicolon between clauses is accompanied by a conjunctive adverb (such as *however*) or a transitional expression (such as *on the other hand*) that signals the exact relationship between the clauses.

> A written speech tends to be very formal; an extemporaneous speech sounds more natural and spontaneous.
> A written speech is suitable for many occasions; however, it is likely to be very boring when read on social occasions.

Note: Remember that when a conjunctive adverb or a transitional expression is used *as an addition to* a main clause, it is often set off by commas.

> A written speech is suitable for some occasions; it is, *however,* likely to be very boring when read on social occasions.

This "addition" to the main clause can be moved to numerous places within the sentence.

A written speech is suitable for some occasions; it is likely, *however,* to be very boring when read on social occasions.

OR

A written speech is suitable for some occasions; *however,* it is likely to be very boring when read on social occasions.   [Note that when the conjunctive adverb immediately follows the semicolon, the semicolon absorbs the first comma.]

Caution: Be especially careful to use a semicolon between two main clauses not joined by a coordinator when direct quotations are involved.

"Prepare only an outline for a talk," the instructor suggested; "don't memorize a set of words."

14b Use a semicolon to separate a series of elements which themselves contain commas.

The four types of speeches we studied were the written speech, which is read to the audience; the memorized speech, which is first written down and then learned verbatim; the extemporaneous speech, in which a plan, but not the exact words, is often sketched out as a guide; and the impromptu speech, which is made without preparation or advance thought.

14c Do not use a semicolon between parts of unequal grammatical rank.

A semicolon should not be used between a clause and a phrase or between a main clause and a subordinate clause.

NOT   He gave an extemporaneous speech; usually the most effective kind.

BUT   He gave an extemporaneous speech, usually the most effective kind.   [A comma, not a semicolon, is used between the clause and the phrase.]

NOT   The speech sounded entirely natural; although it had been carefully planned.

BUT   The speech sounded entirely natural, although it had been carefully planned.   [A comma, not a semicolon, is appropriate between the main clause and the subordinate clause.]

Semicolons Between Main Clauses

Exercise 14–1

NAME _____   SCORE _____

DIRECTIONS   In the following sentences insert an inverted caret (**V**) between main clauses and add the semicolon. In the blank, copy the semicolon and any conjunctive adverb or transitional expression that follows it. Be sure to include the comma with the expression if there is one. Write *C* if the sentence is correctly punctuated.

> EXAMPLE
> You may think that the application process ends when you
> leave the interview;however, you still have more to do.   *; however,*

1. At your interview, you thank the interviewer for talking with you; however, you should also write a thank-you letter.   *; how ever*

2. You want the company to know that you are considerate; your thank-you letter shows this.   *; your*

3. Your letter need not be lengthy; indeed, a letter that rambles on will annoy the reader.   *; Indeed*

4. A thank-you letter can remind the reader who you are, can continue your contact with the firm, and can give you a chance to say more.   *C*

5. Interviews always seem too short once home; you usually think of several points you should have made.   *; you*

6. The thank-you letter is an opportunity to give more information; otherwise, the company will never know those additional facts about you.   *; otherwise*

7. You want the company to think that you will be a competent employee; use this letter to show how your skills meet the company's needs.   *; meet*

8. A thank-you letter should not sound pushy; it should not demand a response; it should not be "cute."   *; ... "cute"*

9. Once you mail your letter, sit back, wait patiently, and remember that no news is good news.

10. Six weeks may seem a long time to wait for the company's response nevertheless, companies often find it necessary to keep you waiting that long.

Semicolons and Commas

Exercise 14–2

NAME _____ SCORE _____

DIRECTIONS   In each sentence use an inverted caret (**V**) to mark the spot where a comma or a semicolon should go. Insert the correct punctuation mark in the sentence and also write it in the blank. (One of the sentences will require two commas or semicolons.)

EXAMPLE
The most widely used speech is the extemporaneous type⌄it is planned

  but not memorized.   —— ; ——

1. The extemporaneous speech is planned and rehearsed however, the actual wording varies from presentation to presentation.   _____

2. The speaker may prepare as much for an extemporaneous speech as for a written or memorized one but the speech itself never has a final, unchanging set of words.   _____

3. Since the phrasing does vary each time the extemporaneous speech is presented, the speaker is not as likely to sound monotonous, preachy, and uninvolved as he or she might in giving a memorized or written speech but the speaker still has the advantage of a carefully planned and rehearsed presentation.   _____

4. The extemporaneous speech can be adapted to the mood of the audience to whom it is presented therefore it is the safest kind of speech to plan for most occasions.   _____

5. The extemporaneous speech is a life-saver if any of these conditions occur: the audience is enthusiastic people look lost or puzzled or someone interrupts by coming in late or asking a question.   _____

6. The speaker may or may not use notes in an extemporaneous presentation in either case the speaker has the advantage of more freedom of movement than he or she would have with a written speech.   _____

7. "What are you going to talk about for your oral report," my instructor asked "and what type of presentation do you plan to use?" _____

8. "In an extemporaneous speech I plan to discuss the advantages that advertising offers C.P.A.s and lawyers" I replied. _____

9. My instructor seemed happy that I was going to speak extemporaneously nevertheless, he cautioned me to make certain that I was well prepared. _____

10. Although an extemporaneous speech may not be written down, it is however, carefully thought out. _____

15

Use the apostrophe to indicate the possessive case (except for personal pronouns), to mark omissions in contractions, and to form certain plurals.

Remember that the apostrophe, in most of its uses, indicates that something has been omitted.

> children's books   [books *of* or *for* children]
> don't   [do *not*]
> the class of '86   [1986]

15a The main use of the apostrophe is to indicate the possessive case (including that of acronyms). Add either an 's or an ' to form the possessive of nouns and some pronouns.

> speaker's duty   [singular possessive; duty of one speaker]
> speakers' duty   [plural possessive; duty of two or more speakers]
> everyone's duty   [singular possessive of a pronoun]
> Mars' terrain OR Mars's terrain   [singular possessive of a singular noun ending in *s*]
> men's shoes   [plural possessive: 's added to plural of *man*]
> chairman of the board's presentation   [singular possessive noun phrase; 's added to last word in phrase]
> sister-in-law's car   [singular possessive noun phrase; 's added to last word in phrase]
> sisters-in-law's cars   [plural possessive noun phrase; 's added to last word in phrase]
> Sam's and Jane's offices   [Sam and Jane have different offices.]
> Sam and Jane's office   [Sam and Jane have the same office.]
> IBM's computer   [possessive of an acronym]

Do not use the apostrophe with the pronouns *his, hers, its, our, yours, theirs,* or *whose* or with plural nouns that are not in the possessive case.

> *Whose* project is this—*yours* or *theirs*?

Form the singular or plural of a word first; then indicate possession:

> gallery→gallery's paintings   galleries→galleries' paintings

15b Use an apostrophe to indicate omissions in contractions and in numbers. Remember to place the apostrophe exactly where the omission occurs.

> *It's* [It *is*]   the duty of the president of the class of '86   [1986]   to open the time vault.

Caution: The use of contractions is not common in writing unless a conversational tone is sought. For instance, contractions are often used in business letters to make the tone less formal.

15c An apostrophe plus s ('s) may be used to form the plural of lower-case letters, figures, symbols, abbreviations, and words referred to as words.

> final *k's* OR k*s*
> 1990*'s* OR 1990*s*
> V.F.W.*'s* OR V.F.W.*s*
> and*'s* OR and*s*

Caution: An apostrophe is never used for plural nouns that are not in the possessive case.

> They put up *signs* to direct *visitors* to the right *buildings* [not *sign's, visitor's, building's*]

Apostrophes and the Possessive Case   Exercise 15–1

NAME _____ SCORE _____

DIRECTIONS   Rewrite each of the following word groups as a noun or a pronoun preceded by another noun or pronoun in the possessive case.

EXAMPLES
the salary of everyone

everyone's salary

the businesses owned by the Davises

the Davises' businesses

1. the history of our company

2. the ships of Columbus

3. the income of their stockholders

4. a technical report by Alice Stevens

5. problems of today

6. slowdown of industry

7. reception given by my brothers-in-law

8. the formulas of the alloys

9. an address by the governor of Idaho

10. the position of the women

11. a store belonging to Joan and Randolf

12. the reunion of the Coopers

13. decisions made by one

14. the floor plan of the shopping mall

15. the tax report of Mr. Jones

16. entries in the index

17. the column of the editor-in-chief

18. the reports of Martha and Emory

19. the interpretation of the rules

20. the designs on the dish

Mastering Apostrophes: A Review

NAME _____ SCORE _____

DIRECTIONS   In the following sentences add all the apostrophes that are needed. Then in the blank enter each word, number, or letter to which you have added an apostrophe. Be careful not to add needless apostrophes. If a sentence is correct, write *C* in the blank.

EXAMPLE
The purpose of Mr. Garcia's speech was to justify the increase

in the electrical rates.   *Garcia's*

1. In the 1980s the price of all persons electric bills will increase sharply.   *persons'*

2. Mr. Garcia hoped to show the reasons for this increase and to explain the power companys outlook for the future.   *Company's*

3. "The power company," he said, "must increase its electric rates to keep up with the demand for more power to run the many machines and appliances required for modern living."   *C*

4. "Todays home is not like the home of the 1950s when fewer electrical appliances were available," Mr. Garcia pointed out.   _____

5. "Its true that people have to pay for the operation of the various appliances they dont want to do without," Mr. Garcia continued.   _____

6. He saved his best arguments for last, hoping to convince his audience of everyones need for electricity.   _____

7. "There are no ifs about the use of electricity in the modern home; its a necessity, not just a convenience," Mr. Garcia insisted.   _____

8. "The Smiths and the Joneses of this country are hooked *on,* as well as *up to,* electricity," he explained.   _____

9. "Our childrens needs for power will be even greater," Mr. Garcia suggested, "because of the inventions and developments that will occur in the next few decades." _____

10. Then Mr. Garcia discussed the amount of electricity required to run the appliances found in most homes and presented experts opinions of how people can conserve electricity and still enjoy their stereos, VCRs, washing machines, and microwave ovens. _____

16

Use quotation marks to set off all direct quotations, some titles, and words used in a special sense. Place quotation marks in proper relationship to other marks of punctuation.

16a Use quotation marks (" ") before and after all direct (but not indirect) quotations.

INDIRECT QUOTATION   He asked me if I would speak at the company's board meeting. [*If, whether,* and *that* frequently introduce indirect quotations.]

DIRECT QUOTATION   He asked me, "Will you speak at the company's board meeting?" [The indirect quotation is made a direct quotation.]

DIRECT QUOTATION   The program for the meeting noted that I was going to discuss "the effects of government regulations on the textile industry." [*The* is not capitalized because only a phrase is being quoted.]

Note: If a prose passage that is quoted would require more than four lines of typing or if more than three lines of poetry are quoted, indent the passage ten spaces from the left margin and do not use quotation marks within the passage.

Use single quotation marks (' ') for quotation marks that appear within other quotation marks.

According to Robert Crandall's article, the "EPA is beginning to experiment with various forms of 'pollution rights' in implementing the Clean Air Act." [The sentence in double quotation marks is quoted from Robert Crandall's article; *pollution rights* appears in quotation marks in the article.]

16b Use quotation marks for minor titles (short stories, short poems, essays, songs, episodes of radio or television series, articles in periodicals).

The article "Speak Up for Success" appeared in a recent issue of *Weekend Worker.*

Note: The title of the periodical, *Weekend Worker,* is italicized. (See also Section **10.**)

16c Quotation marks are occasionally used to indicate that words are being used in a special or an ironic sense.

"Work" for him means anything he dislikes doing. [See also **10e.**]

Note: Either quotation marks or italics may be used in definitions such as the following: "Jargon" means anything a nontechnical reader is likely to find unclear or confusing.

16d Do not use quotation marks to emphasize a *yes* or *no* in indirect discourse.

NOT   He felt that he couldn't say "no."

BUT   He felt that he couldn't say no.

16e Place the comma and the period inside quotation marks; place the semicolon and colon outside quotation marks; place the dash, question mark, and exclamation point inside the quotation marks when these marks apply to the quoted matter and outside when they do not.

"Well," he said, "I'm ready to finish the article."

The speaker pointed out that "big business is now beginning to speak out against overregulation"; indeed, it is more doing than speaking out.

Have you read "Is Government Regulation Crippling Business?"   [The question mark applies to the quoted matter as well as to the entire sentence.]

Have you read "Arsenic and Old Factories"?   [The question mark does not apply to the quoted matter.]

Quotation Marks

NAME _____ SCORE _____

DIRECTIONS   In the sentences below insert all needed quotation marks. In the blanks enter the quotation marks and the first and last word of each quoted part. Include other marks of punctuation used with the quotation marks, and place them in proper position—either inside or outside the quotation marks. Do not enclose an indirect quotation. Write *C* in the blank to indicate a sentence that is correct without quotation marks.

EXAMPLE

Gray Lanier's oral report entitled "How Much Regulation Is Too Much?" was of special interest to the business majors in the audience.

"How...much?"

1. Gray began her report with what she termed essential background information.

"Essential ... information."

2. She pointed out that seventy-five years ago business was concerned about the government's stand on monopolies.

"Seventy-five ... monopolies."

3. "Then a decade or so later," Gray explained, "The main issue that disturbed business was unionism."

_____

4. "What is the major concern of business today?" Gray asked.

_____

5. "Clearly, it is federal regulation," Gray responded to her rhetorical question.

_____

6. For decades the public screamed, "Give us protection from big business!"

_____

7. "After reading an article like 'Is Government Regulation Crippling Business?' one sees how strong big business's response has been," Gray stated.

_____

8. Gray went on to report that a bureaucracy of eighty thousand people was established to protect consumers and workers from injury.

C

_____

9. "The many agencies created by the government to act as the public's voice have had much success, especially in the area of pollution controls, Gray said.

_____

10. "But," Gray went on, "business also has its side, as exemplified in its complaint, The standards set by government agencies are too confusing and costly to result in significant benefits to the American consumer.

_____

17

Learn to use the period, question mark, exclamation point, colon, dash, parentheses, brackets, slash, and ellipsis points in accordance with conventional practices [For the use of the hyphen, see Section **18.**]

17a The period follows declarative and mildly imperative (command) sentences, indirect questions, and most abbreviations. (See 11a.)

Dr. Lee was asked if he would discuss ways to integrate visual equipment into an oral report.

17b The question mark follows direct (but not indirect) questions.

What did Dr. Lee say?
She asked me what Dr. Lee said.

17c The exclamation point follows emphatic interjections and statements of strong emotion.

What an interesting presentation Dr. Lee made!
"Bravo!" some people in the audience responded.

Caution: Do not use exclamation points to make your writing sound exciting or important. Rather, use exclamation points sparingly, and only to follow those sentences that do express strong emotion.

17d Meaning *as follows*, the colon formally introduces a word, a phrase, or a clause (but especially a list or series) that explains or identifies something mentioned in the clause preceding the colon. The colon is also used to introduce a quotation that runs for two or more sentences and to separate figures in scriptural and time references.

Dr. Lee explained the importance of visual aids in an oral presentation: either they are absolutely necessary to save words, or they add interest and variety to the speech.   [The second main clause explains the first one.]

Dr. Lee named the purposes of adding visual aids to a speech: clarity, variety, and reinforcement.   [The list explains purposes.]

Dr. Lee explained: "Visual aids save many words in an oral presentation. They often show in one picture or graph what would require fifteen minutes of speaking to explain."   [The colon, rather than the comma, is used because the quotation runs for more than one sentence.]

Caution: Avoid unnecessary colons, especially between verbs and their complements, prepositions and their objects, or after *such as*.

NOT   Three reasons for using visual aids are: clarity, variety, and reinforcement.

BUT   Three reasons for using visual aids are clarity, variety, and reinforcement.

OR   Visual aids add three things to an oral report: clarity, variety, and reinforcement.

The colon is also used between chapter and verse in scriptural references and between hours and minutes in time references.

Exodus 5:23
6:15 P.M.

17e The dash is used to set off a parenthetical element for emphasis or clarity, to set off an introductory list or series, and to mark an interruption or break in thought.

Clarity, variety, and reinforcement—these are three purposes of visual aids. [The dash sets off an introductory series.]

These three purposes—clarity, variety, and reinforcement—are served by visual aids. [The list sets off a parenthetical element for emphasis.]

Dr. Lee recommended—in fact, more than recommended—that we practice our oral presentations with the visual aids included. [The dash marks an interruption or break in thought.]

17f Parentheses set off supplementary, incidental, or illustrative matter. They also frequently enclose figures or letters used for numbering.

Dr. Lee urged all of us to learn how to operate the various kinds of projectors (all available in our department) while we are studying oral reports.

We could use (1) opaque projectors, (2) film strip projectors, or (3) slide projectors.

Note: Three marks of punctuation are used to set off matter which might be called parenthetical—that is, supplementary, incidental, or illustrative. The most commonly used are commas, which cause the reader only to pause and so see the parenthetical matter as closely related to the main idea of the sentence. Less frequently used are parentheses (which diminish the importance of the matter they set off). Dashes—which create a sharp visual break in the sentences—tend to emphasize what they set off. (Dashes or parentheses rather than commas may be necessary for clarity when the parenthetical matter itself includes commas.)

The computer, unlike any other labor-saving machine, affects every aspect of modern business practice. [Commas would be used by most writers to set off this parenthetical matter because the parenthetical material within commas is so closely related to the rest of the sentence.]

The computer (unlike any other labor-saving machine) affects every aspect of modern business practice. [Parentheses minimize the importance of the parenthetical matter.]

The computer—unlike any other labor-saving device—affects every aspect of modern business practice.   [Dashes emphasize the parenthetical matter.]

Many factors—such as length of workday, time of shift, and occupational hazards—affect most people's attitudes toward their jobs.   [The dashes are needed for clarity to enclose the parenthetical matter that contains commas. Parentheses could also be used, but they would deemphasize the list, whereas dashes emphasize it.]

17g Brackets set off editorial comments, additions, or substitutions included within quoted matter. They may also serve as parentheses within parentheses.

When you need to insert an explanation in a quotation, enclose your explanation in brackets to show that your words are not a part of the quoted matter.

Dr. Lee explained, "They [visual aids] can cause difficulties if you have not practiced using them ahead of time."

"Many insecure managers believe that [employees] should be constantly criticized to keep them on their toes."   [For clarity, the bracketed *employees* replaces the pronoun *they* which appeared in the original sentence.]

A person in the audience yelled, "I seen [sic] it with my own eyes."   [*Sic* indicates something that was said or written which is not the standard word expected.]

17h The slash is used between terms to indicate that either term is applicable to mark line divisions in quoted poetry, and to separate the elements in dates. (See also **16a**).

Most technical writing departments have an opaque and/or overhead projector available for classroom use.

Note: No space precedes or follows the slash when indicating options.

Those who believe in the necessity of work would disagree with Ezra Pound's lines "Sing we for love and idleness, /Naught else is worth the having."

Note: One space precedes and follows the slash that marks breaks between lines of poetry.

11/24/48   MEANING   November 24, 1948

Note: No space precedes or follows the slashes in dates.

17i Ellipsis points (three spaced periods) indicate omissions from quoted passages.

Dr. Lee explained, "Visual aids **. . .** often show in one picture or graph what would require fifteen minutes of speaking to explain."

If ellipsis points are used to indicate that the end of a quoted sentence is being omitted, and if the part that *is* quoted forms a complete sentence itself, use the sentence period *plus* ellipsis points.

Dr. Lee asked if he would discuss ways to integrate visual equipment. . . .

Internal Marks of Punctuation   Exercise 17-1

NAME _____ SCORE _____

DIRECTIONS   In each sentence use a caret (∧) to mark the spot where punctuation should be inserted. Then write the correct punctuation mark in the sentence at that spot and also in the blank. Some sentences will require punctuation in two places; in that case, write both marks of punctuation in the blank. This exercise includes not only the punctuation marks discussed in Section **17** but also the comma (Section **12**) and the semicolon (Section **14**).

EXAMPLE
Clarity, as well as visibility, is important in planning visual aids for an
oral report.   , ,

1. Readers can study a visual aid used in a written report as long as they need to audiences have only a short time to understand a visual effect in an oral report.   _____

2. Since the audience has only a short time to study it the visual should be kept simple.   _____

3. The speaker can simplify the visual aid in several ways; by eliminating all but the absolutely necessary information, by using block diagrams, and by labeling graphs rather than using symbols or difficult abbreviations.   _____

4. The speaker can also simplify by showing only trends not exact numbers in a graph.   _____

5. A clear simple table is far better in an oral presentation than is a table with many columns in small print.   _____

6. Most visuals in books are too complex to be clear to an audience therefore you should resist the temptation to make transparencies of them just as they are.   _____

7. To make a transparency based on a chart found in a book, you must eliminate a great deal of information and rewrite the remaining information in large letters.   book,

8. One other criterion is important in creating good visual aids audience control.   _____

9. Effective visual aids will help you to control an audience on the other hand, poorly made ones distract from your speech. _____

10. Even well-planned visuals can distract from your presentation if they are in front of an audience for an entire speech consequently, they should be removed after, or covered before and after, you have made use of them. _____

11. Visual materials that are passed around the audience can, as you might guess, be especially distracting. _____

12. You cannot control the visuals you pass around the audience examines them and ignores what you are saying. _____

13. Only a visual then that can be quickly removed when you are finished with it gives you audience control. _____

14. If you can change or add to the material presented in a visual you have even more control over the visual and, consequently, over the audience. C _____

15. In addition to movies, slides, and transparencies, there are several simpler devices for displaying visual aids for example, blackboards, posters, and flannel boards. _____

16. Blackboards some people ignore such obvious kinds of visuals are a readily available visual aid. _____

17. Blackboards offer the speaker many advantages they are easy to use; they do not require much preparation; and they hold the audience's attention as you write and draw on them. C _____

18. They do have one major drawback they may require a great deal of your time during the oral presentation. _____

19. Blackboards will present difficulties if you do not draw or write legibly, if you cannot draw and talk at the same time, or if you talk to the blackboard instead of to the audience. _____

20. Still the blackboard, even in this technological age, is one of a speaker's best methods of presenting visual aids. _____

Mastering Punctuation: A Review   Exercise 17–2

NAME _____   SCORE _____

DIRECTIONS   In the sentences below use a caret (**∧**) to indicate where the correct end marks *or* internal punctuation marks—periods, question marks, exclamation points, colons, dashes, parentheses, brackets, and slashes—should go. Insert the punctuation mark in the correct place in the sentence and write it in the blank. In several sentences more than one kind of punctuation mark is possible.

> EXAMPLE
> There are, according to Professor James Connally, certain criteria
> for judging the value of visuals∧visibility, simplicity, and control.   *: or —*

1. Visibility is an obvious criterion if your audience cannot see your visual aid, they cannot gain anything from it.   _____

2. There are certain visuals for example, a small photograph, a typed page, and a page from a book that are too small to be seen beyond the first row.   _____

3. Transparencies and large hand-lettered posters can be seen by the audience if the speaker prepares his her visuals correctly.   _____

4. There is a simple rule for lettering letters should be at least 1 inch high for each 25 feet of distance between the visual and the audience.   _____

5. No rule for the size of other elements drawings, photographs, and graphs can be given.   _____

6. The best advice that can be given is that you should set up the visuals note the list in sentence 5 and move to the back row to see whether they are clearly visible from that distance.   _____

7. "Can you see your visuals from the back row" I was asked by my instructor after I had set them up.   _____

8. "No" I shouted back to her.   _____

9. "Remember the instructions I gave you," she said "If you cannot see the visuals then the audience can't either"   _____

10. In my self-evaluation I wrote, "I wonder what my audience would have thought if I had used the ones visuals I first prepared."   _____

Mastering Punctuation: A Review   Exercise 17–3

NAME _____ SCORE _____

DIRECTIONS   For each of the following items, write a sentence using the punctuation that is needed to illustrate the item. If you need help punctuating your sentences, refer to the rule or rules indicated in parentheses.

EXAMPLE
a list in the middle of a sentence (**17e**)

Three main criteria — visibility, clarity, and control — determine the worth of a visual effect.

1. a list or series following a main clause (**17d**)

2. a break or interruption of the thought in the middle of a sentence (**17e**)

3. supplementary or illustrative information in the middle of a sentence (**17e, 17f**)

4. a quotation of two or more sentences introduced by an expression like *he said* (**17d**)

5. a nonrestrictive clause (**12d**)

6. a declarative sentence with a quoted direct question (**16e, 17b**)

7. two main clauses not joined by a coordinating conjunction (**14a**)

8. a quotation with an editorial comment or explanation inserted (**17g**)

9. an indirect quotation (**16a**)

10. a sentence that has a quotation within a quotation (**16a**)

SPELLING AND HYPHENATION   sp 18

18

Learn to spell and hyphenate words in accordance with the usage shown in an up-to-date dictionary.

If you are a poor speller, one who regularly misspells enough words to have your classwork or professional work graded down, you should begin a definite program for improving your spelling skills. There are many excellent spelling manuals available today that make use of the latest psychological studies to present words in a logical, easy-to-learn order. You may also find the following procedures helpful:

(1) Learn the rules of spelling that are presented in this section of the book.

(2) Proofread your papers carefully at least once for misspelled words only.

As you write a rough draft, it is often difficult, and always distracting, to look up a great number of words; but you can put a check or some other identifying sign above those words you have any doubts about so that you can look up their spelling when you proofread.

(3) Keep a list of the words you misspell.

The words that you misspell on your writing assignments should be recorded in the Individual Spelling List at the end of the *Workbook*. Since most people have a tendency to misspell certain words repeatedly, you should review the list frequently.

(4) Write by syllables the words you misspell; then write the definitions of the words; finally, use the words in sentences.

> e•nig•mat•ic   puzzling or baffling
>
> The report was *enigmatic* until I looked up words that I did not know the meanings of.
>
> pro•pen•si•ty   a natural inclination or tendency
>
> My supervisor has a *propensity* for making spot-checks.

(5) Learn to spell these words, which are commonly used in business and professional writing.

absence	address	appropriate	attendance
accommodate	annual	argument	attorney
accomplish	answer	arrangement	balance
achievement	apparatus	article	basically
acquainted	apparent	attach	beginning

brochure
bureaucracy
business
calculator
calendar
catalog
category
characteristic
college
committee
competition
concede
congratulate
consensus
convenience
correspondence
correspondent
courteous
decision
defendant
dependent
description
desirable
development
difference
disadvantage
dissatisfied
division
efficient
eligible

eliminate
envelope
equipment
especially
essential
excellent
experience
familiar
February
financial
foreman
fundamental
generally
government
guarantee
height
incessant
identify
immediately
indispensable
influential
initiate
insistence
interrupt
judgment
knowledge
labeled
laboratory
library
lien

maintenance
management
maneuver
manual
medicine
mortgage
necessary
noticeable
occasion
occurred
opinion
opportunity
original
pamphlet
parallel
possess
practical
precede
prefer
prepare
presence
prevalent
probably
procedure
proceed
professional
prominent
quantity
questionnaire
receipt

receive
recognize
recommend
reference
referred
repetition
rescind
resistance
respectfully
restaurant
salary
schedule
secretarial
separate
serviceable
similar
sincerely
stationary
stationery
strategy
succeed
superintendent
technician
technique
tendency
thorough
unusual

(6) Invest in a good spelling dictionary.

A spelling dictionary is a small, inexpensive book that gives only the spelling and syllable breaks for each word. It will make looking up words faster and easier.

Misspelling Caused by Mispronunciation

Exercise 18-1

NAME _____ SCORE _____

18a To avoid omitting, adding, transposing, or changing a letter in a word, pronounce the word carefully according to the way the dictionary divides it into syllables.

The places where common mistakes are made in pronunciation—and spelling—are indicated in **boldface**.

OMISSIONS	candidate, everything, government
ADDITIONS	athlete, laundry, drowned
TRANSPOSITIONS	perform, children, tragedy
CHANGE	accurate, prejudice, separate

DIRECTIONS   With the aid of your dictionary, write out each of the following words by syllables, indicate the position of the primary accent, and pronounce the word correctly and distinctly. (Different dictionaries sometimes vary in the way they divide words into syllables. You may find that in a few cases your word divisions differ from someone else's.) In your pronunciation avoid any omission, addition, transposition, or change.

EXAMPLE
similar   _sim·i·lar_ _____

1. interest   _____

2. used   _____

3. family   _____

4. especially   _____

5. candidate   _____

6. temperament   _____

7. professor   _____

8. hindrance   _____

9. prescription   _____

10. receipt   _____

11. congratulate   _____

12. sincerely   _____

13. mirror   _____

14. privilege   _____

15. pamphlet   _____

16. surprise   _____

17. environment _____

18. February   _____

19. perhaps   _____

20. scissors   _____

21. recognize   _____

22. supposedly _____

23. escape   _____

24. asked   _____

25. knowledge   _____

Confusion of Words

NAME _____ SCORE _____

18b Distinguish between words that have a similar sound or spelling. To be sure of the spelling, check the word's meaning in the context of the sentence.

affect—effect   quiet—quit—quite
loose—lose   to—too—two

(See the spelling checklist in the Appendix.)

DIRECTIONS   In the following sentences cross out the spelling or spellings in parentheses that do not fit the meaning, and write the correct spelling in the blank at the right. Consult your dictionary freely.

> EXAMPLE
> (Their, ~~There,~~ ~~They're~~) loan did not go through.   *Their*

1. With the growth of large corporations the success rate of small businesses is bound to (altar, alter). _____

2. Economic ups and downs have less of an (affect, effect) on diversified conglomerates. _____

3. People find this change hard to (accept, except). _____

4. Today, managing a successful cottage industry (presence, presents) many potential problems. _____

5. People who think they can make a living making and selling crafts are often in for (quiet, quit, quite) a surprise. _____

6. The (principal, principle) difficulty they encounter is finding a market for their goods. _____

7. Many people are not (holey, wholly, holy) convinced that individually crafted goods are worth the higher prices their makers charge. _____

8. A pessimist might (prophesy, prophecy) the eventual death of handmade goods. _____

9. Others find this forecast (to, too, two) gloomy. _____

10. Some theorists think that greedy consumerism often (precedes, proceeds) an economic recession. _____

11. Too much credit card buying can signal a (week, weak) economy. _____

12. But most consumers are not (conscience, conscious) of these early warning signals. _____

13. Is there any (advise, advice) to offer the average businessperson? _____

14. Traditional theories (passed, past) over some factors that contributed to the most recent recession. _____

15. This represents one (instants, instance) of the complex nature of a global economy. _____

16. By the time experts could evaluate all the data, it was (all ready, already) too late. _____

17. But an economy never becomes truly (stationery, stationary). _____

18. Even so, the reasons for its shifts continue to (elude, allude) analysts and investors. _____

19. (It's, Its) one thing to talk about economic instability and quite another to pinpoint its causes. _____

20. Some people would rather complain (then, than) try to find solutions to the problems. _____

21. Everyone seems to have (ideals, ideas) about how to improve the economy. _____

22. But ideas do little to lift the (morale, moral) of people whose businesses collapse. _____

23. (Whether, Weather) a cottage industry or a large corporation, profits still matter. _____

24. The desire to compete can (led, lead) people into new business ventures. _____

25. Those who do not overestimate their potential for success will be the ones who do not (loose, lose). _____

Addition of Prefixes

Exercise 18–3

NAME _____ SCORE _____

18c Add the prefix to the root word without dropping letters. (The root is the base word to which a prefix or a suffix is added.)

un-	+	necessary	=	unnecessary
mis-	+	spell	=	misspell
dis-	+	agree	=	disagree

DIRECTIONS   In the blank at the right enter the correct spelling of each word with the prefix added. Consult your dictionary freely. Some dictionaries may hyphenate some of the following words. (See also **18f(3)**.)

EXAMPLES

mis-	+	quote	*misquote*
pre-	+	eminent	*preeminent*
1. re-	+	activate	_____
2. pre-	+	occupation	_____
3. over-	+	run	_____
4. under-	+	developed	_____
5. un-	+	necessary	_____
6. dis-	+	appoint	_____
7. mis-	+	management	_____
8. re-	+	generate	_____
9. pre-	+	dominate	_____
10. dis-	+	trust	_____
11. un-	+	witnessed	_____
12. under-	+	developed	_____
13. mis-	+	shaped	_____
14. re-	+	consider	_____
15. pre-	+	caution	_____
16. un-	+	forgettable	_____
17. dis-	+	possessed	_____
18. mis-	+	apply	_____

19. re-   +   order   _____

20. dis-   +   solve   _____

Addition of Suffixes—Final *e*

Exercise 18–4

NAME _____ SCORE _____

18d(1) Drop the final *e* before a suffix beginning with a vowel but not before a suffix beginning with a consonant.

bride	+	-al	=	bridal	fame	+	-ous	=	famous
care	+	-ful	=	careful	entire	+	-ly	=	entirely

Exceptions: due, duly; awe, awful; hoe, hoeing; singe, singeing. *After c or g the final e is retained before suffixes beginning with a or o: notice, noticeable; courage, courageous.*

DIRECTIONS   Write the correct spelling of each word with the suffix added. Consult your dictionary freely. Write *(ex)* after each answer that is an exception to rule **18d(1)**.

EXAMPLES

argue   +   -ing   *arguing*

dye   +   -ing   *dyeing (ex)*

1. sure   +   -ly   _____

2. become   +   -ing   _____

3. value   +   -able   _____

4. outrage   +   -ous   _____

5. argue   +   -ment   _____

6. reverse   +   -ible   _____

7. resource +   -ful   _____

8. manage   +   -ment   _____

9. like   +   -ly   _____

10. advise   +   -able   _____

11. arrange +   -ment   _____

12. extreme +   -ly   _____

13. hope   +   -ing   _____

14. judge   +   -ment   _____

15. excite   +   -able   _____

16. sincere +   -ly   _____

17. use   +   -age   _____

18. write   +   -ing   _____

19. knowledge   +   -able   _____

20. live   +   -ing   _____

Addition of Suffixes   Exercise 18–5

NAME _____ SCORE _____

18d(2) When the suffix begins with a vowel (*ing, ed, ence, ance, able*) double a final single consonant if it is preceded by a single vowel that is in an accented syllable. (A one-syllable word, of course, is always accented.)

    mop, mopped   [Compare with *mope, moped*]
    mop, mopping   [Compare with *mope, moping*]
    con·fer̓, con·fer̓ red   [Final consonant in the accented syllable]
    ben·e·fit; ben̓·e·fited   [Final consonant not in the accented syllable]
    need, needed   [Final consonant not preceded by a single vowel]

DIRECTIONS   In the blank at the right enter the correct spelling of each word with the suffix added. Consult your dictionary freely.

EXAMPLE
control   +   -ed   *controlled*

1. cut   +   -er   _____

2. mirror   +   -ed   _____

3. commit   +   -ing   _____

4. fat   +   -en   _____

5. meet   +   -ing   _____

6. big   +   -est   _____

7. travel   +   -er   _____

8. proceed   +   -ed   _____

9. occur   +   -ence   _____

10. rot   +   -en   _____

11. begin   +   -ing   _____

12. equip   +   -ed   _____

13. unforget   +   -able   _____

14. pour   +   -ing   _____

15. prefer   +   -ed   _____

16. stop   +   -ing   _____

17. label   +   -ed   _____

18. control   +   -able   _____

19. attach   +   -ed   _____

20. transmit   +   -ing   _____

Addition of Suffixes—Final *y*

NAME _____ SCORE _____

18d(3) Except before *ing*, a final *y* preceded by a consonant is changed to *i* before a suffix.

defy	+	-ance	=	defiance	happy	+	-ness	=	happiness
modify	+	-er	=	modifier	modify	+	-ing	=	modifying
heavy	+	-er	=	heavier	pretty	+	-er	=	prettier

To make a noun plural or a verb singular, final *y* preceded by a consonant is changed to *i* and *es* is added. (See also **18f.**)

duty	+	-es	=	duties	deny	+	-es	=	denies
ally	+	-es	=	allies	copy	+	-es	=	copies

Final *y* preceded by a vowel is usually not changed before a suffix.

annoy	+	-ed	=	annoyed	turkey	+	-s	=	turkeys

Exceptions: *pay, paid; lay, laid; say, said; day, daily.*

DIRECTIONS   Enter the correct spelling of each word with the suffix added. Consult your dictionary freely. Write (*ex*) after each word that is an exception to rule **18d(3).**

EXAMPLES

boundary + -es   *boundaries*

pay + -d   *paid (ex)*

1. monkey + -s   _____

2. try + -es   _____

3. accompany + -es   _____

4. chimney + -s   _____

5. bury + -ed   _____

6. lay + -ed   _____

7. fallacy + -es   _____

8. hungry + -ly   _____

9. lonely + -ness   _____

10. donkey + -s   _____

Formation of the Plural

NAME _____   SCORE _____

18d(4) **Form the plural of most nouns by (1) adding *s* to the singular form of the noun, (2) adding *es* to singular nouns that end in *s, ch, sh,* or *x,* or (3) changing a final *y* to *i* and adding *es* if the noun ends in a *y* and is preceded by a consonant (see also 18d(3)).**

boy⟶boys	fox⟶foxes	mystery⟶mysteries
cupful⟶cupfuls	Harris⟶Harrises	beauty⟶beauties
Drehmel⟶Drehmels	calf⟶calves	reply⟶replies
	[*f* changed to *v*]	

A few nouns change their form for the plural: *woman⟶women; child⟶children.* And a few nouns ending in *o* take the *es* plural: *potato⟶potatoes; hero⟶heroes.*

DIRECTIONS   In the blank enter the plural form of each word. Consult your dictionary freely.

EXAMPLES
day   *days*
scratch   *scratches*

1. beach _____
2. half _____
3. genius _____
4. company _____
5. hero _____
6. brown _____
7. stitch _____
8. contract _____
9. wolf _____
10. stiletto _____

11. business _____
12. potato _____
13. stress _____
14. question _____
15. policy _____
16. machine _____
17. leaf _____
18. batch _____
19. alloy _____
20. arbitrator _____

Confusion of *ei* and *ie*

NAME _____ SCORE _____

18e When the sound is *ee* (as in *see*), write *ei* after *c* (*receipt, ceiling*), and *ie* after any other letter (*relieve, priest*); when the sound is other than *ee*, usually write *ei* (*eight, their, reign*).

Exceptions: *either, neither, financier, leisure, seize, species, weird.*

DIRECTIONS Fill in the blanks in the following words by writing *ei* or *ie*. Consult your dictionary freely. Write (*ex*) after any word that is an exception to rule **18e**.

EXAMPLES
dec*ei*ve

*ei*ther *(ex)*

1. rec____ve

2. bel____f

3. ch____f

4. s____ge

5. conc____ted

6. gr____f

7. y____ld

8. l____sure

9. misch____f

10. sl____gh

11. th____f

12. gr____ve

13. spec____s

14. c____ling

15. rel____ve

16. h____ght

17. w____ght

18. f____nd

19. n____ther

20. w____rd

Hyphenated Words   Exercise 18–9

NAME _____ SCORE _____

18f In general, use the hyphen (1) between two or more words serving as a single adjective before a noun (except when the first word is an adverb ending in *ly*), (2) with compound numbers from twenty-one to ninety-nine and with fractions, (3) with prefixes or suffixes for clarity, (4) with the prefixes *ex-*, *self-*, *all-*, and *great-* and with the suffix *elect*, and (5) between a prefix and a proper name.

(1) a *know-it-all* expression
(2) *sixty-six, one-half*
(3) *re-collect* the supplies   [to distinguish from *recollect* an event]
(4) *ex-wife, self-help, all-important, great-grandmother, major-elect*
(5) *mid-July, un-American*

DIRECTIONS   Supply hyphens where they are needed in the following list. Not all items require hyphens. Write the correctly hyphenated phrase in the space provided.

EXAMPLES
a well spent bonus
a well-spent bonus
a bonus well spent
a bonus well spent

1. a high rise apartment

2. ex President Townes

3. a four foot barricade

4. a commonly used adjective

5. a long distance call

6. a twenty five year old building

7. Senator elect Johansen

8. He is forty five.

9. western style jeans

10. a two thirds vote of the Senate

11. students who are career minded

12. the clumsily written report

13. three fourths of the voters said no

14. the all seeing eye of the camera

15. dust covered shelves

16. The officer re searched the suspect.

17. long lasting results

18. an all inclusive study

19. the self paced training program

20. She is my great aunt.

21. results that are long lasting

22. The shop specializes in teen age fashions.

23. a two part process

24. The process had two parts.

25. The up and down pattern of the New York Stock Exchange

19

Learn the ways an up-to-date dictionary can help you select the words that express your ideas exactly.

An up-to-date desk dictionary is a necessary reference tool for any student or professional person. (A desk dictionary is based on one of the unabridged—complete, unshortened—dictionaries, such as *Webster's Third New International,* usually found on a stand in the reference area of the library). An up-to-date dictionary not only will show you how words are spelled and hyphenated, but it provides other information. For example, (1) it shows you how to pronounce a word like *harass;* (2) it explains what a word like *fancy* originally meant and gives the various meanings of the word as it is used today; (3) it lists the forms of a verb like *sing;* (4) it gives the synonyms and antonyms of a word like *oppose;* and (5) it may provide usage labels for words like *poke, nowhere,* and *irregardless* (see **19b**). A desk dictionary may also supply you with miscellaneous information, such as a brief history of the English language, the dates and identities of famous people, geographical facts, and lists of colleges and universities in the United States and Canada. The purchase of a current desk dictionary is one of the best investments you can make.

19a Learn to use an up-to-date dictionary intelligently.

Study the introductory matter to find out what your dictionary's guides to abbreviations and pronunciation are; to know what plural and tense forms your dictionary lists; to learn what attitude your dictionary takes toward usage labels (dictionaries vary in the kinds of labels they use, and some dictionaries label more words than others do); and to understand the order in which the meanings of words are listed—that is, in order of common usage or of historical development.

Most words (and most meanings of words) in dictionaries are unlabeled; that is, they are appropriate on any occasion because they are in general use in the English-speaking world.

Avoid choosing words with the labels discussed in **19b–g** unless you are certain that they are appropriate to your chosen reading audience and your purpose.

19b Informal Words

There is one class of words—labeled *Informal* or, sometimes, *Colloquial*—that is commonly used and understood by most writers and speakers. Words in this class are appropriate in speaking and in informal writing and are usually necessary in recording dialogue, since most people speak less formally than they write. But, in general, in most of your college and professional writing, you should avoid words labeled *Informal* or *Colloquial*.

INFORMAL The writer *lifted* the passage from a report he was studying.

STANDARD OR FORMAL The writer *plagiarized* the passage from a report he was studying.

Except in dialogue, contractions are usually not appropriate in formal writing, though they may be used (in moderation) in business letters when a conversational tone is sought.

INFORMAL *There's* hardly anyone who *doesn't* respond to a good oral presentation.

STANDARD OR FORMAL *There is* hardly anyone who *does not* respond to a good oral presentation.

19c Slang

These words are popular expressions that either change their meanings rapidly or pass out of use quickly. (Labeled *Slang* in the dictionary.)

SLANG She really *blew* the sale.

APPROPRIATE She *lost* the sale.

19d Regional Words

These are words used by people in one section of the country; consequently, readers outside the region where a given word is current may misunderstand their meaning. (Labeled *Dialectical*, *Regional*, or *Colloquial* in the dictionary.)

REGIONAL The company car is *right* nice.

APPROPRIATE The company car is *very* nice.

19e Nonstandard Words and Usages

Nonstandard may lead your reader to think of you as uneducated. (Labeled *Nonstandard* or *Illiterate* in the dictionary or omitted entirely.)

NONSTANDARD He *ain't gonna* get the raise he expected.

APPROPRIATE He *is not going to* get the raise he expected.

19f Archaic and Obsolete Words

These words are no longer used in ordinary writing and tend to mark the writer as being pretentious or a snob. (Labeled *Archaic*, *Obsolete*, *Obsolescent*, or *Rare* in the dictionary.)

OBSOLETE The *eldritch* computer no longer served their purpose.

APPROPRIATE The *ancient* computer no longer served their purpose.

19g Technical Words and Jargon

These words are appropriate only for a specialized audience. When the occasion demands the use of a word that is labeled as belonging to a particular profession or trade—for example, an address to a medical convention might call for technical language or even jargon—the word may be judged appropriate because the audience will understand it. But in general speaking and writing, you should depend on the multitude of unlabeled words that most audiences or readers can be expected to understand.

19h Choose words and combinations of sounds that are appropriate to clear prose writing.

A poetic style is generally not appropriate in college essays or professional reports. Usually such writing seems wordy, vague, and even ridiculous.

FLOWERY He was a *tower of power* in our community, a *blazing meteor in a prosperous enterprise.*

PLAIN BUT CLEAR He was a *powerful* man in our community, a *remarkably successful businessman.*

Use of the Dictionary   Exercise 19–1

NAME _____ SCORE _____

The full title, the edition, and the date of publication of my dictionary are as follows: _____

1. Abbreviations   Where does the dictionary explain the abbreviations it uses?

_____

Write out the meaning of each of the abbreviations that follow these entries:

languish, *intr. v.*   _____

hustings, *pl. n.*   _____

nohow, *adv., Dial.*   _____

agro-, *pref.*   _____

2. Spelling and pronunciation   Using your dictionary as a guide, write out by syllables each of the words listed below, and place the accent where it belongs. With the aid of the diacritical marks (the accent marks and symbols), the phonetic respelling of the word (in parentheses or slashes immediately after the word), and the key at the bottom of the page in the introductory matter, determine the preferred pronunciation (that is, the first pronunciation given). Then pronounce each word correctly several times.

charisma   _____

practically   _____

jurisdiction _____

technical   _____

Write the plurals of the following words:

ox   _____

index   _____

medium   _____

tomato   _____

Rewrite each of the following words that needs a hyphen:

bookkeeper   _____

halfhearted   _____

sideglance   _____

3. Derivations   The derivation, or origin, of a word (given in brackets) often furnishes a literal meaning that helps you to remember the word. For each of the following words, give (a) the source—the language from which it is derived, (b) the original word or words, and (c) the original meaning.

	Source	*Original word(s) and meaning*
nefarious	_____	_____
pseudonym	_____	_____
steadfast	_____	_____

4. Meanings   Usually words develop several different meanings. How many meanings are listed in your dictionary for the following words?

subject, *n.*   _____   grace, *v. tr.*   _____   around, *adv.*   _____

tortuous, *adj.*   _____   of, *prep.*   _____   junk, *n.*   _____

Does your dictionary list meanings in order of historical development or in order of common usage? _____

5. Special labels   Some words have technical, or field, labels. These words are likely to be understood by people involved in a particular field of study or occupation, but their definitions may be unknown to people outside the field. Based on your dictionary's label of the word, what field would be likely to use

Use of the Dictionary   Exercise 19–1 (continued)

each of the following words? (If the label is abbreviated and you are unfamiliar with it, consult your dictionary's list of abbreviations.)

sphygmograph   _____

lintel   _____

molto   _____

dactyl   _____

amniocentesis   _____

6. Usage labels   For each italicized word in the items below, consult your dictionary to see if the meaning of the word as it is used here has a usage label (such as *Slang* or *Informal*). If it does, enter the label in the blank and rewrite the entire expression in standard English. If it does not, leave the blanks empty.

	Usage label	*Standard English usage*
tardiness *bugs* me	_____	_____
finalized the contract	_____	_____
he *reckons* so	_____	_____
a *foxy* lady	_____	_____
speaker *don't* see	_____	_____
bust the window	_____	_____
suspicion nothing	_____	_____
tough luck	_____	_____
most everyone	_____	_____

7. Synonyms   Even among words with essentially the same meaning (synonyms), one word usually fits a given context more exactly than any other.

To differentiate precise shades of meaning, some dictionaries include special paragraphs showing groups of closely related words. What synonyms are specially differentiated in your dictionary for the following words?

confirm, *v.* _____

sly, *adj.* _____

8. Capitalization   Check your dictionary; then rewrite any of the following words that may be capitalized.

leo _____   psychology _____

socialism _____   misanthropist _____

holland _____   italian _____

9. Grammatical information   Note that many words may serve as two or more parts of speech. List the parts of speech—*vt., vi., n., adj., adv., prep., conj., interj.*—that each of the following words may be.

panel _____

off _____

open _____

check _____

right _____

10. Miscellaneous information   Answer the following questions by referring to your dictionary, and be prepared to tell in what part of the dictionary the information is located.

In what year was Elizabeth Cady Stanton born? _____

Where is Transylvania? _____

What is a CRT? _____

Does your dictionary give a history of the English language? _____

20

Choose words that are precise, appropriate, and specific.

To communicate clearly, you must choose your words carefully, using words that express your ideas and feelings *exactly*.

As you learned in **18b** and in Section **19,** there is a great difference in meaning between two words like *accept* and *except*, even though they sound nearly the same. There is also a great difference in meaning between *famous* and *notorious*—two words that suggest fame but in very different senses. Imagine how few products your company would sell if you used *notorious* for *famous* in your advertising copy.

> Our styling spray is *notorious* the world over for its effects on men's hair.

Obviously, the audience for your advertisement would envision undesirable results from using your company's product.

To be exact requires more than choosing words that are correct. You must also choose words that are specific enough to be clear and that are appropriate for the audience you are addressing. If you say that your company's styling spray makes hair "look nice," you may know what you mean, but such a general description is not likely to give your audience a clear picture of your product's effect. And if you say that the styling spray "imparts aesthetic enhancements to one's coiffure," you will probably lose your audience midway through your first sentence. Exactness, then, means that your words are correct, specific, and appropriate for your audience and purpose.

20a(1) Choose words that express your ideas precisely.

Remember that a wrong word is very noticeable to your reader and may, like a misspelled word, discredit your entire letter, report, or essay.

> WRONG WORDS   I urge you to *adapt* my proposal in its *entity*.

> CORRECT WORDS   I urge you to *adopt* my proposal in its *entirety*.
>   OR   I urge you to *adopt* my *entire* proposal.

20a(2) Choose appropriate words.

Technical terminology that is appropriate for a reader familiar with your field may be meaningless to others. Technical jargon, or field talk, should be confined to presentations made to people within your own specialized area. When writing or speaking to a general audience, always clearly define any technical terms that you use, and use only those technical terms for which no ordinary word or explanation is available.

> TECHNICAL   Our word processor uses diskettes that can *store 130,000 bytes of information.*

CLEAR   Our word processor uses diskettes that can *contain 75 typed pages of information.*

Appropriate words, then, are words that your audience is likely to be familiar with. Never use a fancy term like "ocular enhancers" when you mean simply *glasses.* Avoid other heavy, ornate language unless you want to be considered snobbish and pretentious. In short, choose the simple and familiar word or phrase whenever possible.

20a(3) Choose specific words.

Words like *big, interesting, exciting, wonderful,* and *good* are too general to communicate an idea clearly to your reader. Giving exact details is essential in technical-report and business-letter writing—think how disastrous it would be if a doctor told a patient to take a *couple* of sleeping pills *every now and then.* Whenever possible, choose the specific word or phrase that communicates the exact quality you have in mind.

GENERAL   Mr. Chomsky's report was *interesting.*

SPECIFIC   Mr. Chomsky's report *explained the government regulations that apply to the labeling of drugs.*

GENERAL   Learning to be a sales representative requires *a lot of things.*

SPECIFIC   Learning to be a sales representative requires that you *get to know the product well, understand its main selling points, and determine the specific needs of your customers.*

20b Use idiomatic expressions correctly.

Exactness also includes the choice of idiomatic language. Idioms are expressions whose meaning differs from what the meanings of the individual words would lead you to expect. Native speakers are able to use idioms without thinking, but for someone unfamiliar with an expression such as *kick the bucket,* idioms can be confusing.

You use many idiomatic expressions every day without considering their meaning, especially phrasal verbs—for example, "I ran *into* an old friend" and "She *played down* the importance of money." In these examples and in other such expressions, the choice of the particle (*into, down*) accounts for the expression's being idiomatic. While most of us would not make the error of writing "I *ran over* an old friend" when we mean that we *met* an old friend, we might slip and use the unidiomatic *comply to* rather than the idiomatic *comply with.*

UNIDIOMATIC   The product did not *comply to* the company's standards.

IDIOMATIC   The product did not *comply with* the company's standards.

20c Choose fresh expressions instead of trite ones.

Trite expressions, or clichés, are idiomatic expressions that have been used so often that they have become meaningless. At one time readers would have thought the expression "tried and true" was effective, a fresh and exact choice of words. Today, readers have seen and heard the expression so often that they hardly notice it, except perhaps to be bored or amused by it. In your reader's eyes, clichés can also mark you as a lazy, uncaring writer, one who will not make the effort to find a fresh way of saying something. Although clichés are common in most people's speech and may even occur at times in the work of professional writers, such words and phrases should generally be avoided because they no longer convey ideas exactly.

TRITE   *Last but not least*, our sales people will have to *put their shoulders to the wheel* or our competitors will *blow us away* in the next quarter.

EXACT   *Last*, our sales people will have to *work hard* or our competitors will *outdistance us* in the next quarter.

Exactness   Exercise 20–1

NAME _____ SCORE _____

DIRECTIONS   In the following sentences cross out the word choice in parentheses that would be incorrect, trite, or inappropriate in an essay written for a general audience. Write the exact or appropriate word choice in the blank. Consult your dictionary freely.

EXAMPLE
Most speakers dress (appropriately for, ~~apropos of~~) the

occasion.   *appropriately for*

1. It is (clear, plain as day) that first impressions *do* make a difference.   _____

2. Our skills, not our wardrobe, are the (predominant, predominate) thing we want business associates to remember.   _____

3. If your clothes look too trendy, they (detract, distract) from your appearance.   _____

4. Your customer will feel uncomfortable (talking, rapping) with you if you are dressed inappropriately.   _____

5. While jeans and a sweatshirt may not be out of place at a service station, they would (gross out, offend) the clients of a real estate agent.   _____

6. Furthermore, a neat, well-groomed appearance (attributes, contributes) to your own confidence.   _____

7. Looking professional is the (*sine qua non*, essential element) in winning a customer's confidence.   _____

8. The way you talk can also (imply, infer) things to your customer.   _____

9. In some (instants, instances) you can offend your customer if you use inappropriate language.   _____

10. You should be (aware, cognizant) that slang makes some people think you do not take them seriously. _____

11. You should be (conscious, conscience) of the impact your way of speaking has on your readers. _____

12. Like slang, too many jargon terms can (blow, ruin) your chances of making a good impression. _____

13. (Obfuscating, Clouding) the issue with big words impresses few people, even experts. _____

14. Mannerisms such as gum chewing and nail biting can also (irritate, bug) customers. _____

15. The (less, fewer) distractions you give your customers, the more successful you will be in your job. _____

21

Avoid wordiness in your essays, reports, and letters.

Wordiness results from inexact word choice (see also Section **20**). Few writers, in their first drafts, are likely to make the best choices in phrasing. Therefore, to insure exactness and to eliminate wordiness, writers must carefully proofread and then revise their first drafts.

Today
~~In today's society~~ workers are concerned not only with protection from hazardous

working conditions ~~and situations~~ but ~~they are~~ also ~~concerned~~ with the quality of the

it
workplace. They ~~ask and~~ demand that work be more than safe; they also want ~~work~~

to be interesting.

21a Use only those words or phrases that add meaning to your writing.

Most wordiness in composition results from a writer's attempt to achieve an elevated style, to write sentences that sound impressive. Many unnecessary phrases inevitably show up in the compositions of writers who never use one exact word when they can instead write a long, impressive-sounding phrase. The temptation to use impressive words leads to monster sentences. Readers, however, are likely to spot the pretentiousness and may dismiss the content of the writing as foolish even when it is not.

No one wants her or his ideas to be laughed at, but the quickest way to get that response is to write something like "Immediately if not sooner it would be prudent when in the presence of combusting materials for all employees and staff to exit and leave the nearby premises by the most expeditious means possible as soon as they are physically able to do so." What did the writer want to say? "In case of fire, immediately leave the building by the nearest exit." By the time the reader finishes the first sentence, the paper (and the reader) might well be ashes. In other words, be direct.

Here is a sampling of verbose phrases and pretentious words, along with their briefer, more straightforward counterparts.

Wordy	*Concise*
to be desirous of	want OR desire
to have a preference for	prefer
to be in agreement with	agree
due to the fact that	because OR since
in view of the fact that	because OR since

Wordy	*Concise*
in order to	to
at this point in time	now
in this day and age	today
with reference to	about
prior to	before
in the event of	if
subsequent	after
substantial	big, large
inadvertency	error
promulgate	issue
domicile	home, house
remuneration	pay
disclose	show, uncover
utilize	use
circa	about
sequent	following
i.e.	that is
e.g.	for example
along the line of	about
consensus of opinion	consensus
during the time that	while
for the purpose of	for
have the need for	need
in due course	soon
in many cases	often, frequently
few and far between	seldom
under the circumstances	because
in some cases	sometimes
in most cases	usually
in spite of the fact that	although

Another source of wordiness, particularly in student compositions, is the writer's lack of confidence in his or her opinions. Expressions such as "I think," "it seems to me," "in my opinion," and "would be" (for *is*) may be appropriate in writing about issues that are genuinely controversial, but more often they can be omitted. If you do not express your ideas confidently, your reader's confidence in them will be diminished, too.

WORDY   *It seems to me that* one reason for boredom among workers *would be* their mistaken belief that a job, to be satisfying, must be free of routine tasks.

CONCISE   One reason for boredom among workers *is* their mistaken belief that a job, to be satisfying, must be free of routine tasks.

21b Restructure sentences whenever necessary to avoid wordiness.

Often you can combine two main clauses through subordination (see **1f** and **24a**) to avoid wordiness.

WORDY   Many people feel that everyone except them has escaped routine chores, and as a result of this feeling they become dissatisfied with their work.

CONCISE   Many people become dissatisfied with their work because they feel that everyone except them has escaped routine chores.

Often wordiness is caused by beginning a sentence with *there* or *it*. When you restructure the sentence without the *there* or *it*, you eliminate the wordiness.

WORDY   *There are* many causes of worker dissatisfaction.

CONCISE   Worker dissatisfaction has many causes.

21c Eliminate needless repetition of words and ideas.

Repetition of the same word in several sentences, unless for emphasis (see Section **29**), results in monotonous writing. The use of pronouns and synonyms helps to avoid excessive repetition.

REPETITIOUS   Even creative *writers* face a number of routine chores. *Writers* must sit down at their desks each day and work a certain number of hours at their *writing*. *Writers* must revise again and again the same piece of *writing*.

BETTER   Even creative *writers* face a number of routine chores. *They* must sit down at their desks each day and work a certain number of hours at their *writing*. *They* must revise again and again the same piece of *manuscript*.

Combining sentences, using a colon if appropriate, can also eliminate needless repetition.

REPETITIOUS   There are two major causes of wordiness in writing. *These two causes are* needless repetition and the use of meaningless words and phrases.

CONCISE   There are two major causes of wordiness in writing: needless repetition and the use of meaningless words and phrases.

OR

The two major causes of wordiness in writing are needless repetition and the use of meaningless words and phrases.

Several popular expressions are always repetitious: "each and every," "any and all," "various and sundry," "if and when," "combine together," "return back," "red in color," "triangular in shape," "city of Cleveland," and "a total of two."

REPETITIOUS   *Each and every* job involves a certain amount of routine.

CONCISE   *Every* [OR *Each*] job involves a certain amount of routine.

REPETITIOUS   A *total of three people* complained about boredom.

CONCISE   *Three people* complained about boredom.

In introducing quotations, many inexperienced writers tend to overwork forms of the verb *say*. Remember that verbs besides *say* can introduce quotations effectively—for example, *explain, point out, note, describe, observe, believe, feel,* and *think.*

REPETITIOUS   Albert S. Glickman, a researcher on work and leisure, *says,* "Work and leisure are part of one life." Glickman also *says* that "we need to improve the net quality of life." He *says* we are inexperienced in handling our leisure time by *saying:* "So far we haven't had much experience in the use of free time."

BETTER   Albert S. Glickman, a researcher on work and leisure, *believes* that "work and leisure are part of one life." Glickman *says,* "We need to improve the net quality of life." He *feels* that we are inexperienced in handling the leisure part of our lives: "So far," Glick *points out,* "we haven't had much experience in the use of free time."

Avoiding Wordiness and Needless Repetition   Exercise 21-1

NAME _____ SCORE _____

DIRECTIONS   Cross out needless words in each of the following sentences. For each sentence that requires no further revision other than capitalization or punctuation, write *1* in the blank; for sentences that require additional changes in wording, write *2* in the blank and make the needed revision.

EXAMPLE   *2*

~~The reason why~~ /the audience relaxed ~~was~~ because the speaker

seemed calm and confident.   ___*1*___

1. Each and every speaker feels nervous before a presentation.   _____

2. In order that you might appear calm to your audience, do not

   rush your opening.   _____

3. Walk slowly to the lectern, without hurrying.   _____

4. Prior to beginning your speech, arrange your notes or

   manuscript on the lectern.   _____

5. Also, take time as well to survey and look at your audience.   _____

6. It is obvious that you should establish eye contact with your

   audience before you begin to speak.   _____

7. Greet your audience in an appropriate way and manner;

   then open your speech on a positive note.   _____

8. There is one thing you should not do in your opening

   sentence, and this is to apologize to your audience.   _____

9. In the event that you have had delays in getting to the speak-

   ing engagement, do not tell the audience about your hard-

   ships.   _____

10. It is recommended that an audience be at ease in your presence, not concerned with inconveniences you experienced. _____

11. Many people feel that all speeches should have a humorous introduction, and because of this they always begin their presentations with a joke. _____

12. If you begin with a joke, it is important to remember that a joke should be not only funny but it should also be appropriate to the topic of the speech. _____

13. Nothing gets a speech off to a worse beginning than a joke that the audience listening to the speech does not find funny in quality. _____

14. Most speech textbooks say to begin with a joke only if it has been tested. They also say that you should avoid a humorous beginning if you do not tell jokes well. And they say that you should be prepared to continue your speech immediately if the audience does not laugh at your joke. _____

15. If the point of your joke is not appropriate to the purpose of your speech, your audience may spend the next few minutes trying to figure out the reason why you included it. _____

22

Include all words necessary for clarity or emphasis.

Note: Since writers often omit words that are needed to complete a parallel construction, Section **22** may profitably be studied together with Section **26**.

22a Include all necessary articles, pronouns, conjunctions, and prepositions.

Note: Use a caret (∧) to mark the place *below* the line where an omitted word, phrase, or mark of punctuation is to be inserted. Write the insertion *above* the line.

DIRECT QUOTATION   My speech teacher pointed out, "Your body language often communicates as much as your words do."

INDIRECT QUOTATION   My speech teacher pointed out ∧*that* body language often communicates as much as words do. ∧ [The word *that* generally introduces an indirect quotation; without *that*, *body language*, rather than the entire clause, seems to be the object of *pointed out*.]

Avoid using intensifiers like **so** and **such** without a completing *that* clause; do not write *The speaker was* **so** *tense* or *The speaker was* **such** *an interesting person*. Either omit the *so* or *such* or explain the meaning of the intensifier with a *that* clause.

The speaker was so tense/∧ *that he made his audience uncomfortable.*

Note: The word *that* may be omitted when the meaning of the sentence would be clear at first reading without it.

The speaker was so tense he made his audience uncomfortable.

Omitting a preposition can result in unidiomatic phrasing.

The speaker believed ∧*in* and made use of gestures during oral presentations.   [*Believed in* (an idiom) means something quite different from *believed*. Without *in*, the sentence says that the speaker *believed gestures*—not what the writer intended.]

The type ∧*of* gestures used by the speaker emphasized certain points.   [Without *of*, *type* seems to be an adjective modifying *gestures*.]

Do not omit an article from a list of items that requires both *a*'s and *an*'s in order for it to make sense.

Effective body language includes *a* use of gestures, *a* movement on stage whenever

an

appropriate, and expressive face.
　　　　　　 ∧

22b Include necessary verbs and helping verbs.

used

Speakers have always and will continue to use gestures during their presenta-
　　　　　　　 ∧
tions.　[Without the *used* the sentence would mean "Speakers *have* always *continue* and *will continue* to use gestures during their presentations." *Have continue*
is an error in tense form.]

22c Include all words necessary to complete a comparison.

　　　　　　　　　　　as　　　　　　 *those of*

The speaker's gestures were as good if not better than any other speaker I had
　　　　　　　　　　　　　　 ∧　　　　　　 ∧
observed.

other

Body language is as important as any part of the speech.
　　　　　　　　　　　　　　　 ∧

Avoiding Omissions   Exercise 22-1

NAME _____ SCORE _____

DIRECTIONS   In the following sentences insert the words that are needed to complete the sense; then write those words in the blanks.

EXAMPLE
Many people do not understand that oral reports $\overset{are}{\wedge}$ something

they will present frequently.   *are*

1. Giving an oral report makes most people more nervous

   than preparing a written.   _____

2. Accomplished speakers may be nervous, they never let

   their uneasiness show.   _____

3. Good speakers understand the importance and know

   how to use gestures to keep their audience's attention. _____

4. An outline and list of visual aids will help you keep your

   speech well organized.   _____

5. People often ask what type outline is best for presenta-

   tions.   _____

6. You will find the gestures you use in ordinary conversa-

   tion will be the most convincing.   _____

7. Remember, too, speaking too fast and not pausing for

   breath will make your report hard to understand.   _____

8. Voice coaches counsel their students deep breathing

   will help them relax and speak distinctly.   _____

9. Eye contact, however, has and always will be the best

   way for you to let your audience know you are sincere.   _____

10. If you cannot look at your audience, they will feel left

    out, and will not know how they are reacting.   _____

SENTENCE UNITY   su 23

23

Make sure that all parts of a sentence are clearly related and that the subject, or central focus, of the sentence is clear.

Errors in unity are so common and so varied that it is impossible to show more than a sampling of them. (Often the instructor marks this type of mistake with a *K*, indicating that the sentence is awkward and needs to be entirely rewritten.) Most mistakes of this type stem from (1) a failure to establish a clear relationship between clauses in a sentence or (2) a tendency to overcrowd a sentence with adjectives and adverbs, thereby losing focus and confusing the reader.

23a Establish a clear relationship between main clauses in a sentence: develop unrelated ideas in separate sentences. (See also Section **24.**)

UNCLEAR   Creighton Alexander lost his audience after only three minutes of speaking, and his face never showed a change of expression.

CLEAR   Because his face never showed a change of expression, Creighton Alexander lost his audience after only three minutes of speaking.

OR

Creighton Alexander's face never showed a change of expression even though he lost his audience after only three minutes of speaking.

OR

Creighton Alexander lost his audience after only three minutes of speaking. His face never showed a change of expression.

23b Keep the central focus of a sentence clear.

Adding too many phrases or clauses to the base sentence (*subject–verb–complement*)—even when they are relevant additions—will make the focus of the sentence unclear.

UNCLEAR   Creighton Alexander, with his shifting eyes and rigid body, which showed his nervousness all too clearly, while he stood as if planted behind the lectern, failed to establish any rapport with his audience.   [The focus of the sentence—*Creighton Alexander*—has been lost.]

CLEAR   Creighton Alexander, with his shifting eyes and rigid body, failed to establish any rapport with his audience.

23c Do not mix constructions.

MIXED   When speakers ramble and stumble causes their audience to lose the thread of the argument.   [adverb clause + predicate]

REVISED   When speakers ramble and stumble, they cause their audience to lose the thread of the argument.   [adverb clause, main clause]

MIXED   It was a long speech but which was quite interesting.

REVISED   It was a long speech, but it was quite interesting.

OR

It was a long speech which was quite interesting.   [noun + adjective clause]

Note: Sometimes a sentence is flawed by the use of a singular noun instead of a plural one: "Many who attended the sales meeting brought their own cars." [NOT car]

23d Avoid faulty predication.

Faulty predication occurs when the subject and predicate do not fit each other logically.

ILLOGICAL   Because the speaker was enthusiastic kept the audience interested.   [A *because* clause is not a noun or a pronoun and thus cannot function as a subject.]

LOGICAL   The speaker's enthusiasm kept the audience interested.   [*Enthusiasm* is a noun and can serve as the subject.]

OR

Because the speaker was enthusiastic, the audience stayed interested.

23e Avoid faulty *is-when* or *is-where* definitions.

ILLOGICAL   Gesturing is when a speaker uses his hands to clarify or emphasize certain points.   [*Gesturing* is an act, not a time.]

LOGICAL   Gesturing is the speaker's use of his hands to explain or emphasize certain points.

Unity of Sentence Structure

Exercise 23-1

NAME _____ SCORE _____

DIRECTIONS   In the blanks enter *1* or *2* to indicate whether the chief difficulty in each sentence is (1) the linking of unrelated ideas or (2) excessive additions to the base sentence. Then revise the sentences to make them unified.

EXAMPLE

~~When you take the time to look,~~ *I*f people are not paying attention to

your talk, you should, ~~and probably would want to,~~ change your

manner of presentation.   *2*

1. The problem may be that you are speaking too softly or that

   the audience cannot hear you.   _____

2. Sometimes, besides talking too softly, another reason people

   also cannot follow you is when you are speaking indistinctly.   _____

3. Slurred speech, one of the least excusable errors in oral

   presentations, which is a lazy way of talking that suggests to

   your audience that you are not really concerned about them,

   may result in the phrase *human beings* sounding like *human*

   beans.   _____

4. Sometimes people have trouble understanding you if you talk

   too rapidly and sometimes a high-pitched voice can irritate

   the audience.   _____

5. The audience went to sleep, and the speaker's voice was so low that he bored them. _____

6. Pitch, rate of speech, and volume are important in establishing rapport with an audience, and look closely at the people you are addressing. _____

7. The conclusion of the speech, which many speakers ruin by suggesting that they are finished and then continuing to talk for another ten minutes, thus trying the patience of the audience, is a part of the speech that you should have clearly in mind. _____

8. One of the most common problems in speeches is when the speaker continues for many minutes after he has indicated that he is coming to an end. _____

9. A speaker should not hurry from the rostrum, and the audience may want to applaud. _____

10. Applause, which usually follows a few seconds of silent eye contact with your audience but which is not expected in certain situations, such as a company briefing, should be accepted from the rostrum, not from your seat. _____

24

Use subordination to show exact relationships between ideas. Use coordination to give ideas equal emphasis.

In Section **1** you learned that short, choppy sentences may often be combined. When one of the short sentences is made into a sentence addition or modifier, the writer is using subordination. A writer uses subordination, or sentence combining, not only to improve style but also to show more clearly the relationships between ideas.

24a Instead of writing a series of short, choppy sentences, combine the sentences by expressing the main idea in the main or base clause and the less important ideas in subordinate clause or phrase additions.

CHOPPY	A question-and-answer period may follow your speech. Be sure to be courteous and correct in your responses.
SUBORDINATION	*If a question-and-answer period follows your speech*, be sure to be courteous and correct in your responses.
CHOPPY	Repeat the question. Answer it concisely and carefully.
SUBORDINATION	*After repeating the question*, answer it concisely and carefully.
CHOPPY	Andrea Joseph accepted questions from many people. The people were seated in various parts of the room.
SUBORDINATION	Andrea Joseph accepted questions from many people *who were seated in various parts of the room.*

24b Instead of writing loose, strung-out compound sentences, express the main idea in a main clause and make the less important ideas subordinate. Use coordination to give ideas equal emphasis.

STRUNG-OUT	A hostile person in the audience tried to harass Andrea with questions she was not qualified to answer, so Andrea replied simply, "I do not have the information to answer your questions at this time."
SUBORDINATED	When a hostile person in the audience tried to harass her with questions she was not qualified to answer, Andrea replied simply, "I do not have information to answer your questions at this time." [The writer emphasizes Andrea's reply.]
COORDINATED	A hostile person in the audience tried to harass Andrea with questions she was not qualified to answer, and she replied simply, "I do not have the information to answer your questions at this time." [The writer gives equal emphasis to the harassment of Andrea and her reply.]

24c Avoid excessive subordination.

Too many subordinate clauses in a sentence can make the focus of the sentence unclear. (See also **23b**.)

UNCLEAR   Andrea, who had never had to deal with a hostile member of an audience before, showed composure, particularly considering the circumstances, which included an overheated room and inadequate lighting, when she answered the person's question quickly but politely and then went on to respond to other questions.

CLEAR   Andrea, who had never had to deal with a hostile member of an audience before, showed composure when she answered the person's question quickly but politely and then went on to respond to other questions.

Subordination and Coordination   Exercise 24-1

NAME _____ SCORE _____

DIRECTIONS   Combine each of the following groups of choppy sentences by using either subordination or coordination.

EXAMPLE

A woman in the audience asked a foolish question. Andrea did not make fun of her

or of her question.

When a woman in the audience asked a foolish question, Andrea did not make fun of her or of her question.

1. Andrea was asked a few questions outside her field. She did not pretend to be an expert in all areas. She acknowledged her inability to answer those questions.

2. Andrea kept track of the time during the question-and-answer period. She answered all questions concisely.

3. Some people requested additional information. Andrea did what she promised to do. She mailed it promptly to them.

4. Andrea had anticipated many of the questions she was asked. She had brought additional charts and tables. These helped her answer the questions clearly.

5. Andrea was well prepared for the question-and-answer period. She enjoyed this part of her presentation.

25

Place modifiers carefully to indicate clearly their relationships with the words they modify.

While most adverbial modifiers may be moved to various places in a sentence without affecting the clarity of the sentence, adjectival modifiers usually must be placed either just before or just after the words they modify. (See also **1d.**)

ADVERBIAL   *When you think about the number of hours you will spend working,* you realize how important a choice of careers is. [Notice that the *when* clause may be moved to the end of the sentence or to the middle, after the main verb *realize*, without affecting clarity.]

ADJECTIVAL   Most people *who hold full-time jobs* can expect to spend ten thousand days of their lives working. [Notice that the *who* clause cannot be moved anywhere else in the sentence without affecting clarity.]

ADJECTIVAL   *Optimistic about the future,* most high-school and college students expect to achieve recognition and status in their occupations. [Notice that the verbal phrase may be placed either before or after the word it modifies—*students*—but nowhere else in the sentence without affecting clarity.]

25a Avoid needless separation of related parts of a sentence.

MISPLACED   Fifty percent of all college seniors expect to become wealthy who were *interviewed in 1978.*

CLEAR   Fifty percent of all college seniors who were *interviewed in 1978* expect to become wealthy.

AWKWARD   You will find that most students are, *when you analyze their expectations,* determined to have successful careers. [Even an adverbial modifier should not be placed so that it awkwardly splits parts of the verb.]

CLEAR   *When you analyze their expectations,* you will find that most college students are determined to have successful careers.

INFORMAL   Perhaps students *almost* expect too much from their careers.

CLEAR   Perhaps students expect *almost* too much from their careers.

25b Avoid dangling modifiers.

Dangling modifiers do not refer clearly and logically to another word or phrase in the sentence. (Most dangling modifiers are misplaced verbal phrases.) To correct a dangling modifier, either rearrange and reword the sentence base so that the modifier clearly refers to the right word or add words to the sentence to make the modifier clear by itself.

DANGLING   *Not wanting to waste forty years of their lives*, students' concern about their careers is not surprising.   [The verbal phrase illogically modifies *concern*.]

CLEAR   *Not wanting to waste forty years of their lives*, students, not surprisingly, are concerned about their careers.   [The verbal phrase logically modifies *students*.]

OR

Since most students do not want to waste forty years of their lives, their concern about their careers is not surprising.   [The verbal phrase is made into a clear subordinate clause with *students* as its subject.]

DANGLING   *Once unheard of*, many people today change their careers.   [The verbal phrase illogically modifies *people*.]

CLEAR   *Although the practice was once unheard of*, many people today change their careers.   [The verbal phrase is made into a clear subordinate clause.]

OR

Once unheard of, changing careers is common today.   [The verbal phrase logically modifies *changing*.]

Note: A dangling modifier usually cannot be corrected by simply moving it to the end of the sentence.

DANGLING   *Having mastered one job or skill*, another one may be tried.   [The verbal phrase illogically modifies *one*.]

DANGLING   Another one may be tried, *having mastered one job or skill*.   [The verbal phrase still illogically modifies the subject, *one*.]

CLEAR   *Having mastered one job or skill*, a person may try another.   [A subject, *person*, is supplied for the verbal phrase to modify.]

**Avoiding Misplaced Parts
and Dangling Modifiers**   Exercise 25–1

NAME _____ SCORE _____

DIRECTIONS   In each of the following sentences either a misplaced part or a dangling
modifier is in italics. Rewrite the sentence or add the words needed so that the reference is
clear and logical.

EXAMPLE
Some things have changed during the last few years *about the job market.*

*Some things about the job market have changed
in the last fifteen years.*

1. Liberal arts majors *almost* were certain to have a difficult time finding a
   job during the early 1970s.

2. Graduates with a general education were, *during the late 1960s and early
   1970s,* considered to be too plentiful.

3. *Not specifically trained for any one job,* many businesses refused to hire
   these graduates.

4. Today many businesses are seeking liberal arts majors *that did not hire
   them during the early 1970s.*

271

5. *Offering something valuable to the job market,* the late 1970s began to appreciate graduates with a general education.

6. Liberal arts majors can be molded for particular jobs *who have received a general education* by the companies that hire them.

7. *Able to adapt themselves to different kinds of jobs,* many companies now appreciate graduates with a general education.

8. Many career planning offices are, *so that students will have greater job flexibility,* advising them to train for more than one limited area of work.

9. A field may be overcrowded by the time a student graduates *that seems promising at the moment.*

10. Persons who *only* can do one thing may not be able to find a job in their area of specialization.

26

Use parallel structure to give grammatically balanced treatment to items in a list or series and to parts of a compound construction.

Parallel structure means that a grammatical form is repeated—an adjective is balanced by another adjective, a verb phrase is balanced by another verb phrase, a subordinate clause is balanced by another subordinate clause, and so on. Parallel structure can emphasize ideas (see Section **29**), make relationships clear, and contribute to coherence within and between paragraphs (see also Section **32**).

There are several connectives that frequently call for parallel structure: *and, but, or, nor* and especially *not only . . . but also, either . . . or, neither . . . nor,* and *as well as.* These words and phrases—and sometimes *rather than* or *not*—can be used to give a balanced treatment to items in a list or series or to parts of a compound construction.

Examples in this section are given in outline form to show the parallel structure (printed in italics) and the connectives (printed in boldface).

> Each year more and more women enter traditionally "male" professions:
> > *they become* civil or electrical engineers;
> > *they become* attorneys, public defenders, and judges;
> > **and**
> > *they become* professors of physics and computer science.

26a To achieve parallel structure, balance a verb with a verb, a prepositional phrase with a prepositional phrase, a subordinate clause with a subordinate clause, and so on.

> People no longer believe
> > *that it takes* brawn to design a skyscraper
> > **or**
> > *that one needs* muscle to perform open heart surgery.   [balanced subordinate clauses]
>
> > *Gaining equal recognition for equal responsibilities*
> > **as well as**
> > *earning equal pay for equal work*
> concerns women in the work force.   [balanced verbal phrases]

26b Whenever necessary to make the parallelism clear, repeat a preposition, an article, the sign of the infinitive (*to*), or the introductory word of a long phrase or clause.

The number of women demanding equal opportunity is not likely
>   *to* decrease in the future
>   **but**
>   *to* increase during the next decade.

A woman who enters a career wants to be seen
>   *as* a competent worker first
>   **and**
>   *as* a woman second.

Parallel Structure

NAME _____ SCORE _____

DIRECTIONS   In the following sentences underline the connective(s) that call for parallel structure; then make the structure(s) parallel.

EXAMPLE

Today women <u>not only</u> want challenging careers <u>but also</u> ~~to have~~ *want* equal pay and

esteem for what they do.

1. In the 1970s the number of women attending college <u>and</u> who held jobs increased noticeably.

2. Since the early 1900s women's rights have expanded to include voting, education, <u>and</u> having the right to own property.

3. Three major problems facing women are gaining access to education, finding suitable employment after graduation, <u>and</u> to command equal salaries for equal work.

4. In the past women had difficulty enrolling in certain educational curriculums <u>and</u> to find employment in certain professions.

5. Ratification of an equal rights amendment would assure that all people have equal rights under the law <u>and</u> for no one to have her or his rights denied.

Parallel Structure   Exercise 26–2

NAME _____ SCORE _____

DIRECTIONS   To make a topic outline easily readable, a writer should use parallel structure for Roman-numeral and capital-letter headings. The following outline fails to use
parallel structure in five places. Revise these five parts so that all divisions of the outline
will be immediately clear to the reader.

Thesis: The American worker is likely to experience at least three major

kinds of change in his or her job during the next twenty years.

I. Changes in the work schedule

A. Fewer hours

B. Working flexible schedules

C. Companies will use job sharing.

II. Changes in the workplace

A. Less stressful environments

B. Recreational facilities

C. Many routine chores will be handled by robots and computers.

III. There will be many new fringe benefits.

A. Educational opportunities

B. Sabbaticals

C. Providing on-site day-care centers

27

Avoid needless shifts in tense, mood, voice, number, and person. Also avoid needless shifts from indirect to direct discourse.

27a Avoid needless shifts in tense, mood, or voice.

SHIFT IN TENSE During the 1970s women all over the world *became* concerned about their status and *establish* organizations to work for improvements. [The verbs shift from past to present tense.]

CONSISTENT During the 1970s women all over the world *became* concerned about their status and *established* organizations to work for improvements.

SHIFT IN MOOD To understand the recent history of the women's movement, first *read* Betty Friedan's *The Feminine Mystique*, and then you *should examine* what feminists in the 1970s and 1980s have said about women's rights. [*Should examine* is a shift to the indicative mood from the imperative (command) mood, *read.*]

CONSISTENT To understand the recent history of the women's movement, first *read* Betty Friedan's *The Feminine Mystique*, and then *examine* what feminists in the 1970s and 1980s have said about women's rights.

SHIFT IN VOICE First we *will read The Feminine Mystique;* then the writings of contemporary feminists *will be examined.* [The verbs shift from the active to the passive voice.]

CONSISTENT First we *will read The Feminine Mystique;* then we *will examine* the writings of contemporary feminists.

Shifts in tense are especially troublesome. The tendency to shift tenses is particularly strong when you are referring to what others have written, since the customary correct practice is to speak of written observations in the present tense even though they were written in the past.

SHIFT In *The Feminine Mystique* (1963) Betty Friedan *discusses* the lack of fulfillment modern women feel and *showed* that their sense of loss results from their inability to find meaningful occupations outside the home.

CONSISTENT In *The Feminine Mystique* (1963) Betty Friedan *discusses* the lack of fulfillment modern women feel and *shows* that their sense of loss results from their inability to find meaningful occupations outside the home.

27b Avoid needless shifts in person and in number. (See also Section **6**.)

SHIFT IN PERSON   If you study the history of the women's rights movement, *one* cannot help being startled by the changes that have occurred. [The pronouns shift from second to third person.]

CONSISTENT   If you study the history of the women's rights movement, *you* cannot help being startled by the changes that have occurred.

SHIFT IN NUMBER   *Each* woman fighting for equality in the working world feels that *they* have a valid cause.   [The pronouns shift from singular to plural.]

CONSISTENT   *Each* woman fighting for equality in the working world feels that *she* has a valid cause.

27c Avoid needless shifts between indirect and direct discourse.

SHIFT   Women are now saying, "Give us the opportunity to enter the same professions men do" and that they want to be paid the same salaries as men.   [The sentence shifts from direct to indirect discourse.]

CONSISTENT   Women are now saying that they want the opportunity to enter the same professions men do and that they want to be paid the same salaries as men.

OR

Women are now saying, "Pay us the same salaries as men, and give us the same opportunity to enter the same professions."

Avoiding Needless Shifts Exercise 27–1

NAME _____ SCORE _____

DIRECTIONS   In each of the following sentences, indicate the kind of shift by writing *1* if the shift is in tense, mood, or voice; *2* if it is in person or number; or *3* if it is from indirect to direct discourse. Then revise the sentence to eliminate the needless shift.

EXAMPLE
When ~~one~~ *we* look~~s~~ back over history, we realize how much the role of

women in society has changed.   _____*2*_____

1. In most ancient societies women remained at home, and no

   formal education was received by them.   _____

2. Roman women had more legal rights and social freedom than

   other European women did, but their status decreases with

   the spread of Christianity.   _____

3. Examine Old Testament tradition, and you should see why

   the Church affirmed the dominant role of men.   _____

4. Indeed, most of the world's religions questioned the equality

   of women, and could they do any useful work other than

   housework and child rearing.   _____

5. Before the 1800s very few women in the United States

   worked outside the home, and those who did often do so out

   of necessity.   _____

6. When we examine the course of the Industrial Revolution, you find that one of its results was the emergence of women as a significant part of the work force.   _____

7. At first the working conditions in textile mills and in other factories that employed women were reasonably good, but, as time goes by, conditions worsen and salaries drop.   _____

8. The women's rights movement, which began during the first half of the 1800s, makes progress with the introduction of a constitutional amendment granting women the right to vote.   _____

9. Beginning in 1873 the amendment was brought before Congress every year until it finally passes in 1920.   _____

10. Each of the major wars fought by our country has also had their effect on the role of women outside the home.   _____

28

Make each pronoun refer unmistakably to its antecedent.

A pronoun usually depends on an antecedent—a word it refers to—for its meaning. If the antecedent is not immediately clear so that the reader can understand without difficulty, we say that the *reference* of the pronoun is vague. Reference can be vague because *two* possible antecedents appear, or because no specific antecedent has been provided, or because the pronoun refers to the general idea of the preceding sentence or sentences rather than to something more specific.

> *They* claimed that the standard work week *would* be only thirty-five hours by the middle of the 1980s. *They* said *this* because it had decreased continually since 1900.

There are three main ways to correct an unclear reference of a pronoun: (1) rewrite the sentence to eliminate the pronoun; (2) provide a clear antecedent for the pronoun to refer to; and (3) substitute a noun for the pronoun or, in the case of *this*, add a noun, making the pronoun an adjective.

> A *report produced by the American Institute for Research* claimed that the standard work week would be only thirty-five hours by the middle of the 1980s. *The researchers who worked on the report* made *this claim* because the *work week* had decreased continually since 1900.

28a Avoid ambiguous references.

AMBIGUOUS   John wrote to Oliver when *he* got *his* new job.

CLEAR   When John got his new job, he wrote to Oliver.

OR

When Oliver got his new job, John wrote to him.

28b Avoid remote or obscure references.

REMOTE   Oliver studied the job description. A variety of skills and a considerable amount of work experience were required. *It* convinced Oliver that he was not qualified for the position.

CLEAR   Oliver studied the job description. A variety of skills and a considerable amount of work experience were required. The *job description* convinced Oliver that he was not qualified for the position.

OBSCURE   When *Mrs. Mazaki's* company was founded, *she* asked Oliver to join her staff.   [A reference to an antecedent in the possessive case is unclear.]

CLEAR   When *Mrs. Mazaki* founded her company, *she* asked Oliver to join her staff.

28c In general, avoid broad references—that is, the use of pronouns like *which,* *it,* and *this*—to refer to the general idea of a preceding sentence or clause.

BROAD   Oliver was a skillful writer, and he used *it* to get ahead in the new company.

CLEAR   Oliver used his *writing skill* to get ahead in the new company.

BROAD   The new company sent out many proposals. *This* was Oliver's specialty.

CLEAR   The new company sent out many proposals. *This type of writing* was Oliver's specialty.   [One way to correct a vague *this* is to add a noun for the pronoun to modify.]

OR

The new company's need to submit many proposals made use of Oliver's specialty.   [The vague *this* is eliminated by rewriting the two sentences as one.]

28d Avoid the awkward or superfluous use of pronouns.

(1) Avoid the awkward placement of the pronoun *it* near the expletive *it.*

AWKWARD   Although *it* was difficult for Oliver to get a new job, he decided to do *it*.   [The use of the first *it*—an expletive—makes the meaning of the second *it*—a pronoun—unclear.]

CLEAR   Although *it* was difficult for Oliver to get a new job, he decided to *do* so.

(2) Avoid the use of a meaningless *it* or *they* in a construction like the following.

AWKWARD   In the yellow pages *it lists* the names of all insurance companies in the area.   [This construction is wordy as well as awkward.]

CLEAR   The *yellow pages list* the names of all insurance companies in the area.

OR

In the yellow pages are the names of all insurance companies in the area.

AWKWARD   In my business-writing textbooks *they* name two kinds of proposals.

CLEAR   My business-writing textbook names two kinds of proposals.

OR

The author of my business-writing textbook names two kinds of proposals.

Reference of Pronouns   Exercise 28–1

NAME _____ SCORE _____

DIRECTIONS   In the following discussion of leisure time, mark a capital *V* through each pronoun whose reference is vague and write the pronoun in the blank. Then revise the sentence or sentences to clarify the meaning.

EXAMPLE

~~t~~The number of hours spent at work may lessen during

Because   *will*

the coming decade, ~~which will cause~~ people ~~to~~ reeval-

uate their idea of leisure time.   *which*

1. The four-day work week is used by some com-

   panies. This gives employees more leisure time.   _____

2. Increased automation is bound to give employees

   more leisure time. It is hard to say what employees

   will do with it.   _____

3. In Sebastian de Grazia's *Of Time, Work, and*

   Leisure, he explains the ancient and modern at-

   titudes toward leisure.   _____

4. The ancient Greeks had a different notion of

   leisure from ours. We think of using our leisure

   time to accomplish a definite task, like painting

   our house or washing our car. To them it meant

   time to do something enjoyable for its own sake.   _____

5. Many Americans are totally dedicated to the work ethic. This causes them to take a second job if they have very much spare time.   _____

6. When Americans retire from their careers, they often do not know what to do with it.   _____

7. Although it has been a tradition in our country to retire at the age of sixty-five, we are now unsure that it is a good thing.   _____

8. Many people find nothing to give them a sense of fulfillment outside their work, which leads to personal unhappiness.   _____

9. Perhaps we need to adopt the ancient Greek attitude toward leisure. They thought that just thinking, or even doing nothing, could be worthwhile.   _____

10. Automation may well allow us to have three days off during each week and to have twenty or more years of retirement living. We must educate ourselves to use this creatively.   _____

29

Arrange the parts of a sentence, and the sentences in a paragraph, to emphasize important ideas.

The following suggestions will help you stress the main ideas in your sentences and paragraphs.

29a Gain emphasis by placing important words at the beginning or at the end of the sentence—especially at the end—and unimportant words in the middle.

UNEMPHATIC *Leisure time can be a problem*, sociologists tell us.

EMPHATIC *Leisure time*, sociologists tell us, *can be a problem*.   [Note how *problem* gains emphasis.]

29b Gain emphasis by occasionally changing loose sentences to periodic sentences.

In a loose sentence the main idea comes first; periodic sentences place the main idea last, just before the period.

LOOSE Some people find leisure time troublesome, causing them problems such as boredom, anxiety, and stress.

PERIODIC Problems such as boredom, anxiety, and stress trouble some people faced with leisure time.

Caution: Do not overuse periodic sentences; if you do, they will lose their effectiveness.

29c Gain emphasis by arranging ideas in the order of climax—that is, by building from the least to the most important.

UNORDERED Some people regard leisure time as wasteful, as unhealthy, or as a nuisance.

ORDERED Some people regard leisure time as wasteful, as a nuisance, or even as unhealthy.

29d Gain emphasis by using the active voice.

PASSIVE Most people's leisure time *is spent* watching television.

ACTIVE Most people *spend* their leisure time watching television.

29e Gain emphasis by repeating words or structures. (See also Section 26.)

UNEMPHATIC   The prospect of retirement has many unpleasant associations for people who have no interests outside work. It makes them think of boredom. And it may also bring to mind uselessness and loss of self-respect.

EMPHATIC   The prospect of retirement has many unpleasant *associations* for people who have no interests outside their work—*associations* such as *boredom*, *uselessness*, and *loss of self-respect*.

29f Gain emphasis by occasionally inverting the word order of a sentence. (See also 30b.)

NORMAL ORDER   Most people want and need to feel useful and productive.

INVERTED ORDER   Useful and productive is what most people want and need to feel.

Caution: If overused, this method of gaining emphasis will make your style seem stilted and contrived.

29g Gain emphasis by using balanced sentence construction.

A balanced sentence uses grammatically equal structures—usually main clauses with parallel elements—to express contrasted (or similar) ideas. The balance emphasizes the contrast (or similarity).

To use leisure time well is to feel productive; to use leisure time ineffectively is to feel aimless.

29h Gain emphasis by writing the main ideas in sentences that are noticeably shorter than the other sentences.

[1]"Stopping out," or taking a temporary leave from college, is not a new phenomenon, but it is a practice that is gaining popularity among college students. [2]One national survey shows that 95 percent of all college students have seriously considered stopping out during their undergraduate years. [3]Many students would like to leave school temporarily to travel, to work, or just to find themselves. [4]They feel that what they learn during their absence from college will introduce them to the real world, will motivate them to become better students, and will enable them to set realistic goals for their futures. [5]*Certainly stopping out can do all of these things.*

[6]College administrators and many students who have unsuccessfully tried stopping out warn about the disadvantages: getting permanently sidetracked from one's education, finding that travel plans and jobs do not always work out, being tempted to do nothing during the absence from college. [7]*Thus, stopping out is not to be tried on impulse.* [8]It requires careful planning so that a student will not waste a semester or a year, and it requires informing advisors and filling out forms so that the college will know what the student will be doing during the leave and when he or she will return.

Note: These two paragraphs also illustrate the use of the active voice—in all sentences—and parallel structure—in sentences 3, 4, and 6—to achieve emphasis.

Emphasis   Exercise 29–1

NAME _____ SCORE _____

DIRECTIONS   In each of the following, write a sentence that achieves emphasis by means of the pattern given. Then underline the part of the sentence that you wished to emphasize.

EXAMPLE
Place important words at the beginning of a sentence.

<u>How many people</u>, one wonders, look forward to retirement?

1. Place important words at the end of the sentence.

2. Emphasize ideas by means of a periodic sentence.

3. Emphasize ideas by arranging them in the order of climax, from the least to the most important.

4. Use the active voice.

5. Emphasize your idea by inverting the usual word order of the sentence.

6. Emphasize your idea by repeating key words.

7. Emphasize your idea by repeating structures.

8. Write a series of sentences in which the most important idea is contained in a sentence that is noticeably shorter than the others.

9. Use balanced sentence construction to emphasize the similarities between two ideas.

10. Use balanced sentence construction to emphasize the differences between two ideas.

30

Vary the length, structure, and beginnings of sentences to create a pleasing style.

A writer of essays is usually more concerned about variety than a writer of business letters and reports is. In occupational writing, quite understandably, the emphasis is on clarity and simplicity rather than on style. But even the occupational writer, to hold the reader's attention, must avoid too many short, choppy sentences, strung-out compound sentences, or sentences that begin in the same way. In short, business and technical writers, as well as general writers, need to know how to vary their sentence structure to produce writing that is not only clear but also pleasing to read.

30a Vary the length of sentences, using short sentences primarily for emphasis (see **29h**); **also vary the structure of sentences** (see also **1d** and Section **24**).

SIMPLE   A few companies have set up retirement clinics. These clinics help workers prepare for their retirement years.

COMPOUND   A few companies have set up retirement clinics, and these clinics help workers prepare for their retirement years.

COMPLEX   A few companies have set up retirement clinics that help workers prepare for their retirement years.

30b Vary the beginnings of sentences.

(1) Begin with a modifier.

Gradually, workers learn to cope with retirement.

(2) Begin with a phrase.

Through courses and counseling, the clinics help people discover the talents they would like to develop.

(3) Begin with a subordinate clause.

Because more and more people are reaching retirement age, these clinics may become commonplace in the future.

(4) Begin with a coordinating conjunction or a transitional expression when the word or phrase can be used to show the proper relationship between sentences.

More people are reaching retirement age in our country than ever before. *And* [or *In addition*,] many employees are retiring at the age of fifty-five or earlier.

30c Avoid loose, stringy compound sentences. (See also **24b**.)

To revise a loose, stringy compound sentence, try one of the following methods.

(1) Make a compound sentence complex.

COMPOUND   Many older executives have achieved high salaries, and so they are expensive to keep on the payroll, and so their companies force them to retire early.

COMPLEX   Many highly paid older executives, who are expensive to keep on the payroll, are forced by their companies to retire early.

(2) Use a compound predicate in a simple sentence.

COMPOUND   Often people plan ahead, and they save money, and they retire much earlier than the "standard" age of sixty-five.

SIMPLE   Often people plan ahead, save money, and retire much earlier than the "standard" age of sixty-five.

(3) Use an appositive in a simple sentence.

COMPOUND   Many people plan ahead, and they are prudent, and they invest wisely the money they are saving for retirement.

SIMPLE   Many people, prudent individuals, plan ahead and invest wisely the money they are saving for retirement.

(4) Use a prepositional or verbal phrase in a simple sentence.

COMPOUND   The economy is unpredictable, and people saving for retirement know they must take inflation into account.

SIMPLE   In an unpredictable economy, people saving for retirement know they must take inflation into account.

30d Vary the conventional subject-verb sequence by occasionally separating subject and verb with words or phrases.

S-V-C   Some employees are retiring from their present jobs at the age of fifty-five to start a new career.

VARIED   Some employees, *at the age of fifty-five*, are retiring from their present jobs to start a new career.

OR

Many employees, eager to start a new career, are retiring from their present jobs at the age of fifty-five.

Note: This kind of variety must be used with discretion because too frequent a separation of sentence parts makes the writer's style unnatural and even difficult to follow. (See also **25a**.)

30e Occasionally use an interrogative, imperative, or exclamatory sentence to vary from the more common declarative sentence.

Retirement clinics are not commonplace today. In fact, only a very few companies supply them. *But who can say how popular they may become in the next twenty years when the greatest percentage of workers in our history will be reaching retirement age?*

Variety   Exercise 30-1

NAME _____ SCORE _____

DIRECTIONS   Analyze the ways in which the writer has achieved variety in the paragraphs below by answering the questions that follow. When the question asks, "*Which sentence . . .?*" use the sentence's number to identify your answer.

¹Until recently, most people believed that once they chose a profession as young adults they had to stick with it until they retired. ²Now some of them are challenging this assumption. ³Unlike their co-workers who never change fields, these people are abandoning the security of a known routine to explore a new occupation.

⁴Why do professionals such as lawyers, teachers, administrators, and business executives "quit"? ⁵Because they have decided that their comfortable salary and relatively secure position are less important than their desire to feel satisfied with their work. ⁶In their professional occupations they feel bored. ⁷They admit that they are unhappy. ⁸So why not change? ⁹In some respects they are only doing what all of us dream about: following our secret ambitions. ¹⁰However, these people—without any guarantee of success—have had the courage to put their dreams into action. ¹¹What finally has convinced them to risk the change is the thought that if they do not at least try, they will never know if they *could* have succeeded. ¹²That is the best challenge of all. ¹³They want and need to test themselves.

¹⁴These days there are even counselors who help professionals as they make this difficult decision to change their lives. ¹⁵A switch from banking to weaving blankets is dramatic. ¹⁶But if a banker is tired of three-piece suits and has always wanted to move to a mountain resort and restore antique furniture, a career counselor can help determine whether or not the change is likely to be for the best. ¹⁷Of course, not everyone who considers changing careers will actually do so. ¹⁸But for those who take the risk, a happier life may be waiting.

¹⁹I know how difficult it is to make the switch, but it can be done. ²⁰I live in a resort area where many people come to try out their secret ambitions. ²¹My

295

next-door neighbor used to be a social worker in Miami; now he weaves baskets. [22]A couple down the road taught school for years, until they decided that they would rather run a country store. [23]And a former geological consultant raises Christmas trees and rhododendrons. [24]When I ask these people if the expense and the uncertainty of the change have been worth it, I always get the same answer. [25]"Yes!"

ANALYSIS

1. Which sentences are shortest? _____

   Why do you think the writer used them? _____

2. How many simple sentences are there? _____

   How many compound sentences? _____

   How many complex sentences? _____

3. How many sentences begin with something other than the subject? _____

   Which sentences begin with an adverb or an adverb phrase? _____

   Which begin with an adverb clause? _____

   Which begin with a coordinating conjunction or transitional expression? __

   _____

4. In which sentence is the usual subject-verb sequence interrupted by a word

   or phrase? _____

5. Which sentences are not declarative sentences? _____

   What kind are they? _____

Variety

NAME _____ SCORE _____

DIRECTIONS   Write sentences to illustrate the techniques for achieving variety listed below. You may want to continue this book's theme of the world of work.

1. two sentences, the second beginning with a coordinating conjunction

2. a sentence beginning with a subordinate clause

3. a sentence beginning with a verbal phrase

4. a sentence beginning with a single-word modifier

5. a sentence in which the subject and verb are separated by an intervening word or words

Mastering Variety: A Review   Exercise 30–3

NAME _____ SCORE _____

DIRECTIONS   Rewrite the following paragraph so that the sentences flow more smoothly and the style is more varied. Use a transitional expression or two, vary the beginnings of some of the sentences, combine sentences, and add words if you wish.

¹We can find plenty of examples of the worthwhile use of leisure time in our society. ²The arts are attracting many new participants and fans. ³People are painting, writing, dancing, and making music as never before. ⁴Small rural communities are being visited by symphony orchestras and art exhibitions. ⁵Handicrafts are flourishing everywhere. ⁶A majority of the citizens in some towns are involved in making things. ⁷They are making things like pottery, furniture, and macramé items. ⁸People are buying the works that are produced. ⁹Artists of all types are able to make a living from their crafts.

REVISION

31

Base what you say and write on clear, logical thinking. Avoid common fallacies.

Most readers are reasonable people who will listen to what you have to say. How readily they will be persuaded to look at an issue from your point of view, however, depends on how well you present your case. In many respects, informing your reader about an issue is similar to a lawyer's presenting a case to a jury. The more logical the presentation—that is, the more clearly stated and reasonably argued—the more likely your reader will be to listen to your ideas. The more sense a piece of writing makes, the more confidence your reader will have that you know what you are talking about.

31a Learn how to use inductive reasoning in your writing.

When you reason inductively, you reach a conclusion based on the available evidence. For example, if you were writing a memorandum to argue that one of your company's customers should be refused further credit (your conclusion), you would base your recommendation on the customer's poor record of past payment (the evidence). You are reasoning that because the customer has repeatedly failed to meet his obligations in the past, he will probably fail in the future. Note that there is an element of probability, rather than certainty, in inductive reasoning. This requires that you present as much evidence as possible to support the conclusion you want the reader to accept. Inductive reasoning can be a powerful persuasive tool, lending strength and authority to any material you present.

When you use induction, you can arrange your material in one of two ways: you can (1) present the evidence first and then draw the conclusion or (2) state the conclusion first and then develop the evidence that led you to form that conclusion. The first method is effective if you are writing for a reader who is likely to disagree with you: it is best to let this reader evaluate the evidence and then draw the conclusion along with you as you sum up. The second method, presenting the conclusion first and then discussing the evidence which supports it, works well for a reader who is likely to be receptive. Which strategy you select depends on your audience and the effect you wish to produce.

31b Learn how to use deductive reasoning in your writing.

In deductive reasoning the writer argues logically from principles (assertions of truths) rather than from evidence: if A is true and B is true, then it follows that this C *must* also be true. This basic logical structure is called a syllogism. Syllogisms contain three parts: a major premise (usually a generalization), a minor premise (usually a specific fact), and a conclusion that fits both the major and the minor premise. In a deductive argument, you must carefully examine your premises to make sure that they are both true, for even if you reason logically you may reach a wrong conclusion if one of your premises is false. Finally, for your argument to be effective, you must be certain that your premises are ones that your reader can accept.

MAJOR PREMISE   People doing the same job should be paid the same salary.

MINOR PREMISE   Both men and women work at this job.

CONCLUSION   Men and women doing this job should be paid the same salary.

31c Avoid fallacies in your reasoning.

Fallacies are faults in reasoning. Here are some of the fallacies that occur most often in writing.

(1) *Non Sequitur:* A conclusion that does not follow from the premise.

This product outperforms its competitors; therefore it will sell well. [Many superior products do not sell well.]

(2) **Hasty Generalization:** A generalization based on too little, or on exceptional or biased, information.

People dislike changing to new products. [This may be true of some people, but certainly not all.]

(3) *Ad Hominem:* Attacking the person who presents an issue rather than dealing with the issue itself.

It may be true that my competitor makes a superior product, but what has he done for our community? [The competitor's contribution to the community has no bearing on the quality of the product.]

(4) **Bandwagon:** An argument that says in effect, "Everyone else is doing (or thinking or saying) this, so you should."

Everyone likes this make of computer, and you will too. [You will not necessarily *respond* in the same way as the majority.]

(5) **Circular Reasoning:** "Begging the Question"—simply restating an effect as the cause.

He habitually is late because he finds it impossible to be on time. [Being late and finding it impossible to be on time mean the same thing.]

(6) **Red Herring:** Bringing up an irrelevant issue in order to avoid the real issue.

Never mind the workers' demands for better benefits; what we really need is an improved customer service department. [Improving customer relations has nothing to do with meeting workers' demands.]

(7) Post Hoc, Ergo Propter Hoc: "After this, so because of this." Assuming that because one event followed another, the second was caused by the first.

> Last week we redecorated our showroom, and already the number of customers has increased by 25 percent. [The assumption that the redecoration *caused* the increase is not warranted.]

(8) Either ... or fallacy: Asserting that there are only two options when other options exist.

> Our drop in profit last year leaves us with only two options: freeze wages or lay off 25 percent of our employees in order to give raises to the other 75 percent. [In fact, other options exist.]

(9) False Analogy: Assuming that because two things are similar in certain ways they must be similar in other ways.

> Since this computer costs the same as the other model, it will perform all the functions the other does. [Equal price does not necessarily indicate that the two products will be of equal value to the company.]

(10) Equivocation: An assertion that illogically relies on the use of a term in two different senses.

> You have a right to complain, so do what is right and complain. [The word *right* means both "a just claim" and "correct."]

Arguing Logically   Exercise 31–1

NAME _____ SCORE _____

DIRECTIONS   Identify the logical fallacy that weakens each statement, and explain why it is fallacious. Refer to the list of fallacies in this chapter.

EXAMPLE
John has been an accountant for six years; therefore he is

better at his job than the new man we hired last

month.   *Non Sequitur*

Reason: *Being in a job longer does not necessarily mean that a person is more skilled than some- one hired more recently.*

1. We're sorry you found our salesperson rude, but we're sure you understand that this is an extremely busy time of the year for us.   _____

   Reason:

2. Consumers are gullible.   _____

   Reason:

3. Since these two vacuum cleaners are about the same size and weight, either one will do the job.   _____

   Reason:

4. Our company offers higher starting salaries, so the people we hire are better employees.   _____

   Reason:

5. We installed this new record-keeping system in October, and already fifteen files have disappeared.

   Reason: _____

6. It is impossible to give our secretaries additional pay increases because we cannot raise salaries at this time.

   Reason: _____

7. In a free enterprise system we should be free to do whatever we want.

   Reason: _____

8. Why should I accept your criticism of my work when you can't even get your work done on time?

   Reason: _____

9. Only two courses of action are possible: we can accept the added overtime assignments or go on strike.

   Reason: _____

10. Every other homeowner in your neighborhood has one of our insurance policies; you should too.

    Reason: _____

THE PARAGRAPH ¶ 32

32

Write unified, coherent, and adequately developed paragraphs.

We recognize the beginning of a new paragraph in a composition by the indention—about an inch when handwritten and five spaces when typewritten. Although a paragraph may be only one sentence long, most paragraphs require several sentences to adequately develop the central, or controlling, idea. We expect, by the time we finish reading the paragraph, to know what the writer's controlling idea is and to be able to recognize the relationship that each of the other sentences has to the sentence that states or suggests this controlling idea. And, finally, we expect the sentences to flow along smoothly so we do not have to mentally fill in any words or phrases or stop reading after every sentence or two to refocus our attention.

32a Make each sentence in the paragraph contribute to the controlling idea (central thought).

The controlling idea is printed in italics in the following paragraph. Notice that the key word, *flextime*, is echoed in each of the other sentences in the paragraph. (The words that echo *flextime* are printed in boldface.)

> [1]*Flextime is here to stay.* [2]Surveys, like one conducted by *Psychology Today* in 1978, suggest that the American worker strongly approves of **flextime;** fully 78 percent of those questioned by *Psychology Today* wanted to have **some say** in the time they started and finished their workday. [3]Employers, while they acknowledge some problems with **individualized work schedules,** seem equally satisfied with the system; as proof, only two percent of the companies that have tried **flextime** have returned to eight- or nine-to-five schedules. [4]Based, then, on present trends, **flextime** seems certain to replace the rigid work schedules that people have followed since the outset of the Industrial Revolution. [5]Looking ahead to the kind of workplace we will have in the year 2001, William Abbott, editor of the World Future Society's newsletter, *Careers Tomorrow*, says quite confidently, "Workers will schedule their own hours under **flextime.**"

The unity of this paragraph would be destroyed by inserting a sentence that is not a part of the plan called for by the controlling idea. Try reading the paragraph with these sentences inserted between sentences 2 and 3: "People obviously have different biological rhythms. Some people go to bed early and awaken at 6:00 or 7:00 ready for a full day's work. Others cannot fall asleep before 12:00 or 1:00 a.m. and are not really prepared to face the workplace before 10:00 a.m." Although pertinent to the general subject of convenient work schedules, these three sentences, or even one of them, would shift the focus of the paragraph away from the specific controlling idea: *Flextime is here to stay.* To maintain unity in a paragraph, then, you must be conscious of your controlling idea each time you add a sentence.

The sentence that states the controlling idea of a paragraph is called the *topic sentence.* Although a paragraph may have unity without an expressly stated topic sentence, inexperienced writers will find that a clear, specific topic sentence in each paragraph helps them keep their writing well organized. Since the controlling idea gives direction to the other sentences in the paragraph, the topic sentence usually appears early in the paragraph—as the first or second sentence. But it may be placed elsewhere—for example, at the end if the writer wishes to build up to a dramatic closing.

32b Link the sentences in the paragraph so that the thought flows smoothly from one sentence to the next.

A coherent paragraph is one in which the relationship of any given sentence to the ones before it is clear and the transitions between the sentences are smooth. A coherent paragraph is easy to read because there are no jarring breaks—the sentences are arranged in a clear, logical order (for example, by time; from general to specific; from least important to most important; or by location of items being described) and there are smooth transitions between sentences: (1) pronouns are used to refer to antecedents in preceding sentences; (2) key words or ideas are repeated; (3) transitional expressions are used; and (4) parallel structures are used where appropriate.

The following paragraph illustrates the four methods of achieving coherence. The sentences are arranged in order of climax (from least important to most important); the methods of making smooth transitions between sentences are indicated by numbers—1 through 4—that correspond to those cited above.

> There is much evidence that the roles of the sexes are changing. [3] First, and most noticeable, is the change in dress and appearance. Today many young men and women look much alike. [1] Their hair may be similar in style. [1, 4] They may wear the same shirts and pants. [1, 4] They may in fact go to the same unisex hair stylists and boutiques. [3, 2] But more significant evidence of the shift in sex roles is apparent in the job market. While a generation ago no more than one out of ten women with young children was employed outside the home, today one out of three is so employed. [3] And positions that were once considered appropriate only for men are now being filled by women. [3, 2] Conversely, many men today are training to be nurses, secretaries, and flight attendants—positions once considered unmistakably feminine. [3, 2]

32c Develop the argument so that it presents enough information about its central idea to satisfy the reader.

The length of a paragraph varies with its purpose. Thus a one-sentence paragraph or even a one-word paragraph ("Yes" or "No") may say emphatically all that the writer needs to say. Paragraphs that report dialogue are usually short because a new paragraph must begin each time the speaker changes.

Most paragraphs in expository writing tend to vary in length from about seventy-five to two hundred fifty words, the average length being about one hundred words. (And remember that when you write in longhand your paragraph looks much longer than it would if it were typed or set in print.)

32d Learn to use various methods of paragraph development.

The controlling idea of a paragraph may be developed in a number of ways. Most experienced writers use several methods of development in each paragraph without having to think about what they are doing. But as an inexperienced writer, you may need to practice consciously the methods discussed below until you are able to use them automatically and naturally. A study of these methods will help you not only to think of things to say but also to organize your thoughts, since the method of development usually suggests a pattern of arrangement for the sentences in the paragraph.

(1) Use relevant details.

The use of details is the most common method of developing a controlling idea, and almost every paragraph makes some use of it. Pertinent facts and details about the changing roles of the sexes are used to develop the controlling idea of the paragraph illustrating coherence. Notice that the most significant fact is discussed last, a common type of arrangement for this method of development.

(2) Use one striking example or several closely related examples.

A paragraph developed by examples is almost certain to hold the reader's attention. The success of one of the most popular books ever printed, Dale Carnegie's *How to Win Friends and Influence People*, depends primarily on the author's use of hundreds of examples. Because of the interest generated by a well-chosen example, many essays and speeches begin with this type of development. In his book *Megatrends*, John Naisbitt discusses what it takes for a company to be labeled "successful" and offers the following illustration:

> [1]But even among the most successful [companies], Tandem is remarkable. [2]The founder of the fast-growing $100-million-a-year company, James Treybig, emphatically states that the human side of the company is the most critical factor in reaching his goal—the $1 billion mark in annual sales. [3]Treybig frees up 100 percent of his personal time to spend on "people projects." [4]Tandem's people-oriented management style includes Friday-afternoon beer parties, employee stock options, flexible work hours (unlike Intel, where everyone is expected to show up promptly at 8:15 A.M.), a company swimming pool that is open from 6:00 A.M. to 8 P.M., and sabbatical leave every four years—which all employees are *required* to take. [5]Reviews and meetings occur spontaneously with no formal procedures.
>
> —JOHN NAISBITT, *Megatrends*

Examples may be fully developed, like the one above, or simply listed in passing, like the series of examples in the following paragraph used to illustrate the characteristics of workaholics during childhood.

[1]Marilyn Machlowitz, a psychologist for New York Life Insurance Co., has spent the past eight years studying the obsessive worker—first for her doctoral dissertation at Yale, more recently for her book *Workaholics: Living With Them, Working With Them.* [2]From interviews with 165 apparent workaholics, she has found that most exhibit identical characteristics early in their lives. [3]They turn games into imitations of work and go about them with intensity. [4]They set up lemonade stands, run sidewalk carnivals and cash in returnable soda bottles. Later, they sell more Girl Scout cookies, Christmas cards and magazine subscriptions than anyone else on the block. [5]And their teachers love them because they are such hard-working, attentive students.   —"Thank God, It's Monday," *Dun's Review*

(3) Narrate a series of events.

Strong paragraphs are internally consistent—their ideas relate to each other logically. If you are describing an event or a sequence of events, one good way to ensure that your paragraph is strongly unified is to discuss those events in the order in which they occurred. The following paragraph describes the method one businessman employs to make his company successful. Note that the ideas are arranged in chronological order, that is, in the order in which they take place.

[1]When it comes to choosing between business and social activities, Howard Bronson knows where his priorities lie: with his job. [2]Bronson, who heads his own financial public relations firm, is up by four a.m. and has mapped out his day by the time he gets to his Manhattan office at 6:45. [3]He works at a furious pace, often skipping lunch, until about 6:30 in the evening. [4]Then, after dinner, he puts in another hour and a half of reading before turning in at 12:15.

—"Thank God, It's Monday," *Dun's Review*

(4) Explain a process.

Paragraphs that are organized around a process explain how something is done or made. Like the narrative paragraph, this type of paragraph follows a series of events as they occur through time and thus employs a chronological arrangement. In fact, a reader would likely be confused by a process paragraph that violated the ordinary chronological sequence of a group of events as it described them.

In the following instructions for repairing faucets, the reader would more than likely become confused if the chronological order were jumbled.

[1]Turn the handle [of the pipe cutter] to the right until there is no resistance. [2]Then separate the two wheels. [3]Hold the lower one fast and give the handle a fraction of a turn into the work. [4]Tighten the upper wheel against the lower. [5]Again turn the handle to the right. [6]In this way, the cutter removes a layer of metal.

—MAX ALTH, *Do-It-Yourself Plumbing*

(5) Use cause and effect.

A cause and effect paragraph explains why a particular outcome has occurred. To use this method effectively, you must supply enough evidence to convince your reader that you understand the cause or causes for a particular effect. The following two paragraphs rely primarily on comments from interviews to persuade us that the editors of *Newsweek* have correctly identified two causes for the American worker's lack of commitment to the work ethic.

[1]The problem traces to two main factors: a younger work force—25 per cent of which is under 25 years old—and the nature of work itself in a highly industrialized society. [2]"It's mainly a problem of this younger worker," said Benjamin Aaron, director of the Institute of Industrial Relations at UCLA. [3]"He doesn't want to work to get ahead; he wants to work to get enough money for a while and then he wants to drop out." [4]Or, as Jerry Wurf, president of the American Federation of State, County and Municipal Employees, put it: "The Depression is something they learned about in a history class."
[5]Once on the job, workers all too often find that, however good their wages and working conditions, work is a totally unsatisfying experience. [6]"People my age don't take much pride in this work," says Victoria Bowker, a 27-year-old blueprinter at Lockheed Aircraft. [7]"In the old days, you used to start a job and you used to finish it. [8]Now things have become so diversified you can't see your product; you start something and it goes through 50 million other hands before it's completed." [9]Mike Eckert, a longtime Lockheed employee twice Miss Bowker's age, agrees that things have changed. [10]"Today's management doesn't have any compassion for the person that's down the line," he says. [11]"They treat you like a machine . . . and you can't treat human nature that way." [12]And when a worker begins feeling like a machine, he'll probably resort to one of two alternatives: goldbrick, or start looking for another job. [13]"I'll tell you how attitudes are," UAW vice president Ken Bannon summed up last week. [14]"You will find people who say they would rather work in cleanup and take a cut of 15 cents an hour than work the assembly line. [15]At least on cleanup you have the choice of sweeping the pile in the corner or sweeping the pile by the post."
—"Too Many U.S. Workers No Longer Give a Damn," *Newsweek*

(6) Use classification.

Classification organizes something into categories. For example, the following paragraph on "alternate work schedules" breaks its subject down into the four categories of compressed time, flextime, part-time, and shared time.

[1]Alternate work schedules are rapidly replacing the rigid eight- or nine-to-five workdays of the past. [2]For example, the 10-hour, four-day workweek has been used in industry for many years. [3]This type of compressed-time job schedule allows the worker to enjoy a regular three-day weekend. [4]But surpassing compressed-time scheduling in popularity with workers is flextime, which lets them choose their own hours to begin and end their workdays so long as they work a certain number of hours a week and so long as they are on the job during a mid-day core period. [5]Also, part-time work, which involves one out of every six workers in this country, continues to gain in popularity as people, especially the young, begin to value leisure as much as they do money. [6]And shared-time work schedules, whereby two employees share one full-time position, are saving employers as well as employees from massive lay-offs in an increasingly automated society.

(7) Use an extended definition.

Sometimes you may need to compose a paragraph or even an entire essay to define a difficult term or a term that you want the reader to understand in a special way. The essayist Jon Stewart uses two paragraphs to define a silicon chip for a general audience of readers who may be unfamiliar with the workings of microprocessors and computers.

> [1]The revolution, of course, is that wrought by the silicon chip, that virtually invisible, spiderlike network of tiny electronic circuits etched on a flake of silicon (sand) less than half the size of the fingertip. [2]In the form of microprocessors, or miniature computers, it is invading every aspect of American life—the way we play, work, even think.
>
> [3]This computer-on-a-chip, with amazing powers of memory and computation, has immediate applications almost everywhere from universities to automobile engines, from corporate offices to farms, from hospitals to satellites. [4]Virtually any routine work can be taken over by the devices, which have shrunk to less than 1/30,000 the size of their original predecessors, those giant room-size computers of yesterday. [5]And they grow smaller and more versatile almost daily. IBM recently announced that it can now produce a chip containing 256,000 bits of information, four times as many as are crammed onto the most highly integrated chip today.
> —JON STEWART, "Computer Shock: The Inhuman Office of the Future"

(8) Use comparison or contrast.

In everyday conversation you often explain or evaluate something by comparing or contrasting it with something else. In compositions, too, comparison or contrast is often useful. In general, the people, ideas, or objects to be compared or contrasted should belong to the same class (one type of roommate is compared or contrasted with another type of roommate, not with some other type of person).

The following paragraph compares the importance of three values—work, family, and leisure.

> [1]Along with family life, work and leisure always compete for people's time and allegiance. [2]One or the other is usually the center of gravity, rarely does the individual strike an equal balance among all three. [3]For the New Breed, family and work have grown less important and leisure more important. [4]When work and leisure are compared as sources of satisfaction in our surveys, only one out of five people (21 percent) states that work means more to them than leisure. [5]The majority (60 percent) say that while they enjoy their work, it is not their major source of satisfaction. [6](The other 19 percent are so exhausted by the demands work makes of them that they cannot conceive of it as even a minor source of satisfaction.)
> —DANIEL YANKELOVICH, "The New Psychological Contracts at Work"

(9) Use a combination of methods.

The various methods of developing a controlling idea have been listed and illustrated separately, but almost every paragraph makes use of more than one method. For example, the paragraph developed by cause and effect (see **(6)** above) also uses details, and the paragraph developed by classification (see **(4)**) also uses definition and examples to explain the types of alternate work schedules given.

Note: Since paragraphs do not often include more than twelve sentences, you do not need a detailed or complicated outline to follow. But you may find it useful to jot down the controlling idea and the main points of development before you begin to write a paragraph.

Analyzing Paragraphs   Exercise 32–1

NAME _____ SCORE _____

DIRECTIONS   Analyze the unity, coherence, and development of the following paragraph by answering the questions that follow it. When the question asks, "*Which sentence . . .?*" use the sentence's number to identify your answer.

¹During the 1970s and 1980s both men and women have registered complaints about the role of women in the work force. ²Obviously, a possible reason for women's unhappiness with their jobs relates to their salaries: women generally earn far less than men for the same kind of work. ³Employers who pay women less than men offer many excuses for doing so. ⁴They assert that women are less dependable at work than men. ⁵And they claim that women are absent from work more frequently than men. ⁶Yet many employers have found these prejudices to be untrue. ⁷When placed in positions of responsibility women are as capable of handling the work as their male counterparts. ⁸Furthermore, women supervisors seem to be able to handle uncooperative workers more easily than male authority figures do. ⁹Finally, employers have found that female administrators are capable problem solvers. ¹⁰Although the job market is more open to women than it was one hundred years ago, many working women still find it difficult to advance as rapidly as men holding the same job, despite the increased opportunities.

ANALYSIS

1. Which sentence states the controlling idea of the paragraph? _____

2. What is the major method of development used in the paragraph?

   _____

3. Which sentences show the use of comparison or contrast? _____

4. What is the key term that is repeated throughout the paragraph?

   _____

5. Which sentences use transitional expressions? _____

6. Which two sentences are linked by parallel structure? _____

7. Which sentence is the shortest one in the paragraph? _____

   What is its purpose? _____

8. Which sentence is the clincher, the one that repeats the controlling idea?
   (Not all paragraphs have this kind of sentence.) _____

9. What is the basis for the arrangement of the sentences in the paragraph: is
   it by time, from general to specific, by order of climax, or by location of
   what is being described? _____

10. Which two sentences use an introductory phrase to vary from the usual
    word order of placing the subject first? _____

    Which sentence begins with a single adverb? _____

    Which sentence uses an introductory subordinate clause? _____

The Controlling Idea
and the Methods of Development

Exercise 32–2

NAME _____ SCORE _____

DIRECTIONS   For each of the following four paragraphs list (1) the number of the sentence that states the controlling idea; (2) the main method of development used to support the controlling idea; and (3) an additional method of development used in the paragraph.

PARAGRAPH ONE

[1]Of course, not everyone who works long hours is a workaholic. [2]Many people simply have more work than they can handle on a normal schedule. [3]Others work for companies where long hours are part of the job. [4]Some Wall Street law firms, for example, are notorious for expecting associates to work late into the night; and young lawyers, even when they have no work to do, frequently remain at their desks until their superiors have left the office. [5]There are also a number of people who reluctantly moonlight because they need the money.

—"Thank God, It's Monday," *Dun's Review*

1. Controlling idea _____

2. Main method of development _____

3. Additional method of development _____

PARAGRAPH TWO

[1]Psychologists are also starting to unravel the mystery of why some people turn out to be workaholics while others do not. [2]It is becoming increasingly apparent that the process begins in early childhood. [3]Psychiatrist Lawrence Susser, who treats workaholics on his yacht in New Rochelle, New York, claims that workaholics are the products of "controlling parents"; that is, parents who, rather than simply supporting or setting guidelines for their children, are constantly pushing them to excel. [4]The children fear that unless they live up to these expectations, love will be withheld. [5]Eventually they develop a sort of "inner voice" that prods them in the same manner as their parents did. [6]This voice can be very demanding, Dr. Susser says. [7]It does not let them relax.

—"Thank God, It's Monday," *Dun's Review*

1. Controlling idea _____

2. Main method of development _____

3. Additional method of development _____

PARAGRAPH THREE

[1]Many people mistakenly think that creativity is the ability to think thoughts that no one else has ever thought. [2]In fact, creativity is just a way of looking at the ordinary in a different way. [3]Alex Osborn, one of the pioneers in the study of creativity and imagination, discovered that almost everyone is more creative than he thinks. [4]We usually don't recognize our good ideas as creativity in action. [5]For example, in a large midwestern city a gang of thieves had worked out a coordinated routine that was so smooth and fast that they could break into a clothing store, sweep the clothes off the racks, and be gone before the police could answer the alarm. [6]Then a young detective got an idea. [7]He asked all the clothing merchants in the area to alternate the way they placed the hangers on the rack. [8]He told the store owners: "Turn one hook toward the wall and the next one toward the aisle. [9]Do it that way throughout the store." [10]When police answered the next alarm they found the frustrated thieves removing the garments one at a time. [11]Everyday "shirtsleeve creativity" is simply the adaptation of existing ideas—taking another look at all of the pieces of the situation from a new perspective.   —DALE O. FERRIER, "Shirtsleeve Creativity."

1. Controlling idea _____

2. Main method of development _____

3. Additional method of development _____

**The Controlling Idea
and the Methods of Development**   Exercise 32–2 (continued)

PARAGRAPH FOUR

[1]Even in the past decade, the average U.S. farm worker's productivity has increased 185 percent, while the manufacturing worker has upped productivity by 90 percent. [2]Those figures may not be as high as in the past, or in other parts of the world today, but they certainly compare favorably with the performance of U.S. office workers. [3]In the past 10 years, according to studies done by the Massachusetts Institute of Technology and others, the white-collar worker's productivity has increased a mere four percent. [4]This figure is reached by measuring time spent on work tasks, as well as by counting units (letters typed, reports written, cases handled) where possible. [5]Four percent is the total for the whole past 10 years, not an annual rate of productivity increase.

—RAYMOND P. KURSHAN, "White-collar Productivity"

1. Controlling idea _____

2. Main method of development _____

3. Additional method of development _____

Mastering Paragraphs: A Review

NAME _____ SCORE _____

DIRECTIONS   A paragraph requires planning if it is to have unity and if it is to develop the controlling idea fully. For a paragraph about work, make notes for a controlling idea and the supporting development. (You may find the facts and ideas presented in the exercises of this workbook useful in planning your paragraph.) Think about your paragraph as specifically as possible. Once you have made your list, look it over carefully to make sure that all the points of development clearly support your controlling idea. Then arrange the points in a logical order. Finally, write your paragraph, using your controlling idea in the first or second sentence.

SUGGESTED TOPICS

1. new types of job openings in your major field

2. the best (or worst) use of leisure time

3. possible internships available in your major field

4. the reasons why people work (or why *you* work)

5. proof that people in our society value work too much (or too little)

6. the types of jobs available in your major field

7. the reasons why you chose your major or your potential career

8. the types of writing demanded by your chosen profession

9. the advantages and/or disadvantages of early retirement or "stopping out"

10. the effects of automation or computerization on the job market or on your chosen profession

CONTROLLING IDEA

THE PARAGRAPH

DEVELOPMENT

PARAGRAPH

33

Learn to plan, draft, and revise your compositions effectively.

33a Consider the purpose of your composition.

No matter what type of writing you do, you engage in a process of developing a subject for presentation to a specific audience. As you focus on your subject, you develop a thesis statement which will help you determine what material to include in your essay and the order in which you will present your ideas. This writing process is not a "straight line" that runs from the initial conception of a topic to a final draft. Rather, most writers find they must revise their original draft many times to make it a clear, well-unified piece of writing.

As you write, you process ideas, explore and answer questions, rethink strategies, stop in the middle of discussing one idea to take up another that has just occurred to you and so on. You may decide that your original thesis is not specific enough—or that it is not appropriate for your audience. The writing process is a dialogue between you (the writer) and your ideas; having new ideas grow out of the ones that you are currently working on is not a sign that you are a poor writer or that you do not know what you want to talk about. Rather, it indicates that you are working toward an understanding of exactly what you want to say. For this reason your first draft will probably need reorganizing and polishing before all the ideas can work together in a unified way.

The first question you will need to ask yourself is, "What do I want to accomplish in what I am about to write?" The purpose of your composition will determine how you organize your material, the tone you adopt, even the length of sentences and the complexity of the vocabulary you use. All compositions have a purpose—for example, to inform or to persuade the reader. Be sure you have your purpose firmly in mind before you begin planning and writing.

33b Choose an appropriate topic.

The appropriateness of a topic depends on the writer, the reader, and the occasion. You must know and care enough about the topic to have something interesting to say. But you must also be sure that the topic is acceptable to your intended reader or readers and suitable to the occasion on which it will be read.

If your subject is already assigned, or if your situation controls what you will write about, you will be able to begin your work with a consideration of your audience. However, in college writing your instructors may often ask you to select the subject you will write about, which is for some people the most difficult aspect of the writing process.

One way to find a subject to write about is to draw on your own experience, attitudes, or knowledge. What do you like to do with your time? What issues interest you? What has happened recently that made you stop and examine your own attitudes about the subject? Is there a particular event, place, or person you could share with a reader? Being able to select your own topic usually means you can write a more interesting paper because it will deal with something that you care about.

Often, however, the subject you are asked to write about will be one that is unfamiliar to you. For example, you may be required to write a paper for a European history class; the purpose of the paper will be to demonstrate your command of the subject to your instructor. In few papers of this kind will it be appropriate for you to write an essay which focuses on your pesonal opinions. However, writing about an aspect of the subject that interests you will help you write a stronger essay. To select such a topic, review your notes and the chapters in your textbook for issues that catch your attention, look in the subject catalog, or browse through books and articles on the topic in the library. If you are still unable to settle on a topic, discuss the assignment with other students or talk it over with your instructor.

Many times you will be required to write a paper bound by other constraints as well. For example, although you may be allowed to select your topic, your instructor may give you a length limit of six to eight pages. In this case, you would need to make certain that the topic you choose provides you with enough material to satisfy that requirement. Whatever the restrictions, it will be up to you to choose a topic that meets the requirements.

33c Analyze your audience.

Once you determine the topic for your composition, ask yourself what sort of readers you are writing for. Will they be familiar with the topic you have selected? What areas of the topic may need explaining? What level of technicality will your readers be able to understand? Are there aspects of your audience that you need to keep in mind, such as age or attitude toward the subject? What tone will best appeal to your audience? Will your readers "be on your side" or will you need to convince them to think about your topic from your point of view?

Visualizing your audience as you begin to write will help you focus on and discuss your material most effectively.

33d Explore and focus the subject.

How well you limit the topic depends on your ability to focus on an aspect that you can cover adequately in the time allotted to the writing of the paper. For example, "occupational writing" is a topic that might be covered in a book; it is clearly not limited enough to be discussed adequately in the hour or two most students have for writing an in-class paper. There are several methods of limiting a general topic.

(1) Explore your subject.

Make lists.   Often when you begin working on an essay, you will have so many ideas that they will become disorganized if you try to review them all in your mind. Put this surplus information to work for you: make a list of everything that occurs to you about your topic. At this stage of the writing process you should not worry about imposing any order on your ideas. Just jot them down as rapidly as they come to mind and in whatever order they occur. What matters at this point is that you record the ideas themselves; grammar, spelling, and organization are all things you can concern yourself with after you have some material to work with.

As you write your list, one idea will often lead naturally to another. Jot it down. Interrupt your current train of thought if you suddenly think of an important, new aspect of your topic. Experiment until you learn how the listing method can work most effectively for you.

Ask questions.   Another way to explore your topic is to ask yourself the journalist's questions "*who? what? when? where? why?* and *how?*" Investigating your topic by answering these questions may help you to see your topic more clearly as well as to consider its various aspects. You will force yourself to consider *who* is concerned about the material you are developing, *how* something works the way it does, *why* an event happened as it did, and so forth.

Survey development strategies.   Finally, consider which development strategies can best help you explore your topic (discussed fully in **32d**). These strategies parallel the ways in which we think about almost any subject: narration (retelling an event); process (how to do something or how something works); cause and effect (why something happened); description (what something is like); definition, analysis (why something happened or is the way it is); classification, example, and comparison and contrast (how things differ from and resemble each other). These strategies can serve as prompts to help you think about the various aspects of your topic.

(2) Limit and focus your subject.

Once you have explored your topic you must decide which aspects of it to discuss; that is, you must limit and focus your topic. The following analogy will help you understand the importance of this step. When you use a microscope, you first decide what you want to view under the lens, select the appropriate slide, and place it in the viewing field. Next, you use the rough focusing wheel to bring the object into view, turn the light up or down to sharpen or soften the contrasts in the image, and move the slide around on the viewing stage until the segment you wish to concentrate on is under the lens. Finally, you use the fine focusing wheel to bring this segment into sharp focus.

Focusing and limiting your subject works in much the same way. You must find those parts of the topic that meet the requirements of your reading audience. If, for example, you are writing an essay for your history class about the ways in which medieval monasteries preserved manuscripts, you will not want to include information about the architecture of a typical cloister or about the rivalries among the different monastic orders. Such material might be interesting, but it has little bearing on the subject you have chosen.

The particular focus you employ will be determined by your purpose, your audience, the length of your essay, and the amount of time you have in which to write it.

33e Construct a focused specific thesis statement containing a single main idea.

A thesis statement can make the focus of your essay clear to your reader. It will help you to think more exactly about your topic and to avoid straying from the topic as you write. The thesis statement is to the essay what the controlling idea is to the paragraph. As you discuss the various aspects of your topic, refer to your thesis statement from time to time to make sure that what you are saying relates to your main idea. Furthermore, if you have difficulty developing specific material that relates to your topic, a clear thesis statement can often help you organize your thoughts and explore new aspects of the topic. Finally, once you have formulated a thesis statement you should not think that you cannot change it. As you write you may find that you wish to explore a different or modified version of your topic, in which case you will need to rethink and revise your thesis statement.

Most frequently, thesis statements appear in the beginning paragraph; however, they may appear at whatever point in your essay best suits your purpose. For example, if the conclusion is one which you must prepare your reader to accept, your thesis will appear in the conclusion. Or, if you first need to give your reader background information about the broad aspects of your subject, your thesis statement could appear several paragraphs into your paper. In other types of essays—such as narrative or descriptive writing—a thesis statement is often omitted; in still others, it is only implied. Yet no matter what tactic you choose, a thesis statement can help you give direction to your writing—even if it never appears in the finished essay. Use your thesis statement to help you select the information you will include in your essay.

33f Choose an appropriate method or combination of methods of development for arranging ideas, and prepare a working plan.

A working plan can help you write your first draft more efficiently. The strategies for organizing paragraphs (see **32d**) and exploring ideas (see **33d**) are the same as those you will use to organize and develop your essay. The methods you finally use will be determined by your purpose, audience, subject, and focus; and you may find that a combination of methods will be most useful for organizing your material. But no matter what you choose you will probably want to create a written guide to follow as you work on your first draft. Some writers like to create a highly structured, formal outline and use it almost like a map; other writers feel that such a detailed outline inhibits them, that it stifles the development of their ideas. For these writers, jottings or informal lists work better. The formal outline is helpful, however, if you are working on a long or a complex project. Try both ways; then use whichever one works better for you.

Informal Working Plans   Your informal working plan can be simply an organized list of the topics you plan to discuss. This list may resemble the one you generated as you initially explored your topic (see **33d**) with one important difference—in this new list you will arrange the topics in the order you wish to discuss them. As you generate your working plan, your ideas may overlap; arrange and refine the entries on the list until you have a good picture of the general structure of your essay. Like the other methods for arranging ideas, a working plan can be changed at any time—before or as you write.

Formal Outlines   Roman numerals mark the headings that set forth the main points used to develop the thesis statement. The subheadings (signaled by capital letters) present the specific proof for the main headings. If the composition is very long—ten pages or more—further subheadings (signaled by Arabic numbers and then by lower-case letters) may come under the capital letter divisions.

The outline may or may not have an introduction and a conclusion. If during the planning stage you have in mind a way to introduce your thesis statement, write it down as a part of the outline. Likewise, if an idea for a conclusion or a concluding sentence occurs to you while planning the outline, record it at the time.

SENTENCE OUTLINE

How Not to Choose a Career

Introduction: The choice of a career is one of the most important decisions a person makes in life. Yet many people are poorly prepared for this decision.

Thesis: Students have four major misconceptions about how to choose a career.

I. They think they must make the decision unaided.
   A. Qualified friends and family members can be helpful.
   B. High-school and college counselors have special training to guide students in selecting their careers.
   C. Employment agencies can help students find the jobs that fit their skills and talents.

II. They think that their decisions must be based entirely on reason.
   A. Emotions are important in career planning.
   B. There are many examples of unhappy workers in occupations that seemed to be logical choices.
III. They think that their decisions must never be changed.
   A. The changing job market often necessitates a change in career plans.
   B. Actual work experience often reveals a wrong decision.
IV. They think that their decision must make them constantly happy.
   A. There is a good and a bad side to all decisions.
   B. Other aspects of life also influence happiness.
   C. In any job there is the likelihood of an emotional setback.

Conclusion: If students are aware of these common misconceptions about how to choose a career, they will be better prepared for one of life's most important decisions.

TOPIC OUTLINE

How Not to Choose a Career

Thesis: Students have four major misconceptions about how to choose a career.
   I. That the decision must be made alone, without the help of others
      A. Qualified friends and family members
      B. High-school and college counselors
      C. Employment agencies
   II. That the decision must be based entirely on reason
      A. The importance of emotions in decision making
      B. Examples of unhappy workers in occupations that seemed to be logical choices
III. That the decisions must never be changed
      A. Changing job market
      B. Realization of a wrong choice
IV. That the decision must make a person constantly happy
      A. The good and the bad side of all decisions
      B. The importance of other aspects of life
      C. The likelihood of emotional setbacks

Note these points about sentence and topic outlines:

(1) The thesis is stated as a sentence regardless of the type of outline.
(2) The introduction and the conclusion may or may not be included in the outline.
(3) In both the sentence and the topic outlines, there must be at least two

headings at each level (two Roman numerals, two capital letters) for the development to be adequate.

(4) In the sentence outline, only sentences are used; in the topic outline, parallel structure is used.

(5) In any outline, proper indention is maintained to make the outline easy to read.

Avoid making these four errors in outlines:

(1) *Overlapping headings.* If information in one heading (for example, in II.B.) overlaps information in another (for example, in I.A.) or restates it in different words, then the essay will be repetitious.

(2) *Misarranged headings.* The headings show the order of presentation. If the arrangement is not logical, the paper cannot be coherent. (See also **32b.**)

(3) *Inadequately developed headings.* Usually three main headings (Roman numerals) and at least two subheadings (capital letters) are necessary to supply adequate development.

(4) *Needless shifts in tense or number.* This weakness is more noticeable in the sentence outline than in the topic outline. Usually a needless shift in the outline is carried over to the composition.

33g Write the composition.

Once you have created your informal working plan or formal outline, let it guide you as you write the first draft of your essay. Your most important goal is to get all of your material down on paper; do not worry if the sentences are not as polished as you would like them to be or if you misspell words or make grammatical mistakes. You will concentrate on eliminating the weak spots later on as you revise. Write as rapidly as you can; refer periodically to your working plan or outline to check your progress: Have you strayed from the main focus? Are you covering all the points you wished to consider? Your working plan or outline can also serve as a prompting tool when you cannot think of what to say next. You may want to stop occasionally to look over what you have already written; doing so will help you to gain a better perspective on the overall progress of your essay as well as to reassess the points you plan to cover next. Once you have completed your draft, set it aside for a time—preferably for a couple of days—so that you will be able to look at it from a less biased perspective when you begin to revise.

A composing process that works well for one writer may be a disaster for another. There is no one right way to generate a working draft. Some writers like to "blurt out" the entire essay at one sitting, while others work best when they write their compositions a portion at a time and wait till the revision stages to piece the parts together in a logical sequence. Become familiar with your own writing process so that you can use whatever method enables you to produce the best results most efficiently.

The following is an example of the first page of a rough draft for a composition on "How Not to Choose a Career."

How Not to Choose a Career

As small children most of us easily find our careers in a row of buttons: doctor, lawyer, teacher, police officer, fire fighter, astronaut, dancer. Ten years or so later, when what we want to be in life is a real question, many of us continue to be arbitrary in our choice of careers. We may decide ~~be certain that we want~~ to be accountants even though we have never been good at mathematics, or we may choose to be nurses even though we cannot tolerate the sight of an open wound or an infected eye. ~~We sometimes make the most important decision of our lives without any reasonable guidelines.~~ It is not surprising then, to learn that many of us will be ~~are~~ unhappy with our work, for we ~~have~~ approach ~~approached~~ the choice of a career with a variety of misconceptions.

The first and perhaps most serious misconception that many of us think ~~have~~ about career choices is that we must make the decision alone, unaided. Actually there are many people who ~~not only want to help us make the decision but who~~ can also help us make the right decision: friends, family members, teachers, and guidance counselors.

33g(1) Include an introduction and a conclusion in your composition.

In the average-length student paper—three hundred to five hundred words—the introduction and the conclusion need not be long. The introduction gets the reader interested in the body of the paper; the conclusion should wrap up the points you have made. The introduction need be no more than the thesis statement or a sentence that suggests the thesis statement. The conclusion may be no more than a restatement, in different words, of the thesis; or, if the thesis is only suggested in the introduction, it may be the first forthright statement of the thesis.

Students may use as an introduction a striking example, a shocking statement that is later explained, or a question that leads into the thesis. The writer strengthens the conclusion by suggesting a solution to a problem presented in the essay. In the conclusion the writer should never pose a new point that is not to be explored nor apologize to the reader.

33g(2) Give the composition a title.

Usually a title will occur to you during the planning or the writing of the essay. Certainly you should not spend the time you need for writing the paper sitting and thinking about a title. If you have not thought of a title by the time you finish the composition, use the topic or some form of it—for example, "Common Misconceptions About Career Choices."

When time permits, though, give attention to the title. Choose one that is provocative, that will make a reader want to read your essay. But never sacrifice appropriateness for cleverness; above all else, the title should suit the content of the essay. In general, it is best to avoid long, wordy titles or declarative-sentence titles that tell the reader too much about the essay.

Many instructors prefer the title on a separate page, along with your name, the course name and section number, the date, and the paper number. Remember that the title should not be punctuated with quotation marks or italics (underlining) unless you are referring to a literary or artistic work and that the title should be followed by an end mark of punctuation only if it is a question or an exclamation. (See also **8c.**)

33h Revise the composition.

Many inexperienced writers make the mistake of thinking that revising is the same thing as proofreading, which it is not. Very few people can produce a well-written essay in only one draft. In fact, most writers will find that they revise in one way or another throughout all the stages of the writing process: they reorganize their writing plan as they jot down ideas, they consider and discard ideas and topics even before they begin to write, they rephrase or refocus their thesis statement, and so forth. But the majority of your revisions will be made once you have completed the first draft of your essay; in fact, some writers will tell you that they spend more of their time revising than creating a working draft.

After you have let your draft cool off (at least overnight if not longer), look at it first for overall concerns, since you would be wasting your time to correct mechanics, word choice, sentence structure, spelling, and the like in material that may very well be changed as you reorganize your composition. Have you established the focus of your essay early on? Are the sections of the essay organized in the most logical order? Have you strayed at times from your main point or raised issues that do not pertain to your thesis? As you work on these global revisions, check also to see that you have kept your audience in mind.

Next, apply the same perspective to your paragraphs. Are they well focused? Do they use transitions to move smoothly from one idea to the next and from one paragraph to the next? Have you varied sentence structure and length to provide variety, eliminate choppiness, and improve clarity? Look to see if you have maintained a consistent tone, style, level of diction, and point of view.

After you are satisfied with the order in which your paragraphs appear and with their general content, turn your attention to the sentences themselves. Are they clear? If not, examine the structure of each, the words you have used, and the relationship of the ideas to the other sentences in the paragraph. Identify those sentences that use the passive voice and make them active. Look for weak repetitions of words and phrases, for clichés, for redundancy: strengthen these weak spots with more effective words and phrases. Finally, check each of your sentences for errors in mechanics, spelling, and punctuation.

Approached in this manner, revision will be a powerful tool that can help you make your writing forceful and persuasive. In fact, many writers feel that revision is the most important part of the writing process, the part where they clarify, sharpen, and strengthen their writing—deleting, adding, and reorganizing again and again until their composition communicates their ideas clearly to a specific audience. The following suggestions for proofreading may help you to revise your composition.

(1) Wait at least one day, if possible, before you proofread your first draft. Then you will be more likely to spot weaknesses and mistakes.

(2) Proofread at least three times: once for organization; a second time, out loud, for style; and a third time for grammar, punctuation, and spelling. If you have serious problems with grammar, punctuation, or spelling, proofread still another time for the error or errors you most frequently make.

(3) When proofreading for errors, slow your reading down. To make yourself go more slowly, actually point to each word with your pencil as you read. If you have real difficulties with spelling, try reading each line from right to left instead of the usual left to right so that you will notice words individually.

(4) Read your writing assignment to someone else and ask your listener to stop you when something does not make sense or does not sound right.

(5) Type your written work. Even if you do not type well enough to make the final copy, type at least one draft of your work. Typing the manuscript forces you to take a close look at what you have written. (Many writers do most of their editing while they are typing.)

The Essay

Exercise 33–1

NAME _____ SCORE _____

DIRECTIONS   Choose a topic from the list of suggested subjects in Exercise 32–3 (p. 321) or a topic of your own for an essay of three hundred to five hundred words. (If you choose to write about work, you may find the facts and ideas presented in this workbook useful in planning your essay.) You may use the following page for a working plan or outline as your instructor directs. Then write a first draft of the composition. Revise it carefully according to the suggestions in **33h.** (Save your rough draft for future reference.) Follow your instructor's directions with regard to the placement of your title, and number the pages of the paper, using Arabic numerals, beginning in the upper right-hand corner of page 2.

TOPIC

WORKING PLAN OR OUTLINE

35

Write effective letters and résumés, memos, and reports.

Success in business depends a great deal on good communication skills, both person-to-person and written. Many times the only way that a business associate or client will know you will be on paper, so it is essential that what you write communicates clearly and sounds professional. Misunderstandings resulting from poorly written business documents cost money and lose clients. In addition, many business documents are legally binding, and for this reason it is essential that they say clearly and precisely what you mean. Finally, effective business communication eliminates extra work; no one who is busy wants to spend extra time trying to figure out what the writer of a letter, memo, or report "really meant." In the world of work, effective writing pays off: it fosters goodwill; it creates a favorable impression of the company; and, ultimately, it results in increased profits.

35a(1) Use an acceptable format for the letters you write.

Business letters are usually typed on only one side of white, unlined, $8\frac{1}{2}$ x 11 inch paper. Standard business envelopes measure about $3\frac{1}{2}$ x $6\frac{1}{2}$ inches or 4 x 10 inches. (Letterhead stationery and envelopes vary in both size and color.)

Check to see if your company or organization has a policy about letter format. Most companies use either full block (see p. 338), modified block (see p. 340), or indented formats for regular correspondence, though an indented format is often used for personal business correspondence such as thank-you notes, congratulations, and the like.

A business letter has six parts: (1) heading, (2) inside address, (3) salutation, (4) body, (5) closing, which consists of the complimentary close and signature, and (6) added notations.

The *heading* gives the writer's full address and the date. If letterhead stationery is used, the date is typed beneath it flush left, flush right, or centered, depending on your format. If plain stationery is used, the address of the writer followed by the date is placed toward the top of the page—the distance from the top arranged so that the body of the letter will be attractively centered on the page—flush with the left- or right-hand margin, as in the letters on pages 338 and 340. Notice that the heading has no end punctuation.

The *inside address*, typed two to six lines below the heading, gives the name and full address of the recipient.

The *salutation* (or greeting) is written flush with the left margin, two spaces below the inside address, and is followed by a colon.

When the surname of the addressee is known, it is used in the salutation of a business letter, as in the following examples.

Dear Dr. Davis:	Dear Mayor Rodriguez:
Dear Mrs. Greissman:	Dear Ms. Joseph:

Note: Use *Miss* or *Mrs.* if the woman you are addressing has indicated a preference. Otherwise, use *Ms.*, which is always appropriate and which is preferred by many businesswomen, whatever their marital status.

In letters to organizations, or to persons whose name and sex are unknown, such salutations as the following are customary:

Dear Sir or Madam:	Dear Mobil Oil:
Dear Subscription Manager:	Dear Registrar:

For the appropriate forms of salutations and addresses in letters to government officials, military personnel, and so on, check an etiquette book or the front or back of your college dictionary.

The *body* of the letter should follow the principles of good writing. Typewritten letters are usually single-spaced, with double spacing between paragraphs. The first sentence of each paragraph should begin flush with the left margin (in full block or modified block) or should be indented five to ten spaces (in indented format). The subject matter should be organized so that the reader can grasp immediately what is wanted, and the style should be clear and direct. Do not use stilted or abbreviated phrasing:

NOT	The aforementioned letter	BUT	Your letter
NOT	Please send it to me ASAP.	BUT	Please send it to me as soon as possible.

The *closing* is typed flush with the left-hand margin in full-block style. In modified block and indented style, it is typed to the right of the letter, in alignment with the heading. Here are the parts of the closing:

Complimentary close: This conventional ending is typed, after a double space, below the last paragraph of the body of the letter. Among the endings commonly used in business letters are the following:

FORMAL	LESS FORMAL
Very truly yours,	Sincerely,
Sincerely yours,	Cordially,

Typed name: The writer's full name is typed four lines below the closing.

Title of sender: This line, following the typed name, indicates the sender's position, if he or she is acting in an official capacity.

> Manager, Employee Relations
> Chairperson, Search Committee

Signature: The letter is signed between the complimentary close and the typed name.

Notations are typed below the closing, flush with the left margin. They indicate, among other things, whether anything is enclosed with or attached to the letter (*enclosure* or *enc., attachment* or *att.*); to whom copies of the letter have been sent (*cc: AAW, PTN*); and the initials of the sender and the typist (*DM/cll*).

MODEL BUSINESS LETTER: full block format (all parts flush with the left margin)

N.W. 321 Harrison
Pullman, WA 99163 } HEADING
December 21, 1985

Mr. Richard Law
Prestige Kennels
401 State Street } INSIDE ADDRESS
Cincinnati, OH 65432

Dear Mr. Law:} SALUTATION

Will it be possible for me to board my Old English sheepdog from
January 28 to 31? Your kennel was recommended to me by my
brother-in-law, James Duncan, who has boarded his corgi with you
many times.

I will be visiting the Cincinnati area and will be unable to keep my
dog with me while there. Brandy is a five-year-old female who is very
docile; however, she is a big dog and it is important that an outdoor
run be provided where she can exercise.

BODY {

Could you please tell me whether you have room for my dog, what
your kenneling facilities are like, the cost for the four days, and, if
you have a groomer, how much it would cost to have my dog washed
and brushed out.

Because I will be leaving Pullman on my trip on January 8, I would
appreciate hearing from you as soon as possible so that I can complete
my planning.

Sincerely yours,} CLOSING

Elaine Freeman

Elaine Freeman} SIGNATURE (WHEN WRITING BUSINESS LETTERS
INCLUDE YOUR TITLE)

MODEL BUSINESS ENVELOPE

```
Elaine Freeman
N.W. 321 Harrison
Pullman, WA 99163


                    Mr. Richard Law
                    Prestige Kennels
                    401 State Street
                    Cincinnati, OH 65432
```

35a(2) Write effective application letters and résumés.

The first real business writing that you do may be the letter and résumé you prepare when you look for a job. Obviously, you want to take particular care that these documents represent you well; a future employer will judge you on how professionally you present yourself in these samples of your written communication skills.

Both your application letter and your résumé should show the reader that you are suited to fill the job for which you are applying. The letter first identifies the exact job for which you wish to be considered, then discusses your skills *as they relate to* the requirements of the job itself, and finally requests an interview. Your letter should refer to the company by name several times in the body and should call your reader's attention to the résumé that you will have enclosed.

Never send an application letter without an accompanying résumé or a résumé without an application letter. These two documents work *together* to persuade the reader to ask you to come for an interview. Be especially careful to make your letter and accompanying résumé look professional; do not send out material that contains corrected typographical errors or that looks poorly arranged on the page. Neither your résumé nor your application letter should exceed one page in length (unless you have been working for a long time and have a great deal of experience related to the job for which you are applying).

Note: It is thoughtful to send a thank-you letter after an interview (see p. 356).

MODEL APPLICATION LETTER: modified block format (heading and closing may be placed in the center or near the right margin)

Box 734 Wellborn Hall
University of Oregon
Eugene, OR 98731
November 9, 1985

Mr. David Miller
Personnel Manager
Magill Corporation
Box 8712
Minneapolis, MN 55440

Dear Mr. Miller:

IDENTIFY POSITION
SOUGHT AND HOW
LEARNED ABOUT

I believe that my background—a degree in Marketing and Management, experience in retail sales, and familiarity with computer software—qualifies me to be a productive member of the Magill Corporation's sales department. Please consider my application for the position of field representative trainee which you advertised in The Oregonian on February 12.

INDICATE MAJOR
QUALIFICATIONS
FOR JOB

Double majors in Marketing and Management, along with a minor in Computer Science, have provided me with a strong and diverse background for sales work. In particular, I have learned to apply theory to the practical use of computer technology in small business management. My training will enable me to show my clients how to make the best use of Magill's software packages such as FastCalc and Ready Ledger.

REFER TO RÉSUMÉ
INDICATE MAJOR
QUALIFICATIONS
FOR JOB

My activities and work experience show that I enjoy working with people and can handle responsibility effectively. From my résumé you can see that I have learned to adapt to and work effectively in different situations: counseling underclass marketing majors, designing efficiency surveys, and working as a waitress. That I worked to pay all of my college expenses demonstrates my initiative and determination to meet the goals that I set for myself. I will bring the same hardworking attitude to Magill Corporation.

REQUEST
INTERVIEW

I would appreciate the opportunity to meet with you and discuss the ways I can meet Magill's needs. Since you will be on the University of Oregon campus the week of March 25, could you please contact me at the above address or phone me at (503) 342-9817 after 3 p.m. to schedule an interview?

Sincerely yours,

Marilyn J. Prey

Marilyn J. Prey

Enclosure: Résumé

Business Letters

NAME _____ SCORE _____

DIRECTIONS   Using the full or the modified block style, write a letter of application for a job in your field, a letter of complaint about a product you bought that is not performing satisfactorily, and a letter ordering a product that you would like to purchase by mail (use a catalog advertisement or the "For Sale" column of a newspaper or magazine for the product information). Do your planning of the letter in the space provided below, but type or neatly handwrite your letters on white bond paper.

PLANNING SPACE

PLANNING SPACE (CONTINUED)

Your résumé gives a brief overall picture of your qualifications for the job you are seeking. It provides more specifics than you can, or should, discuss in your application letter. Although a résumé may be organized in a number of ways depending on which material you wish to emphasize, it should cover the following categories:

1. Personal Data: name, mailing address, and phone number (with area code)
2. Educational Background
3. Work Experience
4. Honors and Activities
5. References

The material you include in your résumé should illustrate the ways in which you are qualified to fill the position you are applying for. Do not try to list everything about yourself; pick and choose carefully. Consider designing a résumé specifically aimed at the particular job you are applying for. A customized résumé stands out when it is reviewed because it addresses the employer's particular needs. It shows that you have thought carefully about the job and the company.

An excellent way to put together an effective résumé is to make lists of all your qualifications using a separate sheet of paper for each category. Write down everything you can think of about yourself—jobs held, classes taken, honors, activities, and so forth. Then go back and fill in details: dates, supervisors' names, job responsibilities. After you complete your brainstorming, *then* go back and mark those items that you want to include in the résumé you are developing for this particular job. Within each category, arrange information in order with the most recent first: May 1985–present, December 1984–May 1985, and so forth.

Type a neat first draft of your résumé to see how it looks on the page. Do not crowd material too closely together; let information stand out surrounded by some blank space so the reader will easily notice each important aspect of your background. Finally, type a clean copy; if you make an error, do not correct it but retype the page until everything is perfect. Errors and corrections make a résumé look sloppy and unprofessional. Especially if you are not an excellent typist, you may want to have your résumé professionally printed. Choose good stationery—white or a dignified off-white shade such as beige or light gray—and consider buying matching blank paper and envelopes for your application letter.

The following tips will help you prepare a well-organized résumé.

TIPS ON RÉSUMÉ WRITING

1. Don't forget to include your name, address, and telephone number; unless relevant to the job, personal data such as age and marital status are better left out.

2. Mention your degree, college or university, and pertinent areas of special training.

3. Think about career goals but generally reserve mention of them for the application letter or interview (and even then make sure they enhance your appeal as a candidate). Your interest should be to match your qualifications to the employer's goals.

4. Even if an advertisement asks you to state a salary requirement, any mention of salary should usually be deferred until the interview.

5. Whenever possible, make evident any relationship between jobs you have had and the job you are seeking.

6. Use an acceptable format and make sure thc résumé is neat, orderly, and correct to show that you are an efficient, well-organized, thoughtful person.

7. Be sure to ask people's permission before listing their names as references.

MODEL RÉSUMÉ

Marilyn J. Prey

College Address
Box 734 Wellborn Hall
University of Oregon
Eugene, OR 98731
Phone (503) 342-9817
Before May 15, 1986

Permanent Address
Rt. 1, Box 966
Phoenix, AZ 87650
Phone (602) 659-3096
After May 15, 1986

Position Sought

Entry level position as sales representative with a computer firm.

Education

Bachelor of Science Degree in Marketing and Management University of
Oregon, expected May 1986.

Grade Point: 3.43/4.00
Major Courses: Consumer Behavior, Managerial Strategies, Business Law,
                    Accounting
Minor Courses: COBOL, PASCAL, FORTRAN
Related Courses: Business Communications, Technical Writing

Employment (provided 100% of college costs)

Programming Intern, ReadyWare Software, Portland, Oregon
        Debugged specialized accounting packages
        Developed application recordkeeping package for dentist
        Advised clients
        May-August 1985

Sales Representative, Brandes ComputerWorld, Eugene, Oregon
        Demonstrated various software packages to the public
        Developed effficiency evaluation survey
        October 1984-May 1985

Honors and Activities

Phi Kappa Phi Scholastic Honorary
Alpha Lambda Delta Freshman Honorary
TRW Scholarship, 1984
Team leader, College of Business orientation, 1984-present
District Five Representative, Faculty-Student Senate, University of Oregon,
    1984-1985

References

Placement Bureau
University of Oregon
Eugene, OR 98733

The Résumé

Exercise 35–2

NAME _____ SCORE _____

DIRECTIONS   Write a résumé for a summer job, a permanent job, or an internship. Tailor your résumé to meet the specific requirements of the job for which you are applying. Use the space below to list your qualifications, to list the job requirements, and to write a rough draft of your résumé. Type a final copy of your résumé on white bond paper.

JOB REQUIREMENTS

MY QUALIFICATIONS

ROUGH DRAFT OF RÉSUMÉ

35a(3) Write effective business letters.

Letter of Inquiry   Many business letters are requests for information. Such letters should be direct and should give sufficient background so that the person you write to can answer your questions fully. If you need the information by a certain date, be sure to say so (and, in any case, a date will help motivate your reader to get back in touch with you promptly). A stamped, self-addressed envelope can also speed up the reply.

The first paragraph of a letter of inquiry should begin with the most important question. It should also give any background information necessary for the reader to understand why you are asking for the information and to focus the answers accordingly. For example, if you were inquiring about stereo systems for your home, you would probably want to mention the price range you have in mind and the options that you want in the system. Otherwise, the reader might not tell you about the right sort of equipment.

The middle section of your letter contains any questions of a specific kind. Arranging them in a numbered list may make them easier for your reader to answer.

Use the final section of the letter to express appreciation (but avoid the phrase "thank you in advance," which is wordy and might strike your reader as presumptuous). This final paragraph is also the place to mention the date by which you need to receive the information.

MODEL INQUIRY: modified block format

Rt. 1, Box 156
Brewster, WA 98812
January 25, 1986

Customer Service Representative
Interface Computing Service
2001 Halvorsen Drive
Diablo, TX 75643

Dear Customer Service Representative:

ASK YOUR MOST IMPORTANT QUESTION FIRST GIVE SOME BACKGROUND INFORMATION

I run a small nursery business with a fairly complicated inventory. For years I have kept track of my nursery stock on paper; now I would like to use a microcomputer and inventory software program to simplify my operations. Could you please tell me more about your Invent inventory software package, which I saw advertised in last month's issue of Seeds magazine?

I would appreciate it if you could answer the following questions:

ASK THE REST OF YOUR QUESTIONS

1. What is the price of this software package?
2. Can you customize it for a nursery business, and, if so, how much more would that cost?
3. Will your software package run on a Commodore 64 computer with a 1541 disk drive?
4. Can you give me the name, address, and phone number of your nearest sales representative?
5. I would like to keep track of the different varieties of nursery stock I sell (seeds, trees, bushes and shrubs, vegetables, roses, and so on). Will I be able to subdivide the categories by variety and Latin name?

REQUEST A REPLY AND GIVE A DATE

Because I will be placing my spring orders within the next month, I would like to have an inventory software package set up and running before the end of March so that I can work all the bugs out of it before the spring rush begins. I would be grateful if you could send me the information within the next two weeks so that I can place my order soon.

Sincerely yours,

L. Tully Reed

L. Tully Reed
Owner

Claim and Adjustment Letters Claim and adjustment letters are letters that you write to ask someone to resolve a problem for you. These letters are similar to inquiries in that you must explain what you want done and must use specific details so your reader will understand exactly what you want. However, the claim letter requires special diplomacy: remember that even though you may be annoyed by the problem you are writing about, you must not offend or anger your reader. A calm reader is more likely to do what you ask. If you must "blow off steam," do it in your rough draft; then edit out all impolite or accusatory tone as you revise. Appealing to your reader's sense of business integrity and fair play will gain a better response than calling names.

The claim or adjustment letter briefly states the problem in the first paragraph, uses the middle paragraphs to give supporting details, and concludes by outlining what you wish the reader to do. As in the inquiry letter, asking that the problem be resolved by a particular date may speed up the reply process.

In writing a letter of this type details are important. For instance, if a jacket that you ordered prepaid has not yet arrived, send a copy of the cancelled check, give the date on which you placed your order, and list the item number, size, color, and price. Or, if the manufacturer refuses to fix a tape deck still under warranty, provide the model name and number and the date of purchase, and send copies of your receipts and warranty registration cards (keep the originals for your records). Be sure to mention each enclosure in the text of your letter so that your reader will know what to look for.

MODEL CLAIM LETTER

Rt. 5, Box 87
Charlotte, NC 27654
May 5, 1985

Customer Service Manager
Efficient Electrix, Inc.
P.O. Box 765
Manhattan, KS 57744

Dear Service Manager:

STATE THE
PROBLEM

I have always found your appliances to be reliable; that's why I purchased your model 543 pop-up toaster last December. But recently the bread will not come out of the toaster the way that it should.

DESCRIBE WHAT
HAPPENED

Starting a week ago, whenever I put a piece of bread in the slot and pushed down the handle one of two things happened: the bread stuck to the wires, refused to pop up, and burned; or the bread flew about 18 inches out of the toaster and landed on the floor. Needless to say, I'm unhappy about the mess and the waste.

STATE WHAT YOU
WOULD LIKE DONE

Because I followed your "Care and Maintenance Suggestions" that came with my 543, I believe the problems stem from a mechanical malfunction rather than from neglect on my part. For this reason, I believe that my toaster should be repaired at no expense to me, especially since it is still covered by warranty. The enclosed copy of my receipt indicates that I have owned this appliance for less than six months.

ASK FOR A
RESPONSE; GIVE A
DATE AND A
REASON FOR
NEEDING IT BY
THAT DATE.

Would you please tell me where to send my toaster to be repaired and how to make sure that I am not charged for the service? Since I use this appliance every day, I would appreciate hearing from you within the next two weeks so that I can have my 543 back in working order soon.

Sincerely yours,

Thelma M. Braker

Thelma M. Braker

Enclosure: sales slip   SEND ALONG COPIES OF NECESSARY
                           INFORMATION

Thank-you Letter   Frequently in business it will be appropriate for you to write a thank-you letter; these types of letters make the reader see you as a considerate person and build good will for your company or organization. When someone has done you a favor, has been more than ordinarily helpful or generous, or has entertained you as a guest, a letter of thanks is in order.

In addition, it is always a good idea to write a thank-you letter to someone who has interviewed you for a job. Not only will such a letter remind the reader who you are, but it will also convey your sincerity and good business sense. It is appropriate to reiterate briefly some important point you made in your interview, but do not belabor the issue. Keep a thank-you letter brief.

MODEL THANK-YOU LETTER

534 Burroughs Lane
East Wenatchee, WA 98765
April 15, 1985

Ms. Edelma de Leon
Rand Inc.
P. O. Box 12543
Lafayette, IN 36752

Dear Ms. De Leon:

Thank you for taking the time to talk with me about my qualifications for the position of sales representative with Rand Inc. I enjoyed learning more about the job and about the new product line Rand will be marketing this fall.

During our meeting you said that you were looking for a person with at least two years' sales experience after college. Although I recognize that such experience can be valuable, I would like you to consider as equivalent training my two years as advisor for the local Junior Achievement Club and my volunteer work with the campus-wide Fight Hunger Drive as a fund raiser and coordinator of sales.

The extensive travel the job requires is anything but a discouragement to me; on the contrary, I would welcome the opportunity. I enjoy meeting new people and seeing new places and would be glad to have the opportunity to do both as a field representative for your firm.

I look forward to hearing from you soon about your decision.

Sincerely yours,

James McKinley

35b Write effective memos.

While business letters generally go to people outside your company, a memo is the standard way to share information within the firm. Clear, effective writing is just as important for people within your firm as for people outside it. Not only is clear communication essential to the company's operation, but what you write will be evaluated by people who are in a position to affect your future.

Often the tone of a memo can be less formal than that of a letter sent to someone outside your company; let the situation itself govern the level of formality you use. It is generally best to be slightly more formal since familiarity can offend some readers, even though they may be people whom you see every day at the office. This is particularly true if you are relatively new in your job or are a trainee.

Memos can be short or lengthy, depending on their purpose, but the basic format remains the same; most companies have printed forms for memos. The heading of a memo lists the names (and usually the titles) of the recipient and the writer, the subject, and the date.

TO: Henry W. Wills, Vice President

FROM: Sarah O. Jenkins, Quality Control Supervisor

DATE: November 24, 1985

SUBJECT: *Product Endurance Test Results*

If a memo is long, headings should be used to label the sections. In fact, some reports may be written in memo form; these begin with a general statement of purpose followed by a summary section outlining what will follow. The remaining sections discuss various aspects of the topic in greater detail. If the content warrants it, a memo report concludes with a recommendation or conclusion section which states what should be done, by whom, and when. The fairly standard structure of most reports is designed to help busy readers grasp the purpose and important points as easily as possible.

MODEL MEMO

INTEROFFICE MEMORANDUM

Reliable Plastics

TO: M. Andrew Simons, Sales Manager

FROM: Jacob Lenz, Production Manager *J.L*

DATE: July 26, 1985

SUBJECT: The Missing Pipe Insulators

Thank you for forwarding Mr. John Rollins's letter about the Rollins Company's incomplete order #234987. I have investigated the problem of the 5,000 missing 3/4" × 8' styrofoam pipe insulators, stock no. 45612. As I understand it, Rollins received the lengths of PVC pipe but not the insulators.

We have experienced production delays this month caused by a malfunctioning foam extruding tube in our Gary plant. We are currently three weeks behind schedule on filling standing orders for all varieties of pipe insulators. Apparently Shipping and Receiving ran the standing orders for July through the computer, sent out what was available, and neglected to inform some of our customers, including the Rollins Company, about the current delay.

The remainder of the order can be shipped on August 15 in time for the deadline the Rollins Company specified in their order last December. Because we plan to run overtime until we are caught up, we can guarantee that Rollins will receive the pipe insulators by the middle of August.

Please tell Mr. Rollins when he can expect his shipment.

JML/mb

Copies to:
Shipping and Receiving: Carmean
Production: Wellborn
Sales: Durham

35c Write effective reports.

Businesses require reports for a variety of purposes: to describe mechanisms and processes; to provide instructions; to relate progress on the development of products or procedures; to analyze systems and procedures; to present proposals; and to record trips, minutes of meetings, and accidents.

35c(1) Learn to write a process analysis.

Process analyses are step-by-step explanations of how something is made, how it works, or how it is done. Reports of this type often include diagrams to help the reader grasp the concepts being discussed. In a process analysis it is very important to consider for whom you are writing; your audience will dictate what level of complexity you will use in your discussion. What follows is a process analysis of how a thermometer works, written for an eighth-grade science class.

HOW A THERMOMETER MEASURES THE TEMPERATURE

A thermometer is usually a glass tube with a small bulb at the bottom end. The bulb contains a liquid, either mercury or alcohol, that rises or falls inside the glass tube. As the illustration shows, the tube is divided into marked segments of equal size called degree markings; these marks are used to show how much the liquid has risen or fallen. The higher the liquid rises in the tube, the hotter the temperature of the solid, liquid, or gas which is being measured is said to be; the lower the liquid falls, the colder the temperature of the solid, liquid, or gas. The temperature is determined by noting the degree marking with which the top of the liquid in the tube aligns.

A COMMON THERMOMETER USING THE FAHRENHEIT SCALE

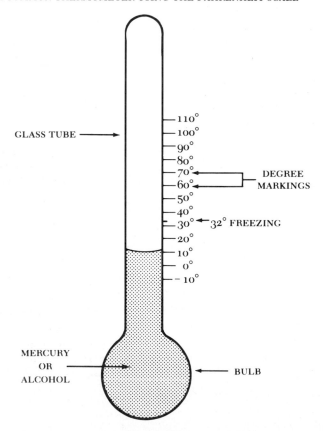

The process by which the thermometer works is quite simple. When what is being measured is hotter than the liquid inside the tube, the liquid expands. Since there is not enough room inside the bulb of the thermometer to contain all of the expanding liquid, some of it rises up the glass tube. The liquid stops rising when its temperature becomes the same as that of the solid, liquid, or gas being measured. The process is reversed when something colder than the liquid in the thermometer's bulb is being measured. A colder temperature of a substance surrounding the bulb of the thermometer causes the liquid inside the bulb to contract. Consequently, the liquid level in the tube falls, and continues to fall until the liquid is at the same temperature as the solid, liquid, or gas being measured.

The Process Analysis Report   Exercise 35–3

NAME _____ _____ SCORE _____

DIRECTIONS Write a process analysis in which you explain clearly and fully how something is made (for example, a contact lens, soap, or pipe tobacco), how something is done (for example, registering at your college, tuning up an automobile engine, or grafting roses); or how something works (for example, the human heart, a single lens reflex camera, or a solar heating system). Specify the kind of audience for whom you are writing and decide how much or how little your audience knows about the topic you have selected.

In the first paragraph, identify the process. In the remaining paragraphs, describe each of the steps in the process.

Consider including a diagram with labels to help clarify the process for your reader. If you use a diagram, make certain that you refer your reader to it in the text of the report.

AUDIENCE

PLANNING SPACE

35c(2) Learn to write a documented report.

Many reports that you will be asked to write may be based on research—on various expected findings or on speculations about a given topic. The use of facts and ideas gathered from sources requires an ability to do three things in addition to the usual planning, writing, and reviewing needed for any composition: (1) paraphrase material taken from sources—that is, report clearly and accurately *in your own words* the ideas and facts that someone else has presented, (2) quote correctly any material that you use exactly as it is stated in the source, and (3) provide documentation for the facts and ideas that you take from sources (the form of documentation varies depending on what guide you are using; the important thing is to follow exactly the format your instructor requests in documenting your research).

Formal reports are generally longer than informal reports, and they usually include additional sections not found in shorter, less complex documents: a letter of transmittal, title page, abstract, executive summary, table of contents, glossary, appendix, notes, and list of works cited.

Note: Not all reports will make use of all of these elements.

The first page of a long report is the *title page,* which gives the full title of the report, the name and title (and sometimes the address) of the person for whom the report was prepared, the name and title (and sometimes the address) of the person who prepared the report, and the date on which the report was completed or is due.

The next page is the *letter of transmittal.* Generally addressed to the person who requested the report, this letter (or memo) introduces the report and sometimes gives the report's conclusions and recommendations.

The *abstract* provides a short summary of the contents of the report. By reading this abstract, a person is able to tell if the report will be useful and which parts of the report he or she needs to read. A report intended primarily for a technical audience often includes an *executive summary* written in nontechnical language for administrators.

The *table of contents* outlines the report's structure so that readers may easily find those sections of the report that they need to read. The simplest way to create a table of contents is to go through the report and list all major headings with their page numbers.

If a report contains illustrations, charts, or tables, these are often listed on a separate page immediately after the table of contents.

If you are writing for an audience who may not understand all of the technical terms that you use in your report, you should include a *glossary,* an alphabetical list that defines the terms. If you include a glossary, you will not need to interrupt your discussion to define terms. You may place the glossary either at the end of the report or after the table of contents.

Supplementary information may be placed in an *appendix,* which would be listed in the table of contents and mentioned in the body of the report. Appendixes are given individual titles and are placed immediately after the last section of the body.

Notes and a bibliography (a list of sources used in the report) appear at the end of the report. Most companies have a preferred style for these, which writers can find by looking at earlier reports in the files. The sample report on the following pages uses the style recommended by the Modern Language Association of America in the *MLA Handbook for Writers of Research Papers*, Second Edition. In this style, sources are cited briefly in parentheses (author and page number) within the text and are then listed alphabetically by author, with full publication data, at the end under the heading "Works Cited." Supplementary comments appear under the heading "Notes"; the reader is referred to these by superscript numbers within the text.

The following documented report was written for an executive who wished to determine whether his company should adopt alternative work schedules. The report presents the findings of a preliminary study. The source material for the first three citations on page 3 of the report is presented below so that you can see how the writer handled both paraphrasing and direct quotations. Study the report to see where the headings are placed and how they are capitalized, how the pages are numbered and where the numbers appear on the typed pages.

SAMPLE SOURCE MATERIAL

(Toffler 246)

> Once we understand this, it comes as no surprise that one of the fastest-spreading innovations in industry during the 1970's was "flextime"—an arrangement that permits workers, within predetermined limits, to choose their own working hours. Instead of requiring everyone to arrive at the factory gate or the office at the same time, or even at pre-fixed staggered times, the company operating on flextime typically sets certain core hours when everyone is expected to show up, and specifies other hours as flexible. Each employee may choose which of the flexible hours he or she wishes to spend working.   —ALVIN TOFFLER, *The Third Wave*

(Wolman 8)

> A typical flextime arrangement allows employees to put in their eight hours anytime within, for example, a 12-hour period, providing they work a mandatory "core period" that provides midday stability.   —JONATHAN WOLMAN, "Work Place 2000"

(Toffler 246)

> This means that a "day person"—a person whose biological rhythms routinely awaken him or her early in the morning—can choose to arrive at work at, say, 8:00 A.M., while a "night person," whose metabolism is different, can choose to start working at 10:00 or 10:30 A.M. It means that an employee can take time off for household chores, or to shop, or to take a child to the doctor. Groups of workers who wish to go bowling together early in the morning or late in the afternoon can jointly set their schedules to make it possible.   —ALVIN TOFFLER, *The Third Wave*

ALTA ENTERPRISES' WORK SCHEDULE:

UPDATING OUR POLICIES

Prepared for
Harold W. Barnes
Development Officer
Alta Enterprises

Prepared by
F. Frederick Skittie
Senior Analyst

July 26, 1985

ALTA ENTERPRISES
1124 48th Avenue
Boulder, CO 33675
(303) 262-3098

July 26, 1985

Mr. Harold W. Barnes
Development Officer
Alta Enterprises
6127 N. Drumheller
Spokane, WA 99205

Dear Mr. Barnes:

Here is the introductory study, which you authorized on January 20, 1985, examining alternatives to the traditional 40-hour work week.

As you will see in this report, Alta Enterprises has several options available in scheduling its employees' working week. In the next phase of our study, we will probably want to contact other companies in our area who already use the options described here: flextime, part-time, shared time, and nighttime shift scheduling.

I believe you will find that this report answers your department's initial questions concerning employee scheduling. If you have any further questions, please call me at (303) 262-3098.

Sincerely yours,

F. Frederick Skittie

F. Frederick Skittie
Senior Analyst
Personnel Department

FFS/mb

Enclosures

ABSTRACT

Alta Enterprises currently structures its working week on the standard 40-hour plan. Other options exist: flextime, part-time, shared time, and nighttime. Adopting one or more or these alternatives would give both our company and our employees greater flexibility. Offering employees a choice of schedules would improve morale and increase efficiency and productivity.

TABLE OF CONTENTS

iv

ALTA ENTERPRISES' WORK SCHEDULE:

UPDATING OUR POLICIES

I.   Introduction

Authorization and Purpose

This report was authorized on January 20, 1985, by Harold W. Barnes, Development Officer for Alta Enterprises, as a preliminary study of the scheduling alternatives to the traditional 40-hour work week currently used at Alta.

The Problem with the 40-Hour Work Week

Not everyone finds the traditional "eight-to-five," five-day work week convenient. In response to the requests of some of our production departments to find ways to meet our employees' needs more satisfactorily, we have begun investigating alternative scheduling plans currently used by some U.S. companies.

Sources of Data

Information for this report was drawn from books and periodicals.

Scope and Limitations

This report represents a preliminary study of innovative work schedules. Because this study is preliminary, the descriptions of each option are brief. In gathering material for this initial phase of our study, we limited our sources to published studies; no interviews were conducted.

Plan of Presentation

After reviewing Alta Enterprises' current policies, this report presents brief descriptions of each of the following scheduling options: flextime, part-time, shared time, and nighttime. Based on the analysis of Alta Enterprises' needs, the report then makes recommendations regarding the steps we should take to complete our study and improve working conditions for our employees.

II. Alta Enterprises' Current Scheduling Policies

Like most companies its size, Alta Enterprises schedules a traditional 40-hour work week, with the working day beginning at 8 a.m. and ending at 5 p.m. Monday through Friday. Until recently, we had given no thought to alternatives; however, more and more people have expressed a need for greater flexibility in their working schedules. We employ many single parents, people who attend the local university part-time, and others who work in areas of our company that routinely conduct tests that run much longer than the regular 8-hour work day.

It has become increasingly clear to us that our current scheduling policy ignores the needs of our employees. Because dissatisfied employees are less productive, and also because this type of dissatisfaction tends to contribute to a high employee turnover rate, we believe that it is necessary to re-evaluate the ways in which we utilize our time.

III. Flextime

Alvin Toffler, in his best-seller about life in the 1980s, The Third Wave, describes flextime as "an arrangement that permits workers, within predetermined limits, to choose their own working hours." Although there may be a set number of core hours when all employees are expected to work—for example, from 10:00

until 2:00—the remaining three or four hours of the work day may be completed

whenever the employee chooses (Toffler 246). The "core period"—from 10:00 to

2:00—insures a stable midday staff (Wolman 8), while the flexible schedule for the

rest of the day gives employees the freedom to plan their days to accommodate

their own and their families' needs.[1] Even more important, perhaps, workers can

schedule their jobs around their biological rhythms: people who awaken early can

report to work by 8:00 while those who stay up late and so awaken late can start

working at 10:00 (Toffler 246). One final advantage of flextime is the improve-

ment in traffic patterns resulting from different starting and finishing times for

workers (Harris 24).

Flextime, which was introduced in West Germany in 1965 as a way to make

the job market more appealing to women with small children, was so successful

that within two years all 12,000 employees of a German aircraft company ex-

perimenting with it were using flextime schedules. Flextime spread rapidly

throughout other European nations as well as in Great Britain. Then during the

1970s multinational firms, like Nestlé and Lufthansa, exported flextime to the

United States. Just a year after its introduction in this country 13 percent of all

United States companies were making some use of flextime scheduling (Toffler

246–47).

Surveys, like one conducted by Psychology Today in 1978, suggest that the

American worker strongly approves of flextime; fully 78 percent of those ques-

tioned by Psychology Today wanted to have some say in the time they started

and finished their workday (Renwick, Lawler, et al. 54). Employers, while

acknowledging some problems with individualized work schedules, seem equally satisfied with the system; as proof, only two percent of the companies that have tried flextime have returned to conventional schedules (Toffler 247). Based, then, on present trends, flextime seems certain to replace the rigid work schedules that people have followed since the outset of the Industrial Revolution. Looking ahead to the workplace in the year 2001, William Abbott, editor of the World Future Society's newsletter, Careers Tomorrow, says quite confidently, "Workers will schedule their own hours under flextime" (Abbott 25).

IV. Part-time

Just as remarkable a variation from rigid work schedules as flextime is the part-time movement that has swept the country during the past twenty years. In 1977 the economist Eli Ginzburg pointed out that 30 percent of all the work in this country was being done by part-time workers (qtd. in Abbot 25). Alvin Toffler summarizes the increase in the number of part-time workers in this way: "In all, there is now one part-time worker for every five full-timers in the United States, and the part-time work force has been growing twice as fast as the full-time force since 1954." Indeed part-time employment has proved so popular with workers that researchers at Georgetown University have predicted almost all jobs in the future will be performed by part-time workers (Toffler 248).

Part-time work has flourished during the last twenty years for a number of reasons. Perhaps most important has been the growing number of working mothers in the job force who need to increase their family's income but who do not want to be separated from their children for the entire day. Part-time work also appeals to the elderly, who have retired from full-time work, and to students and the handicapped, who often cannot work a full eight-hour day (Wolman 1). In addition, there are many people today who simply choose part-time work because it gives them the free time they need to explore other goals—like a hobby, a sport, art, or education. "We are in the midst of a Value Revolution," according to William Abbott. "For many people, the acquisition of material symbols no longer is the primary goal in life" (Abbott 29). Such people will settle for the decrease in pay that comes with part-time work to satisfy their other ambitions (Guyon 1).

Part-time work has become popular with employers because of the high incidence of absenteeism among workers. For example, in automobile plants, where a high percentage of workers invariably have an ailment dubbed "the Friday flu," employers have resorted to hiring part-time workers to fill in. A benefit offered by many companies today—the sabbatical—also causes employers to seek part-timers for the absent workers' positions. Steelworkers today have a thirteen-week sabbatical every seven years as part of their contract; the Rolm Corporation has gone a step further and permits employees with six years of service to periodically take time off with pay. Part-time workers are also needed to fill the spaces left by vacationing employees. The United Auto Workers claim that each day there are 2,368 Ford workers on a personal holiday (Wolman 1, 8). In a variety of situations, then, the part-time worker provides security for large companies so that they can continue to function.[2] As more and more benefits—such as longer vacations, sabbaticals, and educational leaves—are provided, the need for part-time workers increases.

V.   Shared Time

One type of part-time work gaining popularity today is referred to as job sharing. In job sharing a full-time position is simply "split in two" (Wolman 1). With a shared-time arrangement, the job may be split into a four- or five-hour shift for each worker, or it may be divided into full-time work for each for a certain period of time—for example, a six-month work period followed by a six-month free period for each worker (Rich 5).

Job sharing or shared-time work has obvious benefits for both employers and employees. Employers usually get more than an eight-hour day out of each shared job without paying overtime (Wolman 1). Also, with the increasing automation of assembly lines, companies can avoid massive lay-offs by using job sharing (Rich 5). Employees benefit, too, from shared jobs. Working as a team, many are able to have permanent employment and still continue their education. Other people who want the security of a full-time position but who are unwilling to work a full seven- or eight-hour day find job sharing the perfect solution to their problem. Women, in particular, have opted for job sharing, especially those women who need less than a full-time wage (Rich 4–5).

Job sharing is particularly popular in California, where various types of labor ranging from clerical and factory work to teaching are being set up as shared jobs. One of the promoters of job sharing, Barry Olmsted, sums up the rationale for this kind of work schedule: "We want to face reality: most jobs are set up on a 40-hour-a-week basis. Job sharing is an effort to plug part-timers into that framework" (qtd. in Wolman 1).

VI.   <u>Nighttime</u>

Perhaps the most noticeable proof that our country is moving away from the eight- or nine-to-five schedule is the increasing number of people one sees heading for work at odd hours of the evening or night. Alvin Toffler comments that "in the technological nations the number of night workers now runs between 15 and 25 percent of all employees." Manufacturing firms, of course, have long operated 24 hours, using three shifts. But today not only manufacturing but also service- and computer-based companies are employing nighttime workers (Toffler 248).

The advantages of nighttime work for the person who likes to sleep most of the day are obvious. Night shifts also fit the needs of men and women who must take turns caring for their children; one parent is always at home, eliminating the need for sitters or day-care centers.

VII.   <u>Conclusions and Recommendations</u>

From the information gathered so far, it is clear that Alta Enterprises has at least four new options from which to choose if it wishes to restructure its current work schedule pattern. Furthermore, based on the demands of our workers, it would seem that flextime offers both management and workers the greatest possibility to increase morale and production.

For this reason we recommend that Alta Enterprises initiate an in-depth study of flextime, including a review of available published data and consultation with companies similar in size to Alta in order to learn how effective flextime scheduling has been. If, after completing this second stage of our study, flextime continues to look as though it would be an improvement for Alta Enterprises, we would recommend that such a revised scheduling plan be put into effect as soon as possible.

Notes

[1] A variation on this method of scheduling is nighttime, discussed in Section VI.

[2] In many instances the part-time employees also provide companies with a pool from which to fill full-time vacancies when they occur.

Works Cited

Abbott, William. "Work in the Year 2001." The Futurist Feb. 1977: 25–30.

Guyon, Janet. "The American Workplace." The Wall Street Journal 29 Apr. 1981: 1.

Harris, Lillian Craig. "Work and Leisure: Putting It All Together." Manpower Jan.

    1974: 22–26.

Renwick, Patricia A., Edward E. Lawler, and the Psychology Today Staff. "What You

    Really Want from Your Job." Psychology Today May 1978: 53–65.

Rich, Les. "Job-Sharing: Another Way to Work." Worklife May 1978: 4–7.

Toffler, Alvin. The Third Wave. New York: Bantam, 1980.

Wolman, Jonathan. "Work Place 2000," part 2 of "Working in the Year 2000."

    Atlanta Journal-Atlanta Constitution 20 Aug. 1978, sec. C: 1, 8.

The Documented Report

NAME _____

DIRECTIONS   Following the pattern illustrated in "Alta Enterprises' Work Schedule: Updating Our Policies," prepare a documented report on one of the topics listed below. Use the card catalog and the *Readers' Guide to Periodical Literature* or the *Social Sciences Index* at your library to locate information about your topic. Try to use at least five sources in preparing your report. Before you begin writing, identify your reading audience (the person who requested the report) and define the problem to be solved. Remember that the more you know about your intended reader, the better able you will be to communicate clearly and effectively.

SUGGESTED TOPICS

1. Why a person should drop out of college and gain practical work experience.
2. What is wrong with the work ethic?
3. Using the microprocessor in _____ (your field).
4. What to do with your time if you retire early.
5. Some problems with flextime and some solutions.
6. Identifying and helping the workaholic.
7. What types of internships are available in _____ (your major)?

AUDIENCE

STATEMENT OF PROBLEM

APPENDIX

Parts of speech	Uses in the sentence	Examples
1. **Verbs**	Indicators of action or state of being (often link subjects and complements)	Tom *hit* the curve. Mary *was* tired. He *is* a senator.
2. **Nouns**	Subjects, objects, complements	*Kay* gave *Ron* the *book* of *receipts.* *Jane* is a *student.*
3. **Pronouns**	Substitutes for nouns	*He* will return *it* to *her* later.
4. **Adjectives**	Modifiers of nouns and pronouns	*The long* memo is *the best.*
5. **Adverbs**	Modifiers of verbs, adjectives, adverbs, or whole clauses	sang *loudly* A *very* sad song *entirely too* fast *Indeed,* we will.
6. **Prepositions**	Words used before nouns and pronouns to relate them to other words in the sentence	*to* the lake *in* a hurry *with* no thought *beside* her
7. **Conjunctions**	Words that link words, phrases, or clauses; may be either coordinating or subordinating	win *or* lose in the morning *and* at night We won today, *but* we lost last week. Come *as* you are.
8. **Interjections**	Expressions of emotion (unrelated grammatically to the rest of the sentence)	*Woe* is me! *Ouch!* *Imagine!*

Common auxiliaries (helping verbs)

am	could	have	should
am (is, are, *etc.*)	did	have to	used to
going to OR	do	is	was
about to	does	may	were
are	had	might	will
be	had to	must	would
been	has	ought to	
can	has to	shall	

Forms of the verb to be

am	have been	were
are	is	will OR shall be
had been	was	will OR shall have been
has been		

Common indefinite pronouns—those usually considered singular

another	each	everything	nothing
anybody	either	neither	one
anyone	everybody	nobody	somebody
anything	everyone	no one	something

—those considered singular or plural

all	more	none
any	most	some

Relative pronouns

that	which	whoever	whomever
what	who	whom	whose

Common prepositions

across	between	in regard to	through
after	by	like	to
as	for	near	under
at	from	of	until
because of	in	on	up
before	in front of	over	with
beside			

Subordinating conjunction (OR *subordinators*)

after	because	so that	when
although	before	that	whenever
as	if	though	where
as if	in order that	unless	wherever
as though	since	until	while

Coordinating conjunctions (OR *coordinators*)

and	nor	yet
but	or	
for	so	

Conjunctive adverbs

accordingly	henceforth	otherwise
also	however	still
anyhow	indeed	then
besides	instead	therefore
consequently	likewise	thus
first, second, third, *etc.*	meanwhile	
furthermore	moreover	
hence	nevertheless	

Common transitional phrases

as a result	in addition	on the other hand
at the same time	in fact	that is
for example	in other words	
for instance	on the contrary	

Principal parts of some troublesome verbs

PRESENT	PAST	PAST PARTICIPLE
begin	began	begun
blow	blew	blown
break	broke	broken
burst	burst	burst
choose	chose	chosen
come	came	come
do	did	done
draw	drew	drawn
drink	drank	drunk
drive	drove	driven
eat	ate	eaten
fly	flew	flown
freeze	froze	frozen
give	gave	given
grow	grew	grown
know	knew	known
lay	laid	laid
lie	lay	lain
raise	raised	raised
ring	rang	rung
rise	rose	risen
run	ran	run
see	saw	seen
set	set	set
sit	sat	sat
speak	spoke	spoken
steal	stole	stolen
swim	swam	swum
take	took	taken
wear	wore	worn
write	wrote	written

Case of pronouns

SUBJECTIVE	OBJECTIVE	POSSESSIVE
I	me	my, mine
you	you	your, yours
he, she, it	him, her, it	his, her, hers, its
we	us	our, ours
they	them	their, theirs
who OR whoever	whom OR whomever	whose

INDIVIDUAL SPELLING LIST

this list write every word that you misspell—in spelling tests, in themes, or in
my other written work.

WORD (CORRECTLY SPELLED)	WORD (SPELLED BY SYLLABLES) WITH TROUBLE SPOT CIRCLED	REASON FOR ERROR*

* See pages 217–35 for a discussion of the chief reasons for misspelling. Indicate the reason for your
misspelling by writing *a, b, c, d, e, f, g,* or *h* in this column.

a = Mispronunciation
b = Confusion of words similar in sound and/or spelling
c = Error in adding prefix
d = Error in adding suffix

e = Confusion of *ei* and *ie*
f = Error in forming the plural
g = Error in using hyphens
h = Any other reason for misspelling

Individual Spelling List (cont.)

WORD (CORRECTLY SPELLED)	WORD (SPELLED BY SYLLABLES) WITH TROUBLE SPOT CIRCLED	REASON FOR ERROR

Individual Spelling List (cont.)

WORD (CORRECTLY SPELLED)	WORD (SPELLED BY SYLLABLES) WITH TROUBLE SPOT CIRCLED	REASON FOR ERROR